POLITICAL ECONOMY AND
COLONIAL IRELAND

POLITICAL ECONOMY AND COLONIAL IRELAND

The propagation and ideological function of economic discourse in the nineteenth century

Thomas A. Boylan
and
Timothy P. Foley

London and New York

First published 1992
by Routledge
11 New Fetter Lane, London EC4P 4EE

Simultaneously published in the USA and Canada
by Routledge
a division of Routledge, Chapman and Hall, Inc.
29 West 35th Street, New York, NY 10001

© 1992 Thomas A. Boylan and Timothy P. Foley
Typeset in Garamond by GilCoM Ltd, Mitcham, Surrey
Printed and bound in Great Britain by
Biddles, Ltd, Guildford and King's Lynn

British Library Cataloguing in Publication Data
Boylan, Thomas A.
Political economy and colonial Ireland: the propagation
and ideological function of economic discourse in the
nineteenth century.
1. Ireland. Economics. Related to politics. History
I. Title II. Foley, Timothy P.
330. 941509034

ISBN 0–415–06628–X

Library of Congress Cataloging in Publication Data
Boylan, Thomas A.
Political economy and colonial Ireland: the propagation
and ideological function of economic discourse in the
nineteenth century
Thomas A. Boylan and Timothy P. Foley
Includes bibliographical references and index.
ISBN 0–415–06628–X
1. Economics – Ireland – History – 19th century.
2. Economics – Study and teaching (Higher) – Ireland –
History – 19th century.
I. Foley, Timothy P., II. Title.

HB104.B69 1992

330'. 09415' 09034–dc20

To
Noeleen and Molly

'I believe that, next to good Religious Education, a sound Knowledge of Political Economy would tend as much to tranquillize this Country, if not more, than any other Branch of Knowledge that can be taught in Schools.'

(Hugh Hamill, Schools' Inspector, Cork, 1833)

'[Political economy was] the *only* means which existed of rescuing the country from convulsion.'

(Richard Whately, 1848)

'Political Economy is... a science at the same time dangerous and leading to occasions of sin.'

(John Henry Newman, 1852)

'Modern Anglicanism, *i.e.*, Utilitarianism, the creed of Russell and Peel as well as of the Radicals, this thing, call it Yankeeism or Englishism, which measure prosperity by exchangeable value, measures duty by gain, and limits desire to clothes, food, and respectability; this damned thing has come into Ireland under the Whigs, and is equally the favourite of the *Peel* Tories. It is believed in the political assemblies in our cities, preached from our pulpits (always Utilitarian or persecuting); it is the very apostles' creed of the professions, and threatens to corrupt the lower classes, who are still faithful and romantic. To use every literary and political engine against this seems to me the first duty of an Irish patriot who can forsee consequences. Believe me, this is a greater though no so obvious danger as Papal supremacy.'

(Thomas Davis, 1840s)

CONTENTS

PREFACE

This book developed from our ongoing study of Irish political economy, especially of the contributions of John Elliot Cairnes, and our involvement in the international research project 'The Institutionalization of Political Economy: Its Introduction and Acceptance into European, North American and Japanese Universities'. Versions of chapters two and three will be included in the forthcoming volume for Great Britain and Ireland, edited by Istvan Hont and Keith Tribe, entitled *Trade, Politics, and Letters: The Rise of Economics in British University Culture, 1755-1905*, and published by Routledge. We decided to attempt a comprehensive coverage of the propagation of political economy in Ireland at popular as well as at university level. With the exception of the pioneering work of Professor R.D. Collison Black on political economy at Trinity College Dublin and on the Dublin Statistical Society (later to become the Statistical and Social Inquiry Society of Ireland), not only is the field untilled, the very territory is uncharted. This is especially true of what is perhaps the most intriguing area of all, the teaching of political economy to children in the national schools in Ireland in the nineteenth century. As political economy was especially aimed at the lower classes we have addressed the activities of the Statistical Society, in particular its administration of the Barrington Lectures. Central to our study is the role of Richard Whately, Anglican Archbishop of Dublin (1831–63) and former Drummond Professor of Political Economy at Oxford. He founded the Whately Chair at Trinity, he was instrumental in establishing the Statistical Society of which he was president, and, as a commissioner of national education, he introduced political economy into the school curriculum, as well

PREFACE

as writing the textbook *Easy Lessons on Money Matters*. Whately was the great evangelist of political economy in nineteenth-century Ireland.

There was a widespread view that political economy was both little known and little respected in Ireland. Indeed this was seen as yet another explanation for Irish economic backwardness. We argue that in an Ireland divided socially, economically, politically, and denominationally, consensus was sought in the new discipline of political economy, claiming to be scientifically impartial and to be an incontrovertible form of knowledge which transcended all divisions. But political economy *was* ideological, performing the crucial function of defending the socio-economic status quo and, in the words of a schools' inspector in 1833, tranquillising the country. It was a central part of the educational system, formal and informal, and a powerful instrument of social control, achieved not through coercion, but through the intellectual hegemony of a master science. The Great Famine of the mid-1840s was a critical turning point in the reign of political economy and its then inseparable companion, the doctrine of *laissez-faire*. There were vitriolic popular attacks on the discipline, both moral and nationalist. There was increased scepticism concerning both the validity and universality of its laws, and even calls to establish an Irish political economy. There was a concerted attempt by the authorities to defend the honour of political economy, but within a decade there was an increasing awareness that a political economy generated out of English ideas and experiences was unsuitable to Ireland. In the face of an unsparing moral critique, the prestige of political economy faded, its absolutist reign over. Irish resistance, especially to the doctrines of absolute private property in land and the sacredness of contract, was such that various Irish Land Acts had to, in effect, abandon them as the price to be paid for tranquillity. Political economy's mission of assimilating Ireland to England failed; concomitant with its decline was an increased emphasis on Ireland's difference from England. Political economy was unsuccessful as an instrument of empire, and Ireland was to be governed by 'Irish ideas'.

ACKNOWLEDGEMENTS

We have incurred many debts of gratitude over several years in our reasearch for this book and a perfunctory mention here will scarcely serve to discharge them. We want to thank the James Hardiman Library, University College Galway (the Acting Librarian, Ms Pat O'Connell, and especially Ms Maeve Doyle), the National Library of Ireland, the Library of Trinity College Dublin, the British Library, the Bodleian Library, Oxford, the Marshall Library, Cambridge, and the Bancroft Library, University of California, Berkeley. We are also pleased to acknowledge the facilities afforded us by the Research Centre, King's College, Cambridge, the University of San Francisco, and San José State University. We are particularly grateful to the Development Fund in UCG, without whose financial support this project would have been impossible. We are also grateful to the Presidential Research Committee for financial services rendered and to the Social Science Research Centre, also in UCG. Both of us wish to express our gratitude for the Senior Fulbright Fellowships, which eased our paths financially and academically. We also want to thank the Royal Irish Academy and the British Academy for one of their Exchange Fellowships.

We want especially to thank Professor R.D. Collison Black of Queen's University Belfast for his generosity, his encouragement, and his scholarship. Dr Istvan Hont of King's College, Cambridge has been very supportive, as has Dr Keith Tribe of the University of Keele. We are also grateful to Professor Dermot McAleese and Mr Antoin Murphy of Trinity College Dublin, to Professor, and Professor A.W. Coats of Duke University. Gearóid Ó Tuathaigh and Michael Cuddy, Mr Alf MacLochlainn, and Mr P.J. Lawless of UCG, and Professor James Walsh, Dean of the School of Social

ACKNOWLEDGEMENTS

Sciences, San José State University.

We salute Ciara Boylan, age 9, for her heroic services to scholarship in reading Whately's *Easy Lessons on Money Matters* and finding it 'dry'. John Boylan and Jane Foley have yet to manifest an interest in political economy. Most of all we want to thank Noeleen Boylan and Molly Fogarty.

Finally, we are immensely grateful to Imelda Howley and Claire Noone for cheerfully and expertly typing a difficult manuscript.

1

POLITICAL ECONOMY:
'A science unknown in Ireland'

It was widely believed that political economy was little known in nineteenth-century Ireland and, if known, was not highly regarded. There was also a widespread view that the laws of political economy, thought universal in their application, somehow mysteriously contrived not to apply to Ireland. In these circumstances it is not surprising that John Kenneth Galbraith should declare that the Irish had never produced economists of international standing.[1] But Ireland did produce distinguished economists and it is appropriate that many (if not most) of these in the nineteenth century were critical, in different ways, of prevailing orthodoxy. The early Whately Professors in Trinity College Dublin, the so-called 'Dublin School', have been described as 'dissenters', and the leading proponents of the historical and comparative method in the English-speaking world were Irish economists, Cliffe Leslie and John Kells Ingram. Ignorance of and indifference or hostility towards the laws of political economy were added to the already imposing catalogue of causes of Irish economic backwardness. In this respect Ireland was a warning example. In the words of Charles Francis Bastable, one of the most celebrated Whately Professors, 'so far from Political Economy being inoperative in Ireland, no country has furnished more remarkable instances of the action of economic forces, and of the danger of disregarding precepts based on a knowledge of their working'.[2] Among the upper orders of Irish society, from the 1830s onwards, the cultivation of political economy, its widespread dissemination, especially amongst the working classes and the strict application of its principles to the economic life of the country, were seen as absolutely vital to economic progress. This book attempts to describe the

1

production, distribution, and consumption of economic ideas in nineteenth-century Ireland and to consider the ideological functions of these ideas.

We wish to argue that in an economically, politically, and denominationally divided Ireland, one crucial area where consensus was sought was political economy, a discipline claiming scientific impartiality. By the nineteenth century in Britain political economy had become the unchallenged mode of political discourse, the self-knowledge of industrial society, though we argue that in largely agricultural and colonial Ireland, its status was more problematic. In Britain political economy, 'secular', 'descriptive', 'scientific', 'ideologically neutral', had superseded earlier moral, religious, and generally prescriptive discursive modes. Because of denominational division in Ireland, ideological consensus based on religion, traditionally a very powerful agent of social cohesion, was impossible, especially as such division, in large measure, coincided with economic, social, and national differences. Richard Whately, the Anglican Archbishop of Dublin and the central figure in the spread of political economy in Ireland, like most other commentators, saw political economy as second in importance only to religion (even in a crucial sense more important) and as having, in large measure, assumed the position vacated by religion as the great agent of social control. But, we argue, political economy *was* partisan, prescriptive, tendentious. Claiming to be non-sectarian and non-political, it performed a vitally important ideological function for the political and religious establishment in defending existing socio-economic relations, including landlordism, property rights, and in attacking trade unions.

Political economy was especially well qualified as a bonding agency in society as it seemed to provide consensus both at the discursive and at the 'material' economic levels. Interestingly, with the eventual failure of the project, and after the fall of Parnell, which ended many hopes of a political (seen as the quintessential arena of division) solution to Irish problems, consensus was sought at the 'material' level of agricultural co-operation (the foundation of the Irish Agricultural Organisation Society), 'below' the divisiveness of politics, as it were, and at the cultural level, 'above' politics, in the revival of the Irish language (the Gaelic League) and the Literary Revival. In general, the early writings of the Whately Professors and the members of the Dublin Statistical

2

Society (later to become the Statistical and Social Inquiry Society of Ireland) defended political economy as a pure science, just like astronomy or mechanics, and were somewhat embarrassed by the adjective 'political' in its title, and as a consequence they advocated rigorous adherence to the 'laws' of political economy, especially to the policy of *laissez-faire*. These laws were held to be natural laws and hence universal. Indeed as James A. Lawson, a former Whately Professor, put it in 1862, political economy owed its very existence to the 'misfortunes and calamities caused by offending against the laws of nature'.[3] In Britain, in the latter part of the century, this absolutism gave way to relativism, a state of affairs embraced by the new historical school but, in the end, rejected by mainstream British economists who redoubled their efforts to make political economy more scientific. This increased 'scientificisation', even mathematicisation of economic discourse, culminated in a new name, *economics*, indicating that the discipline had, at last, managed to rid itself of its ideological pre-history. But in Ireland, we argue, the movement was, in important respects, in a different direction with increased criticism of the scientific nature of political economy, the universality of its laws, and (a not unrelated matter) the validity of its methodologies. Richard Whately and William Edward Hearn were so dissatisfied with the unscientific name 'political economy' that they coined substitutes, 'catallactics' and 'plutology', thus adding two new words to the English language. But in Ireland, as the century progressed, there was increasing emphasis on what Cliffe Leslie called 'the imperious conditions of time and place', a growing scepticism concerning the universality of political economy, and an increasing awareness that a political economy generated out of English experience and ideas was not appropriate to the very different socio-economic arrangements of Ireland. It was hardly an accident that the leading advocates of the historical method, Leslie and Ingram, came out of Ireland. An increasing emphasis on the historical, the comparative and the institutional, combined with a moral and even political critique seriously undermined the universalist pretensions of orthodox political economy. Several of the early speakers at the Dublin Statistical Society ridiculed John Mitchel's notion of 'Irish political economy', without condescending to name him. The most notable of them, William Neilson Hancock, was later to develop a not dissimilar critique of orthodox political economy, down-

3

grading its scientific character in the name of morality. Indeed the ideas of Leslie and Ingram and the later views of Cairnes were, perhaps, closer to Mitchel's alleged oxymoron than they would have admitted.

In this study of the dissemination and reception of political economy in an institutional context special reference must be made to the extraordinary role in the process played by Richard Whately, Archbishop of Dublin from 1831 until his death in 1863, and previously the Drummond Professor of Political Economy at the University of Oxford. One of his first important actions on appointment to Dublin was to establish and fund a Professorship of Political Economy in Trinity College Dublin in 1832. He retained a keen interest in the Professorship, whose incumbents were chosen, in the Oxford fashion, by competitive examination, and who held office for five years. In the same year he became one of the original commissioners of national education and remained the *de facto* head, and the most influential member, of the Board of National Education for many years. In this capacity he introduced political economy to the school curriculum for which he himself wrote the textbook, *Easy Lessons on Money Matters*, easily the best-selling work in economics in the nineteenth century. In 1847 the Dublin Statistical Society was formed for the purpose of 'promoting the study of Statistical and Economical Science'. The Society's genesis was closely connected with Trinity College and especially with the Whately Professors of Political Economy. Whately himself became the first president of the Society, an office he held until his death. Indeed, according to a subsequent president, Sir John Lentaigne, it was 'mainly through his influence and exertions' that the Society was formed.[4] In 1834 John Barrington, a Dublin merchant, established a trust to fund lectures in political economy, especially for workers, in various cities, towns, and villages throughout Ireland. In 1849 the Statistical Society took over the administration of these lectures, an arrangement which endures to this day. At one period the Barrington Fund was used to train schoolmasters in political economy, a further example of how interconnected were the various bodies involved in the promulgation of the subject.

Whately was by far the most influential propagator of political economy in nineteenth-century Ireland, a task he pursued with evangelical zeal. Before he established the chair at Trinity College, several others, such as Thomas Prior, Samuel Madden, and Robert Burrowes had advocated that political economy (or 'trade') be taught there. But the formal teaching of economics in Ireland dates from the establishment of the Whately chair in 1832 and Whately is seen, quite rightly, as the discipline's founding (and indeed funding) father. Lawson, the third holder of the chair, first used the phrase 'father of economic science in Ireland' with reference to Whately in his address delivered at the opening of the eleventh session of the Statistical Society in 1858 and he repeated it on a number of occasions.[5] Hancock, Lawson's immediate successor in the Whately chair, wrote in 1847 that Whately 'first introduced the study of Political Economy into this University [Dublin], indeed, I may say, into Ireland'.[6] When the president died in 1863 Hancock, in his address to the Statistical Society, said that

> In Dublin, as in Oxford, Archbishop Whately sought to remove prejudice, and to lend the weight of his character and position to the study and teaching of political economy. Besides the lectures in the University, Archbishop Whately attached the greatest importance to the diffusion of the knowledge of the science amongst the poor, and his *Easy Lessons on Money Matters*, so widely circulated and taught, were well calculated to attain this result.[7]

According to Sir Robert Kane, President of Queen's College Cork, Whately had

> by his salutary influence on the courses of the National Schools, and by his munificent endowment of the professorship in Trinity College, secured that means should be afforded of teaching political economy to all classes of society; and in his capacity as Senator of the National University, founded by our beloved Queen, our president has effectually co-operated to introduce, as a portion of undergraduate education the principles of political economy, of jurisprudence, and of statistics, for teaching which professorships have been founded in the Queen's Colleges.[8]

In his presidential address to the Statistical Society in 1877 Lentaigne stated that the Society came into existence as a result of his 'influence and exertions' and that he never ceased 'by every means in his power' to provide the 'knowledge of Social Science, which he considered so important for the well-being of society'.[9]

Richard Horner Mills, the first Professor of Jurisprudence and Political Economy in Queen's College Cork, dedicated his book, *The Principles of Currency and Banking*, to Whately 'whose Liberality and Public Spirit Introduced the Study of Political Economy into Ireland'.[10] According to the Dublin merchant Jonathan Pim, the 'enlightened liberality' of Whately in funding the Trinity chair 'gave the first impulse to the study of economic questions in this country'.[11] Indeed, such was Whately's commitment to the propagation of political economy that instead of a monument to his memory, it was deemed more appropriate, both to the spirit of the man and the age, that 'a permanent endowment for promoting the study of political economy in the University of Dublin' be established.[12]

Writing to Gladstone in 1869, John Bright declared: 'I have great faith in political economy, a science unknown, I suspect, in Ireland.'[13] But in the admittedly partisan view of Whately (and indeed others) much progress had been achieved since 1832 in combating economic ignorance in Ireland. In his presidential address at the conclusion of the first session of the Statistical Society in 1848, Whately praised the increased attention which was being devoted to political economy, asking rhetorically 'for who, twenty years ago, would have thought that such an assemblage of scientific men could be collected for the purpose of promoting the cultivation of Political Economy'? He noted modestly that before the establishment of the Professorship 'very few thought at all of the subject, and the few who did think of it entertained fallacious and erroneous notions relative to it'.[14] Even the learned scholars of Trinity College were ignorant of the subject for, according to Whately, 'not one of the academic heads absolutely knew what the term Political Economy meant'.[15] Even the founding of a chair was 'an enterprise attended with considerable difficulty, owing to the general ignorance of the subject in the University'.[16] Such was the paucity of economic knowledge that Whately almost despaired of finding a 'suitable occupant for the chair.[17]

By 1851 Sir Robert Kane felt that in Ireland, 'where the neglect of economic principles' had been the cause of 'so much individual suffering, and of so much national loss', the 'period of social ignorance and economic error' had 'nearly passed away'.[18] According to Lawson, at the time of the establishment of the Whately chair, 'the very name of political economy was unknown in Ireland. I recollect myself that when it was spoken of even educated men used to ask what it meant.'[19] Concerning political economy, according to Lawson, the founders of the Statistical Society felt that 'we have suffered much from our neglect and ignorance of its ordinary principles'.[20] Writing in 1861 Whately's friend, the eminent economist Nassau Senior, felt that the Irish were still the 'tools of their priests' and that the priests were 'still ignorant of the economical laws on which the welfare of the labouring classes depends'.[21] A few years later, Thomas O'Hagan, praising the work of the Statistical Society, remarked again on Irish backwardness in economic knowledge:

> Economic science, and the inquiries ancillary to the establishment of its principles and their judicious application to the affairs of human life, have only for a very brief period commanded any attention amongst us. They constitute, indeed, almost a new department of knowledge, which has found its special cultivation elsewhere in latter years, but, with ourselves, that cultivation was very long delayed.[22]

As late as 1866 a review of Arthur Houston's book, *The Principles of Values in Exchange*, in the *Irish Industrial Magazine* stated that 'political economy is a subject little cared for in Ireland'.[23]

According to his daughter, Richard Whately did much to rescue political economy from the 'undue prejudices with which it was generally regarded'.[24] It was felt that while most people were simply ignorant of political economy, very many others disregarded its teachings and were prejudiced or hostile towards it. The first Whately Professor, Mountifort Longfield, like several of his successors, felt called upon to defend the honour of his discipline. He devoted the first few pages of his *Four Lectures on Poor Laws* to answering 'an invective against Political-Economy'.[25] A letter to the editor of the *Dublin University Magazine* claimed that Longfield's book was 'well calculated to remove the apathy and the prejudices which have hitherto existed in reference to this science, among those classes of our countrymen to whom a knowledge of its principles... [was of] paramount national importance'.[26] Isaac Butt, Longfield's immediate successor, spoke frequently of 'popular prejudice' and a 'popular hostility' towards political economy, but he believed it was in the decline.[27] Writing in 1851, James Haughton described political economy as being 'attacked unsparingly by a numerous class of reasoners, who find it easier to account for the evils which exist around them on irrational principles, hastily adopted'.[28] There was, as we shall see in chapter six, more reasoned opposition to orthodox political economy in Ireland in the nineteenth century, which saw it as 'immoral', or as opposed to the interests of, for instance, workers, tenants, and even the cause of Irish nationality.

The critique of political economy, especially the doctrine of *laissez-faire* which was seen as inseparable from it, reached a climax in 1847, the year of the Great Famine in Ireland. In that year the Irish Confederation published a booklet, edited by John Mitchel, consisting of extracts from Swift and Berkeley, and significantly entitled *Irish Political Economy*. Mitchel starkly contrasted 'Irish' political economy with what he witheringly called 'English' or 'Famine' political economy. He wrote that

English Professors of political economy have, by perverting and misapplying the principles of that science, endeavoured to prove to us, that to part with our bread and cattle is profitable 'commerce' and that our trading intercourse with their country enriches us immensely whatever the ignorant and starving Irish may say and feel to the contrary.[29]

But many authors, some neither nationalist nor Irish, were in agreement with Mitchel's views. In general, the objections were not to political economy as such but to a political economy which preached *laissez-faire*, the absolute nature of property (especially in land), and the sanctity of contract. There was a general opinion that these principles were suitable to an advanced industrial society such as England but not to an economically and socially backward agricultural one like Ireland. In other words, political economy had a nationality. It was English and it was not appropriate to Irish circumstances. In 1847, the Revd George H. Stoddart, the Secretary of the United Relief Association, wrote that it was

perfect folly to be dancing a Will-o'-the-wisp dance after the abstract principles of political economy, as laid down by Adam Smith, for it ought to be remembered, that he wrote for a country advanced in social position and high civilization.[30]

In his *Coercion in Ireland*, Samuel Laing wrote that the 'absolute rights of property and the sacredness of contract' though sound principles in England, had brought 'unmixed evil' to a poor agricultural country like Ireland.[31] In 1888 'An Irish Liberal', looking back on the Great Famine, wrote that 'Government interference, it was argued, would prejudice private enterprise. The laws of political economy, and the doctrine of *laissez-faire* were equal to all emergencies'. The author added dryly, 'we know what happened'.[32] And, finally, in the early years of this century, Alice Stopford Greene declared baldly that 'Englishmen could not understand Irish conditions. The political economy they advocated for their own country had no relation to Ireland.'[33]

As might be expected, political economists rushed to the defence of the scientificity of their subject and the universality of its laws. Hancock was obviously referring to Mitchel when he wrote that the 'idea of having a science of exchanges peculiar to Ireland, under the name of Irish Political Economy, is about as reasonable as proposing to have Irish mechanics, Irish mathematics, or Irish astronomy'.[34] Hancock had published a book the previous year which he dramatically entitled *Three Lectures on the Question: Should the Principles of Political Economy Be Disregarded at the Present Crisis?* The answer was an unequivocal 'no'. In fact, reading the early contributions to the *Transactions* and *Journal* of the Statistical Society, it becomes obvious that the Society was founded, not so much as a humanitarian response to the Great Famine, though it would be unfair to deny the presence of such an impulse, but in order to defend the laws of political economy then seen as under unprecedented attack.

Longfield attacked the allegation 'that although Political Economy might be a very good thing in other countries, it was not suited to Ireland'.[35] The views being combated by Longfield were that in a country so exceptionally circumstanced as Ireland (especially in time of famine) the laws of political economy should either be completely disregarded or else there should be a relaxation in their application. In 1854 Jonathan Pim claimed that such was the success of the Statistical Society in the seven years of its existence that 'we are no longer told that the rules of political economy may be very good, but that it will not do to enforce them rigidly under all circumstances; that they may do very well for a prosperous country but that in Ireland it is quite another affair'.[36] According to Lawson the Famine in Ireland was a time when people said:

this is no period for the application of the principles of political economy; political economy may do for ordinary occasions, in time of peace, in times when no great national disaster had fallen upon the people; we are now in a particular crisis – the case is an extraordinary one, and therefore ordinary remedies and doctrines ought to be flung to the winds.[37]

In 1866 John Joseph Murphy wrote that 'Ireland is, no doubt a poorer country than Great Britain; but to relax the application of the principles of political economy in the case of a poor country, would be as reasonable as to relax the application of medical science in the case of a patient of weak constitution'.[38] But the victory of the political economists was far from complete. The general view seemed to remain that, in the words of the Limerick Declaration of 1868 (a repeal of the Union manifesto by an assembly of Roman Catholic priests), 'Ireland has had enough of political economy'.[39] Two years later Cairnes could uncontroversially claim that all schemes offered for the settlement of the Irish land question had in common 'a profound distrust of Political Economy.... It is either sneered at as unpractical and perverse, or its authority is respectfully put aside as of no account in a country so exceptionally situated as Ireland'.[40] Four years later R.E. Thompson stated that Gladstone and Robert Lowe 'hold fast to every letter of the old shibboleth, except when it comes to legislation about Ireland. The laws of economy which govern the rest of the world are not in force on the western shore of St George's Channel'.[41] As late as 1884, Bastable felt called upon to reject the 'widely-diffused idea that economic principles are not applicable to Ireland', the idea that 'although Political Economy might be a very good thing in other countries, it was not suited to Ireland'. As we have already noted, Bastable concluded that 'so far from Political Economy being inoperative in Ireland, no country has furnished more remarkable instances of the action of economic forces, and of the danger of disregarding precepts based on a knowledge of their working'.[42]

Attacks on political economy became more virulent in 1847 in response to the Great Famine and in the revolutionary year of 1848. There were demands to ignore the laws of political economy, to relax their rigorous application, and even to construct an Irish political economy. In 1832 the Whately chair was set up to minister to the educated classes. An anonymous review of Longfield's *Lectures* in the *Dublin University Magazine* in 1834 stated that a knowledge of the principles of political economy was of 'paramount national importance' for 'all men of a certain standing in society', by which the author meant the Irish landed gentry.[43] But that very year John Barrington set up his trust fund, for the teaching of political economy to the lower classes. Soon afterwards national teachers were being instructed in the subject and they, in turn, taught it to the children of the poor in Ireland. But with the events of 1847 and 1848 a new sense of urgency, even of panic, was evident. The Statistical Society, founded in 1847, propagated economic ideas to a largely middle-class audience but, by accepting the administration of the Barrington Trust in 1849, the Society earnestly hoped to reach the most disaffected (and so important) audience of all, the working classes. There is also some evidence to show that political economy became, at this time, a much more important part of the national school curriculum than had been the case.

Whately believed passionately in the need to promulgate political economy widely, but especially among the lower orders. The science would be of no real benefit if merely cultivated by 'five or six men of taste and science' and the 'very best theories were but useless until made practical and public'. It had to be 'diffused generally amongst the people, to whom the acquirement of it was of the deepest importance'.[44] In 1833 Whately, writing to a Miss Crabtree (a former parishioner of his), claimed that 'perhaps the sort of thing most wanted now for children and the poor, is some plain instructions in Political Economy'. He wanted Miss Crabtree to 'work up some such instruction into familiar tales and dialogues' after the fashion of Harriet Martineau.[45] By 1854 Jonathan Pim felt that not only was the importance of political economy admitted but that 'instead of being treated as an abstract science, and confined to a few learned professors', it was now 'widely diffused' and was, in fact, a 'popular science'.[46] James Lawson was almost equally sanguine: the popularity of 'social science' was a modern phenomenon, for it was previously unknown 'save to a few studious men in the closet'.[47]

It is unnecessary to catalogue in any great detail the numerous statements from within the educational system on the vital importance of a knowledge of political economy to the people of Ireland and especially to the lower classes. William McCreedy, a head inspector of national schools, reported in 1848 that the topics of political economy were 'all matters of the deepest interest, upon which it is most desirable all men should entertain correct views'.[48] The following year he wrote that an acquaintence with the subject was 'important' and even 'necessary' to all classes of society.[49] His colleague James Patten regretted in his report for 1848 that the answering by the teachers in political economy was not up to his expectation despite the 'great prominence' he had given the matter and the 'importance' he attached to it.[50] In 1853 J. Macdonnell of Larne Model School spoke in even stronger terms:

> The deplorable results that frequently arise from ignorance of the simplest principles of this science make it a matter of the deepest importance to have the rising generation carefully instructed in these principles. It has always formed a part of the education of boys here, but more especially during the past year have I felt myself called on to devote more than ordinary attention to it.[51]

In 1879 J. Moylan (presumably the schoolmaster of Limerick Model School who was appointed a Barrington lecturer in 1873–4) declared his keen disappointment to find political economy 'wholly excluded' from the Intermediate Education programme. 'But certain it is', he wrote,

> that political economy is not getting anything like the amount of public attention commensurate from its importance as a means of correcting popular errors, or as an interesting subject of the curriculum of intermediate or elementary education; so that at the snail's pace at which we are progressing in this regard, it will, I fear, be a long time till political economy will have fulfilled its mission of making popular and rendering irrefutable the simple proposition that the 'wealth of mankind is the abundance of things'.[52]

Needless to mention, the members of the Statistical Society were absolutely convinced of the importance of political economy, especially in Ireland. 'To our own country', wrote Sir Robert Kane, 'the proper appreciation of the dignity and utility of political economy is of paramount importance, and it is most fortunate that in no country are in action more extended or more effectual agencies for diffusing economical information'.[53] Similar ideas were carried to many towns and villages of Ireland by the new Barrington lecturers, prominent among whom were Professors from the recently founded Queen's Colleges. From Galway, for instance, lectures were being given in various parts of the country by not only the Professor of Jurisprudence and Political Economy (Denis Caulfield Heron) but also by the Professor of Logic and Metaphysics (Thomas W. Moffett) and the Professor of Greek (W.E. Hearn). Not only did the Galway papers carry extensive reports of lectures delivered to Galway audiences (often the full texts) but they usually reprinted the accounts in local papers of lectures delivered by Galway Professors at other venues. To take one example, long extracts from lectures delivered by Moffett in such places as Armagh, Ardee, Coleraine, Holywood, Lisburn, and Garvagh were reproduced in the *Galway Vindicator*. An extraordinary amount of space was devoted in these local papers, in the late 1840s and early 1850s, to political economy, and both lecturers and newspapers constantly reiterated the crucial importance, especially at that time, of the subject. Moffett's first lecture at the Galway Mechanics' Institute set out to deal with, *inter alia*, the 'Importance of the Science at the present time'.[54] With reference to this lecture the *Galway Vindicator* reported that Moffett 'insisted on the paramount importance of the diffusion of sound views' on political economy 'to the community at large, especially at the present time'.[55] Referring to the same lecture the *Galway Mercury* wrote that 'Political Economy has now become a science of paramount importance. Its principles should be, to some extent, at least, studied by every individual in society'.[56] On receiving an illustrated address from the committee of the Mechanics' Institute at the conclusion of the final lecture in the series, Moffett reiterated that the 'existing circumstances of the country' had 'invested with vital importance' the subject of political economy.[57]

The closing years of the 1840s, when popular criticism of political economy was at its most intense, also saw the beginning of a powerful official defence of the discipline. Whately himself entered the fray, his Professors at Trinity descended from their chairs to more popular forums, the Statistical Society was founded and sought to influence people through lectures and publications, the Professors in the newly established Queen's Colleges in

Belfast, Cork, and Galway began to spread the good news, the Barrington Lectures under the aegis of the Statistical Society became highly successful, and increased emphasis was placed on the teaching of political economy in the national schools. In his address at the conclusion of the first session of the Statistical Society in June 1848, Whately was impressed by the increased interest paid to political economy. For who, he asked, 'twenty years ago, would have thought that such an assembly of scientific men could be collected for the purpose of promoting the cultivation of Political Economy'? He stressed the importance of the Professors in the cultivation and diffusion of the subject and in creating 'a taste for the study of it'; it was to them the Statistical Society 'owed much of its success'.[58] By 1851 Kane felt that the era of Irish economic ignorance was over. No other country, he said, had 'more extended or more effectual agencies for diffusing economical information', thanks in large measure to Whately. Kane also remarked that the reception accorded the Barrington lecturers throughout Ireland afforded 'most gratifying proof of the desire for economic knowledge'.[59] Looking back on the first seven years of the operation of the Statistical Society, Jonathan Pim said that there had been a remarkable alteration in the public attitude towards political economy. Its importance was now admitted, 'now every one is a political economist'.[60]

Perhaps the most optimistic and even lyrical of all commentators on the success of political economy was James A. Lawson. Addressing the Statistical Society in 1858, he congratulated Whately, whom he had called the 'father of economic science in Ireland', for having a 'very numerous family'.[61] Four years later he wrote that the study of the subject was introduced by the setting up of the Whately chair and it was to it was owed the 'existence of a school of economists now so numerous in this country'.[62] It was also, for Lawson, a matter of 'pride and satisfaction' that the 'two best text-books on the subject of Banking and Currency' were Irish books written by Irish Professors.[63] The Statistical Society and the Barrington lecturers had continued to spread economic knowledge throughout Ireland, 'sowing the seeds of knowledge broadcast over all the land'.[64] In its first ten years, the Statistical Society had been extraordinarily successful, in Lawson's view, in its essential task, the 'diffusion of a sound knowledge of political and social science'.[65] Writing in 1858, he maintained that:

14

at the present moment there is no country in which political quackery or economic or social fallacies would be less likely to pass current than in Ireland; a state of things which stands broadly in contrast with the condition of the country twenty-five years ago.[66]

At the time of the foundation of the Statistical Society the public mind was 'quite unsound' on economic questions and the 'principles of free-trade had not been established'.[67] In the ten years of the Society, Lawson wrote, in a passage worth quoting at length,

We have in some degree contributed to produce in this metropolis and through those parts of Ireland to which our labours extended, something like a sound public opinion upon economic and social questions. We have supplied the wholesome food of rational discussion, instead of the unwholesome diet of party politics, which up to that time was perhaps the most acceptable thing that could be presented. And we have now many of the people well instructed in those truths. I venture to say if a socialist came into the country and propounded any of his levelling doctrines, that there is hardly a child in the national schools that would not establish the fallacy of those doctrines; or if any man preached an inconvertible paper currency or a project for land banks, there is not a town in which our lectures have been delivered that would not furnish persons able to show that such views were contrary to the sound principles of social science.[68]

In his presidential address to the Statistical Society in 1877, Lantaigne drew attention to the importance of the role played by Whately's *Easy Lessons on Money Matters* in disseminating political economy among schoolchildren. These lesson books were 'now in the hands of more than one million readers in Ireland, children on the rolls of schools under the Board' and were read by 'countless numbers throughout the British colonies and the continent of America'.[69] Finally, writing in 1878, when the fortunes of political economy had gone into decline, Hancock stated that the 'systematic teaching of economic science in Trinity College, in each of the Queen's Colleges, in the National Schools, and under the Barrington Lecture Trust, had produced a state of opinion highly favourable to progressive study of economic science'.[70]

Political economy in the 1870s in Britain, in the words of Professor A.W. Coats, 'suffered a considerable loss of public prestige'.[71] It was suggested with reference to the dinner given by the Political Economy Club of London to mark the centenary of the publication of Adam Smith's *Wealth of Nations* in 1776, that the assembled economists 'had better be celebrating the obsequies of their science than its jubilee'.[72] To make matters worse, in the following year, 1877, Francis Galton, the founder of the perhaps not excessively scientific discipline of eugenics, proposed that Section F of the British Association for the Advancement of Science, dealing with Political Economy and Statistics, be discontinued as the subject lacked scientific status. In 1878 the Irish economist John Kells Ingram defended the scientific credentials of political economy, while admitting the existence of widespread scepticism on the question.[73] As we have already noted, in 1879 Moylan greatly regretted the public decline in interest in political economy.[74] The same year Samuel Haughton wrote a brief article entitled 'Causes of slow progress of political economy'. He ascribed the decline in standing of the subject to the excessive claims made on its behalf by its proponents, giving it a pre-eminent position of control over human affairs, usurping all social, political, and artistic values. These writers asserted that 'this science of mere wealth was to be the master, not the servant of man'.[75]

2

THE WHATELY CHAIR OF POLITICAL ECONOMY AT TRINITY COLEGE DUBLIN 1832–1900

The establishment of the Whately Chair of Political Economy at Trinity College Dublin in 1832 represented the first step in the formal institutionalisation of political economy in Ireland. That this process should have commenced at Trinity College was largely inevitable, since this was the only university institution in the country at this time, though in a deeply-divided society it was not a representative body. These social divisions were the result of a sustained policy of colonisation, begun in the twelfth century, but pursued more thoroughly and systematically during the sixteenth and seventeenth centuries. To comprehend the divisions of Irish society resulting from colonisation and the place of Trinity College Dublin within this society, which has been termed 'the first colonial university institution',[1] some attention must be devoted to the historical background. The historical context is of particular significance if the influences which determined the intellectual functions of political economy and the reception afforded to it in a colonial context are to be adequately understood. In this chapter we examine the history of the Whately Chair at Trinity College, in its wider societal context, from its foundation in 1832 to the turn of the century. A number of aspects of this history will be treated in some detail: a brief historical account of Trinity College within the larger framework of Irish society, the establishment of the Whately Chair and the teaching of political economy from the 1830s to 1900 approximately, and the contribution of the Whately Professors to the emerging science of political economy. We conclude the chapter with an account, albeit brief, of the formative influences on political economy at Trinity College during the course of the nineteenth century.

Despite numerous attempts to establish a university at Dublin during the medieval period, these efforts were not attended by any lasting success. While a university institution was established at St Patrick's Cathedral, which received a measure of support from the crown in 1358, by the end of the fifteenth century it was in effective decay, as was a similar institution established by the Irish Parliament at Drogheda.[2] If such an institution were to be successfully established, a substantial endowment from the government or powerful private patrons would be required.

In the event, and consequent to the act which established the diocesan schools in 1559, government plans for university education quickly followed. Originally it was planned to review the institution attached to St Patrick's, but this encountered considerable opposition from the cathedral chapter. After protracted consultations, and partly as a result of the fact that the corporation of the city of Dublin offered an alternative site to locate the new university, a royal charter for the establishment of the University of Dublin was received in 1592.[3] The charter described it as *mater universitatis*,[4] and this was generally interpreted to mean that a number of constituent colleges within the University of Dublin would be established, along the lines of Oxford and Cambridge. Notwithstanding this interpretation, Trinity College was from the outset invested with the powers of a university. A charter in 1613, which provided it with representation in the Irish Parliament, declared that 'the said college was, and was esteemed, a university, and possessed all and singular the rights, liberties, and immunities pertaining to a university'.[5] Shortly after this instruction from James I to the Lord Deputy, regarding 'the settling of a university as well as of the college near Dublin', reference was made to a scheme 'wherein certain bounds may be set of an university which may contain within them such places as have, or in probability may have, learned men in them'.[6] This scheme was the first of a number of projects for adding new colleges to the University of Dublin, none of which was implemented. As a result the University of Dublin and Trinity College remained a single entity, though in theory a distinction between them could be drawn. This distinction between the university and college was a central consideration during the debate on the Irish university question in the nineteenth century.

Nevertheless the charter as drawn up presented a number of difficulties. In the first place the implications of the designation *mater universitatis* were not clarified within the charter. As interpreted later in the nineteenth century the term was taken to imply that a federal university with a number of collegiate institutions, along the lines of Oxford and Cambridge, was the intended structure for the new university. There were certainly close affinities with the older English universities, as reflected in the fact that the constitution of the new college in Dublin was based on that of Trinity College, Cambridge, and that the first three provosts in Dublin were graduates of Cambridge.[7] While the extension of the University of Dublin into a multi-collegiate institution would have provided Irish students with the same facilities as their counterparts in England, the political instability in Ireland during the course of the troubled seventeenth century, coupled with the lack of material resources, acted as major inhibiting factors to such developments. Atkinson has argued that

> [the] real significance of the foundation at Trinity College is that it was the first colonial university institution, equipped to carry out the functions of both a college and a university, and as such the prototype of Harvard (1639), Yale (1701), Columbia (1734) and other institutions overseas.[8]

Second, the foundation of the college was the direct result of government policy. Writing in 1606, Chichester the Lord Deputy, stated that the crown should make every effort to encourage the Irish upper classes to send their sons there, so that they could be 'brought up at the college near Dublin in English habit and religion'.[9] From the outset, Trinity College was clearly perceived as an instrument to implement an official Anglican policy, a role not required of the comparable institutions in England. Finally, the original charter did not provide an adequate endowment for the new institution. The annuity, amounting to £100 in value, which the Lord Deputy succeeded in extracting from Elizabeth I, proved hopelessly inadequate, and in 1598 the provost was forced to go to England and to plead the cause of the college. The reign of James I proved to be more benign in terms of official endowment; in addition to large grants in the plantation of Ulster, the college received an increased annuity amounting to £388 from the Irish exchequer. But even this proved insufficient, and were it not for the contributions of private benefactors the college would have experienced serious difficulties.[10]

In its early curriculum Trinity reflected a trend towards

intellectual and even social radicalism, but by the end of the seventeenth century it had become the central educational institution of the Anglo-Irish, particularly of the gentleman farmer and Church of Ireland cleric, and the intellectual buttress of the social, religious and political values of this ruling elite.[11] During the course of the eighteenth century, however, a number of initiatives were taken which facilitated the introduction of new areas of learning. In 1724 a chair of natural and experimental philosophy was established; this was followed in 1762 by chairs of mathematics and oriental languages, in 1776 by two royal chairs of modern languages, and in 1785 by chairs of chemistry and botany, while in 1791 a chair of Irish was established. The establishment of these chairs did not ensure the active development of these subjects in all cases, but in comparison with the older English universities the pursuit of contemporary studies and an emphasis on modern authors was pronounced. One commentator writing in 1759 stated that 'the Newtonian Philosophy, the excellent Mr Boyle's philosophy, Mr Locke's metaphysics prevail much in the College of Dublin'.[12]

The formal administrative structure of the University of Dublin consisted of the chancellor, vice-chancellor, and the senate, whose principal function was, and remains, the conferring of degrees. In addition there was the council, a body which represented the board, fellows, professors and the senate. In practice the government of the college and university lay in the hands of the board in association with the visitors. This latter group consisted of the vice-chancellor, and the Archbishop of Dublin, *ex officio*. Under the charter they formed the final court of appeal and were required to conduct visitations every three years. In 1811 annual visitations were established, an arrangement which lasted until 1833, when it was abandoned and the visitors were released from any formal obligations to visit at stated intervals.[13]

The board was the centre of power in the institution, and within it was concentrated all judicial, executive, and legislative functions. It appointed to all academic posts, with the exception of the provostship, which was reserved for the crown. It controlled all the finances of the college and university, and appointed all the major executive officers, the vice-provost, librarian, registrar, senior lecturer, and bursar. As a judicial body it was subordinate only to the visitors as a court of appeal.[14] The position of the Archbishop of Dublin as a visitor was clearly one of prestige and influence, which doubtless greatly facilitated Whately's dealings with the college.

To locate Trinity College within the wider Irish society its place within the religious and educational spheres must be outlined. Trinity College Dublin was founded 'for the education ... of youths ... that they may be the better assisted in the study of the liberal arts and in the cultivation of virtue and religion'.[15] The religion in question was that of the Anglican Church, as established in 1560. A central function of the college was to ensure a supply of well-educated clergy to the service of that church. The provost and fellows had to be Anglicans. In its early years Trinity College does not appear to have insisted on religious tests for admitting students, and a small number of Catholic lay students did attend. In 1627, however, Charles I, under royal authority, appropriated the right to make statutes and imposed an exclusively Anglican character on the college. A series of tests and oaths was introduced which prohibited Catholics and dissenters from attending, a situation which was to prevail until the close of the eighteenth century.[16] It was only with the passing of the Catholic Relief Act of 1793 that Catholics and non-conformists were legally entitled to enter and obtain degrees, though professorships, fellowships and scholarships of the college continued to be confined to members of the established church. What later came to be termed the 'Irish university question', which dominated a large part of the nineteenth-century Irish debates, had its beginnings in the latter end of the eighteenth century. This centred on efforts to acquire higher education, in a form acceptable to them, for Catholic and Presbyterian clergy and laity to whom Trinity College, the only university institution in Ireland, was effectively closed.

Four major parties to this involved and singularly protracted issue can be identified. Firstly, there was the British government, which ruled Ireland directly since the Act of Union in 1801. The growth of Irish nationalism, both revolutionary and constitutional, ensured that Irish issues, including the provision of university education, occupied an increasingly prominent position in the agenda of successive British administrations.[17]

Secondly, there was the Church of Ireland which, until its disestablishment in 1869, was the state church and was also the church of the ruling élite. Even after disestablishment it was closely associated with the landed aristocracy and the professions

21

and continued to occupy the dominant position in Irish society and the state. Trinity College was regarded by Irish churchmen as the intellectual centre of their educational infrastructure and in general they were assiduous in maintaining its Anglican character. While this attitude was modified during the course of the nineteenth century, it was not fundamentally changed.

Thirdly, there were the dissenters, who were mainly Presbyterians, located almost exclusively in Ulster and who maintained cultural links with Scotland. Ulster Presbyterians had played a pivotal role in the later eighteenth century in the struggle for national independence, through the United Irishmen movement. But after the ill-fated rebellion of 1798, which led to the abolition of the Irish Parliament and the consequent Act of Union of Ireland with Great Britain in 1801, the Ulster Presbyterians renounced nationalism. But the majority of Presbyterians did not differ from Anglicans and Catholics in demanding strict denominationalism in education. Consequently their demands for an institutionally independent educational structure constituted a central part of the university education question during this period.

Finally there were the Catholics, who constituted three-quarters of the population. By the end of the eighteenth century they were emerging from seventy-five years of economic, social, and political subjugation. The Catholic Relief Act of 1793 was a critical turning point. Full emancipation was not to be achieved until 1829, as a result of sustained agitation under the leadership of Daniel O'Connell. As the nineteenth century proceeded the Catholic population adopted home rule as their central political objective, and with the extension of parliamentary democracy they became the strongest force in Irish politics. These developments were ultimately to lead to a realignment of the social and political configuration of the country, and their implications for university education were no less profound. In response to the demands of the Catholic majority new institutions were established, such as Maynooth College in the 1790s, to cater for the education of the Catholic clergy, the Queen's Colleges in the 1840s, and the Catholic University in 1854. As a result the pivotal position of Trinity College was challenged by these institutional developments. More significantly the social and economic philosophy of the ruling élite was also increasingly challenged by two major forces, which were to influence crucially the direction of political and social developments during the nineteenth century, Irish nationalism and the Catholic Church. It is against this background that Whately's arrival in Dublin in 1831 and his subsequent activities in Ireland and at Trinity must be viewed.

Very shortly after his arrival in Dublin, and notwithstanding the various problems which faced the established church in Ireland at this time, Whately turned his attention to Trinity College, perceiving as a major defect the absence of any teaching of political economy. He immediately set about rectifying this situation. At a meeting of the board of Trinity College on 31 December 1831 a communication was read which contained a proposal for the establishment of a professorship in political economy which was to be held for a maximum period of five years, with the Archbishop providing a stipend of £100 per annum,[18] a payment which he continued to contribute until his death. Examinations for the position were held on 9 July 1832, and on 31 October of the same year the first Whately Professor of Political Economy, Mountifort Longfield, was appointed.[19]

The regulations governing the Whately Professorship were contained in an entry in the *Calendar* for Dublin University for the following year and read as follows:

1 The Professor to be at least a Master of Arts, or Bachelor in Civil Law, who has *regularly* graduated in the University of Dublin, Oxford, or Cambridge.

2 The Professor, from time to time, to be elected by the Provost and Senior Fellows of Trinity College.

3 No person to hold the office for more than five successive years, or to be re-elected until after the expiration of two years.

4 Every Professor to read in Term during any one of the four Academical Terms in every year, in a place appointed by the Provost, A Course of Lectures on Political Economy, consisting of nine Lectures at the least; and also, during every year, to print and present to the Provost, Senior Fellows, and Visitors, one of such Lectures at the least. The Lectures to be free to all graduates. Under-graduates to be recommended by their tutors. Private courses may be superadded at the discretion of the Professor.

5 Every Professor to give public notice of the time proposed for the commencement of every Course of Lectures.

6 Three persons, at the least, are required to constitute a Class.

7 Every Professor neglecting to give notice or, on the attendance of a Class to read a Course of Lectures during the time and in the manner aforesaid, or to print and publish one Lecture at the least forfeits the whole of his stipend or salary for the year or years in which such neglect takes place; the amount of the forfeiture to be laid out in the Funds, and the interest applied to the augmentation of the Professorship in future.

8 The first Professor not absolutely required to read or publish any Course of Lectures during the first year of his election.[20]

Whately's offer of the establishment of a chair of political economy was initially 'received with a caution that verged on suspicion'.[21] This assessment is borne out by the account given by his daughter Elizabeth Jane Whately:

In the year 1832 Archbishop Whately founded the Professorship of Political Economy which bears his name in the University of Dublin. This was an enterprise attended with considerable difficulty, owing to the general ignorance of the subject in the University. It was hard to prevent those to whom the science was new from imagining that it had something to do with party politics which, in his own words, 'had about as much to do with political economy as they had with manufactures or agriculture'.[22]

Whately's concern with the initial appointments appeared to centre on the need to keep party political considerations from intruding on the competition for the Professorship, and indeed from the content of lectures to be given by the successful candidates. Writing to the provost of Trinity in March, Whately commented:

Allow me to repeat what I said in the former occasion that I do hope political party will be excluded from the competition. We have enough and too much of it in almost all departments of life; but the name of Political Economy is too apt to cause its being confounded with Politics, with which it is no more connected than it is with Farming, Commerce or Alms-giving.[23]

Whately again wrote to the provost on the subject in May: 'The question will I hope serve to indicate to the candidates, what I hope you will take care to impress on them the elementary non-political character of the lectures they will be expected to give'.[24] This concern was again in evidence when Whately wrote to the provost as follows:

I earnestly hope the candidate you may select may in every respect do credit to the College, and most especially may redeem the science from the influence of the vulgar error which confounds it with *Politics* and free all connection with political partizanship.[25]

Some years later, in 1848, addressing the conclusion of the first session of the Dublin Statistical Society, Whately recounted, with some obvious amusement, the reception his offer initially received in Trinity College. There was clearly a fear among the college authorities that no suitable candidate for the chair would be available.[26] The provost of Trinity related to Whately that 'in the absence of any person having a full knowledge of the science, a person should be selected ... who should be of sound and safe conservative views'.[27] The Archbishop declared himself to be 'appalled at the introduction of party politics into a subject of abstract science'.[28] Whately maintained a keen and abiding interest in the appointment of candidates to the chair until his death in office in 1863.

As we noted, when the chair was established graduates of the Universities of Dublin, Oxford, and Cambridge were eligible for appointment. The Queen's Colleges were founded in 1845, in Belfast, Cork, and Galway, and it appears that Whately allowed their graduates to compete. In 1861, for instance, John Monroe, who had graduated from Galway in 1857, winning its Senior Scholarship in Metaphysical and Economic Science in 1858–9, and who was later to become a judge in the High Court of Ireland,[29] was a candidate for the Whately Chair.[30] Longfield, Butt, Hancock, and Cairnes were the examiners, incidentally, and among the other candidates was Leonard Courtney, then Fellow of St John's College, Cambridge, who was favoured by Cairnes.[31] Houston, however, was the successful applicant. There is evidence in an unpublished letter of Cairnes, to his wife Eliza, to suggest that after Whately's death the board of Trinity College attempted to exclude graduates of the Queen's Colleges, a development which greatly angered Cairnes, who then occupied chairs in both Galway and London. The letter, dated 24 April 1866, is long but is worth reproducing at length:

You will I dare say not be sorry to hear that I have been relieved of a rather troublesome job I had undertaken, although the way in which this has happened has been such as greatly to disgust me. I forget whether I told you that Houston wrote to me some time ago announcing the intention of the Board of Trinity College to continue the endowment of the Whately Professorship of Pol. Economy, and asking me to take part in the examination for the new Professor. I at once assented, and entered into arrangements with Houston as to the part I was to take. In the course of our correspondence it turned out, almost accidentally, that the Trinity College Board had decided to exclude from the competition students of the Queen's Colleges, who with those of Oxford and Cambridge were admitted to it by Whately. The moment I discovered this, I wrote a letter in the most indignant terms I could command expressing the pain with which I had heard of the intention to 'degrade the Dublin chair from the liberal footing on which it had been placed by its Founder', and begging that my name should be removed from the list of examiners. Houston has written me in reply, entreating me with a great deal of feeble reasoning to reconsider my determination. Of course I have not done so, and will not do so. The proceeding is simply a piece of paltry donnish spite, such as could only be committed by a close Corporation equally unalive to the interests of Science and to their own real dignity. However, I have written Houston a letter which if he sends it in to the Board, will I think drive them pretty nearly mad, and this is but the beginning of their sorrows. Thompson, who has taken up the matter in a spirit that has greatly pleased me is prepared to write a stinging letter to the *Daily News* denouncing this unworthy proceeding in suitable terms. I have written to James McDonnell begging him to bring the affair under Judge Longfield's notice, and I am in hopes that the Judge may also withdraw from the examination, though this is doubtful. Sh^d this happen, the examining staff will be reduced to Butt, and Houston, whose *imprimatur* will not give much *prestige* to the chair. The upshot of all this is that for the present I am relieved from the examination, which I know my pettins will rejoice at – naughty pettins not to have more public spirit.[32]

For whatever reason, it seems unlikely that the board of Trinity College persisted with its new policy, for both Robert Cather Donnell, who occupied the chair from 1872–7, and James Johnston Shaw, his immediate successor (1877–82), were educated at Queen's College Belfast. As noted above, and in keeping with his objective of providing for the dissemination of political economy at all levels of the educational system, on his arrival in Dublin Whately quickly turned his attention to Trinity. He was not the first to make the observation that political economy was a regrettable omission from the Trinity curriculum. The significance of political economy as a distinct discipline and the desirability of its introduction into the curriculum at Trinity College Dublin had been a recurring theme during the eighteenth century. One of the earliest recommendations for the inclusion of political economy or 'trade', as it was then called, appeared in Thomas Prior's pamphlet published in Dublin in 1729 entitled *A List of the Absentees of Ireland* where he argued that the study of trade should be facilitated by the foundation of a chair at Trinity College. A similar recommendation was made by Samuel Madden in his *Memoirs* published in 1733.

These recommendations were not pursued, and towards the end of the eighteenth century the Revd Robert Burrowes, a fellow of the college, again advocated the introduction of political economy. This he did in a pamphlet published in Dublin in 1792 entitled, *Observations on the Course of Science Taught at Present in Trinity College, Dublin, with Some Improvements Suggested Therein.* Burrowes cited Adam Smith's condemnation of 'the course of Education established in most Universities as teaching a species of Learning which has been long exploded by the World', while later scientific discoveries were neglected. Chemistry was one science and 'that Science the object of which

27

is the Wealth of Nations' was the other which were 'in such general repute, that no person can form any pretensions to a Literary Character, or hold almost any communication with the World, without being acquainted with their fundamental principles'. Yet, he added, 'these and other branches of Knowledge of no less importance make at present no part of our Course'. Burrowes suggested that political economy be incorporated as part of ethics, and his proposed curriculum combined an historically based study, in the Scottish manner, 'of the progress of civil Society from the simplicity and rudeness of the earliest time to the refinements of modern cultivation', along with more conventional topics in political economy. Interestingly, his suggested authors were, without exception, Scottish: Robertson, Ferguson, Miller, Steward, and Adam Smith.[33]

Notwithstanding these repeated recommendations for the inclusion of political economy in Trinity's course of studies, the establishment of the first chair in the subject had to await Whately's arrival. In this Whately was greatly facilitated in that his arrival in Dublin coincided with the appointment of Bartholomew Lloyd as provost in 1831. Lloyd is regarded as one of the great reforming provosts in the college's history. Concerning the period between 1794 and 1831, which is viewed as a critical turning point in the history of Trinity College, McDowell and Webb have written:

> For a generation academic society went, as it were, to ground, and lived in a limbo that was characteristic of neither century. Only in 1831, when Bartholomew Lloyd became Provost and inaugurated a series of important and far-sighted reforms, did there emerge clearly in the College that attitude towards scholarship and education which was to characterise the nineteenth century.[34]

The structure of teaching of political economy in Trinity was governed by the regulations, referred to in the previous section, laid down by Whately and modelled on the Drummond Professorship of Political Economy at Oxford. These were a carefully structured set of minimal conditions within which the holder of the chair was to discharge his duties. Commenting on these regulations, one of the earliest holders of the chair, Isaac Butt, complained that, 'the regulations under which this Professorship is placed make it impossible for the person holding it to attempt anything like a regular course of instruction in Political Economy'.[35] R.D. Collison Black, reacting to Butt's comment, accepted this state of affairs as 'almost inevitable' given 'the state of economic knowledge and opinion then prevailing in Ireland', along with

> the general and almost 'popular' character of the instruction given, together with the fact that the short term of office at first attracted young graduates who usually had law rather than political economy in view for a permanent career, prevented the appearance of any strong teaching tradition.[36]

Lloyd's appointment as provost marked 'the beginning of a series of important reforms which affected nearly all aspects of the College's educational activities'.[37] These reforms included: the restructuring of terms and vacation into something resembling their modern form, the introduction of a tutorial system, the establishment of two new chairs (one of which was the Whately Chair), the introduction of the distinction between pass and honours courses, and the setting up of moderatorships. (The title 'moderator', which is unique to Dublin University, is applied to a successful candidate at the BA honours examinations, and the term 'moderatorship' refers to an honours degree programme.) The latter reforms are clearly of interest since they provided the overall structure for the teaching of political economy for the remainder of the century. These reforms were negotiated at board level during the course of 1833 and came into effect in Michaelmas term in 1834. The introduction of the pass–honours distinction resulted in a considerable reduction in the number of prescribed textbooks for those taking pass courses. In contrast, for those taking honours, the changes led to a more comprehensive and advanced course being devised for them in every term of the four-year degree course. The philosophy underlying these changes was relatively straightforward. Pass candidates were to pursue a more restricted and less advanced course than heretofore, but would be expected to have assimilated it thoroughly. Honours candidates, in contrast, would pursue a more comprehensive course than previously prescribed, but a less detailed knowledge would be required.[38] These changes would be reflected, in due course, in the structure of the curriculum for political economy. In addition, the honours courses would become the vehicles for introducing new subject areas into the degree courses. The successful candidates at the final degree examinations, having pursued honours courses, would henceforth be termed moderators, and specialisation within degree courses would, in future, be pursued through the creation of separate moderatorships in individual, or in different groups of individual subject areas. At the time of Lloyd's reform in 1834, three moderatorships were introduced, and over the next fifty years more were added which included political economy as an integral part. We will trace chronologically the principal developments in the teaching of political economy in the period 1832 to 1900, by reference to its position within the overall degree structure, its course contents, where available, and particularly the reading material prescribed by the various holders of the Whately Chair for the different courses in political economy.

As early as 1837, five years after the establishment of the chair, the provost and senior fellows instituted a prize in political economy which was to be awarded on the basis of an annual examination and confined to students in the bachelor classes. The calendar entries concerning the requirements for this prize provide valuable evidence of the reading material which formed the basis for the examinations as prescribed by the earliest holders of this chair. The recommended reading for the prize examinations in 1839, for instance, included Smith's *Wealth of Nations*, Longfield's *Lectures*, Whately's *Lectures* and Senior's *Lectures*.[39] The then Professor, Isaac Butt, also recommended additional works which could be consulted 'with advantage', including works of Say and Ricardo, along with Huskisson's pamphlet concerning the question of currency and the balance of trade. Particularly recommended was Longfield's theory of profit and, not too surprisingly perhaps, the lecture *Rent, Profits, and Labour,* 'published by the present Professor'.[40]

The entry by Professor James Anthony Lawson, the third holder of the Whately Chair, for the same examination in 1842, was somewhat more cautious with respect to individual authors included in the reading list, with Ricardo coming in for particular attention. It stated:

The Professor recommends to Candidates, as works from which the fundamental truths of the science may be correctly and readily gathered, the article 'Political Economy', in the Encyclopaedia Metropolitana; and Longfield's Lectures on

'Political Economy'; and those on 'Commerce and Absenteeism', and Archbishop Whately's Lectures. After these the great work of Adam Smith can be read with more advantage, and, taking care to make such corrections as an acquaintance with the above works will show to be necessary, the Treatise of Mr. Ricardo, M'Culloch's note to Adam Smith, and Chalmer's 'Political Economy' may be then consulted.[41]

Lawson also initiated changes in the structure of the examination in political economy. In addition to an examination in the general principles of the subject, Lawson selected a specific topic each year which would 'constitute a great part of [the candidate's] Examination, and with which it is necessary that the candidates should make themselves especially well acquainted'.[42] This development does not appear to have been maintained by his successor in the chair, but was reintroduced by Professor C.F. Bastable in the 1880s.

In 1847 Professor W.N. Hancock added considerably to the basic course of instruction in political economy by providing two additional private courses of lectures, one for candidates for the prize in political economy, the other for students commencing the study of the science.[43] In the same year J.S. Mill made his first appearance on a reading list, with his *Essays on Some Unsettled Questions of Political Economy*. That year – known in Ireland as 'Black '47', the culmination of the Great Famine – is of immense significance in Irish economic and social history, so it is not surprising to find a number of works on poor laws and the conditions of the labouring classes, along with the *Reports of the Commissioners Inquiring into the Operation of Poor Laws in England* (1834) being included on Hancock's reading lists. Two years later, in 1849, the first European material, in the form of M.P. Rossi's *Cours d'Economie Politique*, was introduced into the reading list. Porter's translation of Bastiat's *Sophismes Economiques* appeared the following year.

During the course of the early 1850s developments in a somewhat distant area of learning within Trinity College led to political economy being included in a new moderatorship. These developments resulted from the appointment of Richard McDonnell as provost in 1852. This left vacant the chair of oratory, which was filled by John Kells Ingram, a man of some significance for Irish political economy, though never occupying a chair in that subject. Ingram extended, with the approval of the board, the scope of the chair of oratory to include English literature, and he was thereafter termed the Professor of Oratory and English Literature. Ingram's lectures were to form the basis for a new moderatorship, but English literature alone was considered too 'soft' an option for a degree course, so the course was 'hardened' by the inclusion of modern history, jurisprudence, and political economy. The political economy course was moved from its location within the ethics and logic course where, according to McDowell and Webb, it would have been placed as a result of Whately's influence.[44] The same authors are of the opinion that the 'prescribed reading' in these various subjects within the moderatorship was not very adventurous: Smith, Mill, and Senior in economics, in jurisprudence selections from Blackstone and Smith on contracts, the history of England and France up to 1789, English literature from Shakespeare and Bacon to Johnson and Goldsmith, with some simple philology. But, nevertheless, they add the comment that with 'Ingram, Anster and Cairnes as lecturers the course must have been quite a stimulating one'.[45]

By 1857, twenty-five years after the founding of the chair, and a year after J.E. Cairnes had succeeded to it, the required reading list was as follows:

Introductory work
    Easy Lessons on Money Matters
    Whately's Lectures on Political Economy
    Professor Hancock's Introductory Lecture

Works on the general principles of the science
    Mr Senior's Treatise on Political Economy, from the Encyclopaedia Metropolitana.
    Dr Lawson's Five Lectures on Political Economy omitting Appendix.
    Dr Longfield's Lectures on Political Economy.
    Adam Smith's *Wealth of Nations*, Book I (omitting Chapter XI to the end, inclusive), Book II, Book IV.
    Mr John Stuart Mill's *Principles of Political Economy*, Book I (omitting Chaps. i, ii, and iii); Book II (omitting Chaps. xviii and xxi); Book V. Essay No. 2, of the essays of the same author.

Ricardo's *Principles of Political Economy*, chaps. vii,viii, xx, xxi, xxv, xxviii.
Labour and Capital, by C. Morrisson

Works on banking and currency
Professor Hussey Walsh's Elementary Treatise on Metallic Currency
Tooke's *History of Prices*, Vol. IV, Chap. i, part 3.
Articles on Banking and Banks, and the Funds in M'Culloch's *Commercial Dictionary*. (To be read in one of the late editions.)[46]

While the above was the material on which examinations in political economy would be based, the structure of the degree programme for undergraduates was contained within a four-year degree course, divided into junior freshman, senior freshman, junior sophister, and senior sophister years respectively. The undergraduate courses for each examination were divided into two parts: one which was read by all students and did not include any courses in political economy (these were presumably the pass courses); the other was read by those aspiring to honours. For the honours course, political economy was combined with history in a separate section, and was taught in Michaelmas term in both junior and senior sophister years. The basic requisite reading for these honours courses was Senior's *Treatise on Political Economy* and Mill's *Political Economy*, Book III along with the first six chapters of Book V.[47] By 1864 a number of changes, worth noting, occurred in the reading material for the prize examinations: Ricardo's works were deleted, and Cairnes's *Character and Logical Method of Political Economy* appeared on the reading lists for the first time. This latter text was to remain on the reading lists in Trinity College for the remainder of the century.

The 1870s saw a number of developments in the subject matter of political economy in Trinity College. Early in the decade, in 1871, a Whately Memorial Prize in Political Economy was established, which was financed from the earnings of the residual funds accumulated for the erection of a bust to Archbishop Whately in St Patrick's Cathedral, Dublin. This prize was to be awarded every five years.[48] The first winner of this prize was a John Dockrill in 1872.[49] More significant, from the point of view of the teaching of political economy, was the fact that in 1873 the moderatorship in English literature, history, jurisprudence and political economy, which had been initiated by Ingram was abandoned[50] and political economy was relocated in a different moderatorship with history and political science. The reading material was extended and included the works of Smith, J.S. Mill, W.T. Thornton, W.N. Hancock, T.E. Cliffe Leslie, J.E. Cairnes, F. Harrison, and G.J. Goschen (this was his first appearance on a reading list). In 1874 additional material was appended to the required reading list for the prize examinations by Robert Cather Donnell, who acceded to the chair in 1872. These included Fawcett's *Manual of Political Economy*, R.H. Mills's *Lectures on Currency and Banking*, A. Houston's *Principles of Value*, and a translation by Cobden of M. Chevalier's *On Depreciation of Gold*.[51] By 1876 Donnell had further extended the reading material for both the political economy section in the moderatorship and for the prize examinations, to include additional material by Cairnes, specifically his articles 'Political economy and land' and 'Political economy and laissez-faire', *Essays in Political Economy* and *Some Leading Principles of Political Economy Newly Expounded*. The list also included Hancock's *Local Government and Taxation in Ireland*, Broderick's *Local Government and Taxation in England*, R.B.D. Morier's *Local Government and Taxation in Germany*, and De Laveleye's *Le Marche Monétaire et ses Crises*.[52] Shortly after this Bagehot's *Lombard Street* and the *Cobden Club Essays* (second series) were added.

Towards the close of the decade, in 1877, Trinity College was added, by the Secretary of State for India, to the list of institutions in which selected candidates for the civil service of India would be permitted to reside.[53] As part of the course for a writership in the civil service of India, preparation for which extended over a two-year period, political economy was included among five nominated subjects for the second year of study. The political economy course included the following works: Smith's *Wealth of Nations*, Mill's *Principles of Political Economy*, Ricardo's *Political Economy*, Northcote's *Twenty Years of Financial Policy*, and Goschen's *Foreign Exchanges*.

When C.F. Bastable succeeded to the Whately Chair in 1882, he broke with precedent by negotiating a life tenure and occupied the position for the next fifty years until 1932. He too introduced a number of changes into the courses in political economy. The required reading for his honours course in the senior sophister year was dominated by Mill's *Principles of Political Economy*, but Marshall made his first appearance on the course, represented by his *Economics of Industry*,[54] while in the moderatorship new works such as L. Cossa's *Guide to the Study of Political Economy*, and F.A. Walker's *Money and Its Relations to Trade and Industry* were introduced.[55] The structure of the prize examinations was also altered. The course of this examination was now divided into two parts, one general, the other based on a special topic which could vary from year to year. The special topic for 1884, the first year of its operation, was 'Crises and Periods of Depression'. The authors included for study for the reorganised prize examinations were: Walker, Jevons (this was his first appearance on a reading list), Bagehot, Goschen, Mill, and Cairnes.[56]

By 1890 Mill's *Principles* had been replaced by Walker's *Political Economy* in the honours course reading for senior sophisters,[57] and for the moderatorship examinations the following additions to the reading material had been included: Ingram's *History of Political Economy*, Toynbee's *Industrial Revolution*, and Bastable's own *International Trade*.[58] By 1900 Marshall's *Principles* was widely used, particularly in the honours course for senior sophisters, and the political economy component of the moderatorship which was now retitled 'Economics and Economic History', reflecting the contracting scope of the subject and the emergence of economic history as a specialisation. The course for the moderatorship consisted, at the turn of the century, of 'a knowledge of (a) Economic Theory and the History of the Chief doctrines; (b) the existing Economic conditions in the United Kingdom; (c) English Economic History'.[59] The reading material included, in addition to the works of Smith, Mill, and Marshall, Nicholson's *Money*, Clare's *Money Market Primer*, Rae's *Contemporary Socialism*, and Ashley's *English Economic History*.[60] By this stage also a third prize, the Cobden Prize, was being awarded every third year to the successful candidate in political economy.

A number of more general observations can be made on the teaching of political economy by the various holders of the Whately Chair in the nineteenth century. The development was mainly to be seen in the continued elaboration and refinement of the course structures in political economy (particularly in the honours courses), in the creation of a number of moderatorships which included political economy as an integral component, and in the institution of a number of competitive prizes in political economy. Certainly by 1857, twenty five years after the establishment of the chair, Isaac Butt's comments were no longer valid. The structure and contents of the different political economy courses were well established and the foundations of a solid teaching tradition were well in place. Unfortunately the Trinity College records do not provide information on the numbers of students taking political economy, and consequently comparisons with other university institutions within Ireland or elsewhere are not feasible. In addition to its ordinary teaching, special courses were offered for particular purposes from the 1870s onwards, such as the Indian civil service examinations. Secondly, a number of observations may be made with reference to the required reading for the various courses. There was a small number of authors whose works dominated for long periods, constituting, as it were, a 'hard core' of essential material. These included Smith, Mill, Senior, and Whately himself, certainly during his lifetime. Ricardo, interestingly, received a much more mixed reception at the hands of the Whately Professors. In addition there was an impressive showing by Irish authors, many of them Whately Professors, such as Longfield, Cairnes, and later Bastable, and to a lesser extent, Hancock and Hussey Walsh. At best this practice attested to the quality of Irish economic writing, while at worst it was little more than a bit of harmless mutual back-scratching among academic and legal colleagues and leading members of the Irish intelligentsia. However, the status and significance of Longfield's and Cairnes's work within the history of economic thought scarcely makes it necessary to defend their presence on university reading lists in Trinity or anywhere else. The presence of works by continental authors, either in their original language or in translation, remained minimal during the course of the nineteenth century. The virtual absence of untranslated works may be explicable largely on linguistic grounds. Finally there was, in most cases, perceptible changes in course structure and content corresponding with the interests, priorities, and indeed abilities of the various holders of the chair. Whately's regulation had the effect, as noted by Black, 'of bringing a succession of fresh minds in contact with the subject and, still more important, of ensuring the publication of their views',[61] and this result was clearly 'foreseen, no doubt, by

Whately'.[62] It must be noted, however, that some of the holders brought fresher and more formidable minds than others to the chair, something which is already perceptible in their different contributions to the development of the teaching programme, but which will become even more pronounced in the quality and status of their published work, which we now briefly examine.

Professor J.K. Galbraith recently declared that 'all races have produced notable economists with the exception of the Irish who can doubtless protest their devotion to higher arts'.[63] This apparently safe generalisation scarcely does justice to some of the estimable men who occupied the Whately Chair at Trinity College Dublin. Galbraith contrived to overlook the fact that since the earlier part of this century, beginning with the work of Seligman in 1903,[64] the holders of the Whately Chair have been recognised by historians of economic thought as constituting an important group of political economists who contributed very significantly to a number of areas of economic theory.[65] Indeed they were later raised to the status of constituting a 'school of thought'.[66] The principal topic around which the 'Dublin School' centred was undoubtedly their formulation of and commitment to a subjective theory of value thirty-five years before its more formal articulation in the hands of Jevons and Menger. However, as Black observes, 'it must be admitted at the outset ... that this claim involves some misuse of the word 'school', which normally connotes a body of disciples of one teacher or a group having a connected system of doctrine in common.[67] Nevertheless that there was a large degree of unanimity and intellectual unity among the first holders of the Whately Chair is not in question. 'What is remarkable', Black notes, is that the 'principles of the Dublin Professors should so steadily have run counter to the trend of received opinion, for from the first labour or cost-or-production theories of value are either refuted or given a very subordinate place by them',[68] and this in a period when the labour or costs-of-production theories of value held the dominant doctrinal position.

Whately himself was hostile to the labour theory of value and advocated the utility approach in the manner of his friend and predecessor at Oxford, Nassau Senior.[69] Whately's own contributions on this topic were rather limited and amounted to no more than a few brief, but interesting comments. Nevertheless, the received view of Whately's personal influence on the selection process of candidates for the chair would account at least for the general 'direction of study' pursued by the early holders of the chair on the topic of value theory. The most significant contribution to the formulation of the subjective theory of value was undoubtedly that of the first holder of the chair, Mountifort Longfield, who must be considered the effective founder of the Dublin School.[70] His was the most complete offering on the subject, and it was contained in his *Lectures on Political Economy, Delivered in Trinity and Michaelmas Terms, 1833*, published in Dublin in 1834. The originality of Longfield's contribution, however, did not secure him a place among the leading theorists of his day. He remained, certainly outside Ireland, firmly ensconced in Seligman's unenviable category of 'neglected economists' of the nineteenth century. Seligman, in fact, referred to him as 'in some respects the most remarkable of all' the writers he had 'discovered'.[71]

Longfield's successors continued to expound and develop the utility or subjective approach to the theory of value. This was certainly true of Isaac Butt, his immediate successor. James Anthony Lawson, who succeeded Butt in 1841, was a firm adherent of the subjective theory and provided, in an Appendix to his *Five Lectures on Political Economy*, published in 1844, a particularly lucid treatment of the subject. William Neilson Hancock, who succeeded Lawson in 1846, provided what has been described as 'one of the most interesting discussions of value theory given by any member of this group of Dublin economists'.[72] The originality of Hancock's contribution is all the more striking considering that he was primarily interested in practical issues, an orientation generally held to be inimical to the production of economic theory. The significance of Hancock's contribution lay in the fact that, in addition to providing considerable clarification of a number of aspects of the subjective theory of value as bequeathed by Longfield, he suggested how distribution theory could be viewed as part of a more generalised theory of pricing, a development which was later to become an integral part of the theoretical core of neoclassical economics in the Walrasian tradition.

Hancock resigned from the Whately Chair in 1851. His successor Richard Hussey Walsh does not appear to fit as comfortably into the tradition of commitment to and continued elaboration of the utility theory of value that characterised the previous four holders of the chair. While there is no compelling evidence to suggest that Walsh was not an intellectual adherent of the Whately–Longfield tradition with respect to value theory, his support was more implicit in form, and consequently its interpretation is more problematic. Ambiguity, however, was never a feature of the thought of Walsh's successor, John Elliot Cairnes, in relation to the subjective approach to the theory of value. Cairnes was never a supporter of this approach, adhering firmly to a cost-of-production theory, and never conceding on this question to either 'his predecessors in Ireland or his successors in England'. We too may ask the intriguing question, posed by Black, whether and how Cairnes reconciled his theories with those in Longfield's *Lectures*, which were prescribed reading for the students he examined.[73] The final representative of the Dublin School was Arthur Houston, who succeeded Cairnes to the chair in 1861. He was faced with the task of synthesising the conflicting doctrines on value then prevailing in Trinity College. In his efforts to achieve such a synthesis Houston displayed considerable analytical ability and developed a number of interesting concepts, some of which have become very familiar, albeit in somewhat different garb, to modern students of economics. When Houston resigned in 1866, the 'marginalist revolution', with its subjective value theory, was a mere six years away. The Dublin School's contribution, even if unacknowledged at the time, must be considered one of, if not the most impressive precursors of that 'revolution' in terms of its coherence and sustained elaboration at the hands of the first generation of Whately Professors.

In addition to their strikingly original contributions to the utility approach to the theory of value, the Whately Professors made distinguished and original contributions to a number of areas of political economy. According to Black 'it may reasonably be claimed that in the past century the economists of Trinity College have been responsible for original contributions to almost every branch of their subject'.[74] While this assessment may err on the generous side, the Dublin economists differed in a number of areas from their contemporaries and anticipated in several instances later developments which were to become integral parts of accepted theoretical orthodoxy. One of these areas, which was closely related to developments in the theory of value, was distribution theory and, as we have seen already, Hancock made several important suggestions as to their conceptual integration. Given the commitment of the early Whately Professors to a utility-based theory of value, with its emphasis on demand, it is not too surprising to find that their distribution theory should be also based on a demand approach, with productivity and scarcity being introduced to explain factor prices. Important contributions in the development of this theoretical approach are to be found in the works of Longfield and Butt. In particular, their contributions to the theory of wages and profits bear striking similarities to the work of the leading European theorists, such as von Thünen and the later Austrian School. It should be noted here that Cairnes was not involved in these developments in the Dublin School, remaining a staunch adherent of the Ricardian analysis. With respect to the theory of rent, the Dublin economists remained, on the whole, within the Ricardian tradition, but they contributed important modifications to this theoretical structure, particularly Longfield and Butt. On this topic Whately himself had, according to Bowley 'the most admirable ideas on rent as the consequence of immobilities of certain factors or groups of factors'.[75] Arguably, even if the Dublin School had never contributed to the subjective theory of value, their contributions to distribution theory should, other things being equal, have earned them a secure place in the history of economic thought, although it is difficult to conceive of their particular input into distribution theory divorced from the theory of value.

Whately Professors also contributed very significantly to the theory of international trade. Longfield, Butt, and Cairnes, and particularly Bastable published important works in this area. Longfield's contribution to this topic deserves the distinction 'of having given the first statement of several points which are now an accepted part of international trade theory'.[76] These included, among others, contributions by Longfield to such topics as the causes of international specialisation, the role of demand in international trade, and the analysis of trade in more than two commodities. Isaac Butt's contribution concerned his advocacy of protection and its effects, and in the course of this analysis contributed an astute and perceptive assessment of the relative strength and limitations of the prevailing classical analysis of this topic. Cliffe Leslie later singled out Butt's unique concern with protection when he wrote, 'in the United Kingdom only a single professor of the science – the late Isaac Butt, who for a time held the chair of Political Economy in the University of Dublin – has shown any leaning towards protection'.[77] In contrast, Cairnes was a firm advocate of the classical orthodoxy in international trade. His principal contributions, in addition to an impressive systematisation of the classical doctrine on trade, included the application of the concept of non-competing groups to the problems of international trade, a seminal contribution to the analysis of the mechanism of international lending and the influence of loans on international trade, along with an examination of the effect of gold discoveries on prices and trade.

Perhaps the most distinguished contributions to international trade theory by a Whately Professor was that of C.F. Bastable. Bastable's contribution to this area of economics can be viewed as an elaboration and development of the classical school of nineteenth-century economics. More specifically, his contributions represented a series of major theoretical extensions to the existing Ricardo–Mill theory of trade, through the introduction of a number of important qualifications. These included, firstly, allowing for varying elasticities of demand in the determination of international values. Secondly, where Ricardo and Mill had assumed constant returns to scale in production for their analysis, Bastable introduced increasing and decreasing returns to scale, thereby greatly extending the scope of the theoretical framework. Thirdly, he provided a more elaborate analysis of the hindrances to competition and other obstacles to free trade than had been supplied by Mill. In addition, Bastable also made a number of improvements and corrections to Mill's analysis of the international payments system, particularly where the source of these payments did not originate in commerce.[78] Just as Cairnes's name is invariably linked with the concept of 'non-competing groups', so too is Bastable honoured in the form of the 'Mill–Bastable condition', which has become an integral part of the analysis of protection. No less an authority than F.Y. Edgeworth, the distinguished Irish economist and holder of the Drummond Professorship of Political Economy at Oxford, and a leading theorist in mathematical economics, had to concede to the correctness of Bastable's analysis concerning the impact of import and export taxes.[79] Edgeworth held Bastable's work in international trade theory in the very highest regard. He considered Bastable's *Theory of International Trade* as 'the best manual on the most difficult part of Economics'.[80]

An aspect of economics which was not of major concern to the early Whately Professors, but which later in the century emerged as an important area of study, was public finance. In this field Bastable produced a number of outstanding works, particularly his *Public Finance*, first published in 1892. Professor G.A. Duncan, who succeeded Bastable in the Whately Chair in 1932, has argued that Bastable's principal intellectual interest was not trade theory but public finance, 'a field in which, for the British Isles, he was a pioneer, and laid the foundations of a systematic study'.[81] This systematic study was contained in *Public Finance*, which Duncan described as 'the best text-book in English for its organisation, synoptic treatment, and sense of proportion'.[82] Other commentators on this work were no less laudatory. Edgeworth, referring to a later edition of the work, described it as 'this now classical work'.[83] Henry Higgs referred to it as 'a work of assured position, which seemed destined to be revived again and again',[84] while L.L. Price, writing in the *Economic Journal*, described it as 'a book which, we venture to think, will take its place among the permanent, as distinguished from the merely ephemeral, products of British economic inquiry'.[85] Clearly Bastable's contribution to both the areas of international trade theory and public finance were substantial and were judged to be so by both contemporaries and successors.

A distinguishing characteristic of the early Whately Professors, apart from Cairnes, was their abiding commitment to an inductivist methodology in political economy. This was true of Longfield's approach to the subject, while his successor Isaac Butt generated a vibrant scepticism with respect to the generality of economic principles, in contrast to the view of many of his contemporaries.[86] The same commitment to an inductive approach is clearly evident in Lawson's *Five Lectures on Political Economy* of 1843. Lawson was critical of Senior's efforts to reduce political economy to an axiomatic basis consisting of four general propositions. Lawson stressed the need for attending to facts with the utmost care and attention, and only then subjecting them to careful theoretical interpretation. The early Whately Professors did not, individually or as a group, call into question the validity of the deductive method in political economy. The 'Ricardian vice' had taken too firm a methodological hold on political economy for that to occur. Their methodological position was that empirically-observed facts should provide the basis for deductive reasoning in political economy, a position which was later in the century given a methodological *imprimatur* in J.N. Keynes's *The Scope and Method of Political Economy* of 1891. The exception among the Whately Professors to an inductivist position was, of course, Cairnes, who produced the most rigorous exposition of the deductive method in political economy written in the nineteenth century. This was Cairnes's *The Character and Logical Method of Political Economy* of 1857, which was based on a course of lectures originally delivered in Trinity College Dublin.[87] This work remained for a uniquely long period the most authoritative statement on methodology in political economy.

The methodological bias towards the inductive approach of the Whately Professors had, arguably, two important consequences for political economy in Ireland. The first was their propensity to conduct investigations in applied or practical areas of economics. This is reflected in the work of several Whately Professors, most notably that of Longfield, Hancock, and Houston; while Donnell concentrated practically all his efforts on applied issues. This, it has been suggested, may have been due to factors other than their methodological position, not least being the economic and social circumstances of nineteenth-century Ireland, which made such studies an obvious, even a compelling duty for professors of political economy to undertake. In addition, the fact that all of the Whately Professors were lawyers by training, and most of them by profession, provided the requisite educational background to address the most pressing issue of the period, the Irish land question, which clearly had both legal and economic dimensions.[88] A second consequence was the extent to which the commitment of the early Whately Professors to an inductive approach influenced colleagues and graduates in Trinity. Two distinguished Trinity graduates in particular must be mentioned, Cliffe Leslie and Ingram. Both were major figures in the English-speaking world as pioneers of the historical school of political economy. They were major critics of the classical method of deduction and stressed the absolute necessity of an inductive approach to the study of economic issues, which in their view could never be separated from the larger social matrix of relations.

3

POLITICAL ECONOMY AT THE QUEEN'S COLLEGES IN IRELAND

(Belfast, Cork, Galway), 1845–1900

After the establishment of the Whately Chair in 1832 at Trinity College Dublin, the most important contribution to the teaching of political economy in Ireland was the foundation of the Queen's Colleges in 1845. Each of the three colleges, at Belfast, Cork, and Galway, had from the outset a chair of Jurisprudence and Political Economy. The founding of the colleges was followed five years later by the establishment of their degree-granting institution, the Queen's University. The decision to establish the Queen's Colleges at this time was not an isolated event. It was in fact an integral part of a new policy of conciliation, implemented by Peel in 1843, to counteract Daniel O'Connell's campaign for repeal of the union between Great Britain and Ireland. The problem which Peel sought to solve by the establishment of the Queen's Colleges, the inadequate provision of higher education in Ireland, had a long history and involved not only questions of education but also of religion, politics, and economics. It was a source of profound periodic disturbance in Irish public debate as it was in Anglo-Irish relations throughout the nineteenth century. To understand the particular circumstances surrounding the establishment of the Queen's Colleges and their subsequent development warrants an examination, albeit brief, of the troubled and protracted history of university education in Ireland.

The university question in Ireland emerged in the last quarter of the eighteenth century. At this time the only university institution in Ireland was the University of Dublin, centred on its single constituent college, Trinity College, which had been established 'for the education ... of youths... that they may be better assisted in the study of the liberal arts and in the cultivation of virtue and

44

religion'.[1] The role of Trinity College was to provide a supply of clergy to the established church. Its members comprised the bulk of the landed aristocracy and the professions, and they were unquestionably dominant socially and politically throughout the nineteenth century. Trinity College was overwhelmingly Anglican and its provost and fellows had to be of that faith. In addition, with the accession of Charles I, students were required to attend Anglican services and all candidates aspiring to degrees had to take the Oath of Supremacy, along with a number of other anti-Catholic declarations. Admission to the college was never formally denied to either Catholics or Protestant dissenters, but they were, in effect, legally excluded. During the course of the 1780s, public debate in Ireland about the university question centred on a number of possible solutions which were put forward for consideration. These included: the 'opening' of Trinity College to Catholics and Protestant dissenters, by the abolition of religious tests; the establishment of a new college or colleges within the University of Dublin; and the foundation of new university institutions independent of the existing university. In the event, nothing was to emerge from the deliberations of the 1780s. However, in the following decade, under the impetus of external events, a number of important developments were to take place.

The external events included the French Revolution and the ensuing war between Great Britain and the new revolutionary regime. One of the results of the French Revolution was the closing down of the Irish Colleges in France and Flanders, which had been the principal locations for the education of the Irish Catholic clergy. With the closure of these colleges the Irish bishops regarded the continued education of Irish clerical students on the Continent with grave apprehension; they feared students would be exposed to the prevailing revolutionary ideas. The government was equally anxious to inhibit the importation of revolutionary notions into Ireland, so a number of major concessions were made to Catholics. The first was contained in a section of the Catholic Relief Act of 1793, which, along with the letters patent granted to Trinity College the following year, permitted Catholics legally to enter and graduate from Dublin University. They were not entitled, however, to enter for fellowships, professorships, scholarships, or prizes, which greatly devalued the concession since few Catholic students were able to finance their way through the degree course.[2]

While acknowledging the concession of 'opening' Trinity College to Catholic laymen, the Catholic hierarchy did not view it as a solution to the problem of educating the Catholic clergy. They pressed for the establishment of a special seminary which would be, for all practical purposes, under their exclusive control. The government, for their own strategic reasons based primarily on their desire to secure the services of the Catholic clergy in maintaining the established order, granted permission for the foundation of a college at Maynooth, to be supported by an annual grant from Parliament.[3] Parliament imposed no restrictions on the admission of students, other than that they should be Catholics, but the bishops did not favour the admission of lay students, even though, for a short period between 1810 and 1817, a lay college was maintained in addition to the seminary. Maynooth became, within a short time, one of the most powerful national institutions in Ireland.

The Protestant dissenters, who were mainly Presbyterian, comprised of middle-class tenant farmers, businessmen, industrialists, and shop-keepers concentrated geographically in Ulster, were now motivated, as a result of the establishment of Maynooth College, to demand a similar arrangement for the education of their clergy. Traditionally, the Ulster Presbyterians had maintained strong cultural links with Scotland, and many of their clergy were educated there. Politically, however, they were out of favour with the government of the day as a result of their espousal of radical and republican principles and hence continued demands for a second university in Ulster fell on unresponsive ears. A plan for a more broadly-based university in Ulster, which was to be accessible to all Protestant denominations, including Anglicans and dissenters, and financed by a sum of £5,000 bequeathed by Lord Rokeby, a former primate, was unequivocally rejected by Parliament in London in 1799. This, in effect, marked the end of an important decade in the history of Irish university education, for the problem would not receive any further serious attention, at Westminister at least, until the 1840s.[4]

The intervening period, from the close of the eighteenth century to the 1840s, was not marked by lack of activity with respect to higher education in Ireland, north or south. In Ulster, the Presbyterians, whose demands had been firmly rejected by Parliament, proceeded to establish, in 1810, a college in Belfast which went a considerable distance in satisfying their educational needs, the Belfast Academical Institution. This resulted from the combined efforts of the local commercial and industrial interests who were anxious to provide, in Belfast, the focal point of Ulster and Irish Presbyterianism, a centre of education at school and university level for both their clergy and laity. The structure of the new Institution reflected these concerns, and contained schools of English, French, mathematics, classics, writing and drawing, as well as a faculty of arts, with professorships in logic, mathematics, classics, *belles-lettres*, natural philosophy, moral philosophy, Irish, Hebrew and oriental languages, and divinity, and a medical faculty which was established later, in 1835.[5] The Institution was, in effect, totally free from religious tests and was founded on the principle that secular could be distinguished from religious education and that students of whatever religious denominations should receive their secular education in common. The establishment of chairs of divinity was not incompatible with the avowed secular stance of the Institution, since these professors were appointed and financed by their respective churches and taught only members of their own faith. For over thirty years the collegiate department of the Institution went a considerable distance in solving the practical difficulties of providing university education for Ulster Presbyterians. But it suffered from two major difficulties: an inadequate level of financial support from the state, and the emergence of a sectarian controversy between orthodox and non-subscribing Presbyterians. The first problem affected both faculties of the Institution, but was less damaging than the second, which was centred exclusively in the arts faculty. It was this latter problem which finally led orthodox Presbyterians to sever their connections with the Institution in 1844 when Sir Robert Peel, in July of that year, announced in Parliament his intention to introduce legislation on the Irish university question.

Meanwhile, in the south of Ireland the agitation for educational reform, particularly for the Catholic laity, itensified during the 1840s under the leadership of Thomas Wyse, MP.[6] It was this agitation, rather than events in Ulster, which finally provoked Peel into addressing the question of university education in Ireland. Wyse, who belonged to the Catholic upper class, was an enthusiastic supporter of O'Connell in the struggle for Catholic emancipation. When this emancipation was granted in 1829 he was one of the first Catholics to enter the Westminster Parliament, having been elected as a Liberal in the general election of 1830. He immediately committed himself to achieving a number of major reforms in Ireland, especially in the area of education. His plan for educational reforms embraced all three levels, primary, secondary, and higher education. By the end of 1830, Wyse had presented a scheme for a national system of education in Ireland, which, though rejected, exerted a decisive influence on the scheme introduced the following year by Stanley, the Irish chief secretary, on behalf of Grey's Whig administration. In 1835 Wyse introduced his second education bill, this time dealing with secondary and higher education. The government of the day, under Lord Melbourne, appointed a select committee, with Wyse as chairman. This committee reported in 1838, and in an impressive document, written by Wyse, they provided the government with a detailed blueprint for the future of Irish education.[7] The Report envisaged five different levels: an elementary school level based on the parish; a secondary school, or academy system at the county level; agricultural and professional schools; four provincial colleges; and the provision for additional or 'supplementary' education, which would be supplied through the work of literary and scientific societies, mechanics' institutes, and libraries.

These last institutions were later to play an important role in the popular dissemination of political economy, throughout the remainder of the nineteenth century.[8] The different levels envisaged in the Wyse proposals were to be under the direction of a board of national education. A central concern of the proposed scheme was the emphasis on the provision of education for the middle classes. This argument was predicated on the premise that the upper classes were catered for by the University of Dublin, that the lower classes had available, by this time, the state-financed national school scheme, but that the middle classes were largely neglected by the state. It was to rectify this deficiency that the Wyse committee proposed the establishment of county secondary schools or academies, particularly the provincial colleges.

The publication of the Wyse committee's report gave rise to considerable agitation in Munster for a college along the lines suggested in the report. This agitation was led by Wyse himself, with the assistance of another member of the Wyse committee, William Smith O'Brien, MP. A Munster college committee was formed in Cork in September 1838, and later Limerick was also involved in the agitation. Between 1838 and 1840 considerable pressure was brought to bear on the government of the day, but by this time the administration of Lord Melbourne was in retreat, and the Munster college movement was a spent force by the time Parliament was dissolved in June 1841. But despite the government's overall lack of response to the Wyse committee's report, its recommendations provided the basis for educational reform throughout the nineteenth century, with its principle of mixed or united education, its advocacy of hierarchical structure, and its emphasis on providing an integrated structure of education for the whole country.[9] The establishment of the Queen's Colleges was also to justify his proposals that the educational problem required an integrated approach, as the college scheme was greatly hindered by the lack of a secondary system which was not introduced until 1878. This, however, was in the future and the decision to establish the Queen's Colleges was yet to be negotiated.

The major problem which faced Peel's administration in 1845 was the higher education of the Catholic laity in Ireland. By this time Wyse's long campaign for educational reform, particularly university reform, had convinced Peel that government action was necessary and that Wyse's scheme of provincial colleges based on the principle of mixed education was attractive. Peel's motivation in pursuing educational reform was, among other things, based on his belief that 'mere force, however necessary the application of it, will do nothing as a permanent remedy for the social evils of Ireland'.[10] He feared in particular that he would lose the support of the middle and upper classes among the Roman Catholics, and he wished to retain their loyalty, at what some members of his administration regarded as too high a price.[11] This was certainly the view of De Gray, Peel's lord lieutenant in Ireland, who disagreed fundamentally with his prime minister's views. De Gray was removed from office in July 1844 and replaced by Heytesbury, who shared Peel's approach to Irish policy. The same year Peel embarked on his policy of conciliation for Ireland, with a view 'of weaning from repeal the great body of wealthy and intelligent Roman Catholics by the steady manifestation of a desire to act with impartiality and to do that which is just'.[12] Specifically the policy of conciliation consisted of three measures, implemented over the next few years, which included the establishment of the Queen's Colleges and later the Queen's University.[13] The first, enacted in 1844, was the foundation of a board of charitable bequests, which effectively replaced an almost exclusively Protestant body which had been established in 1800. The structure of the new board was to consist of thirteen commissioners, five of whom were to be Roman Catholics. Reaction to this measure was very unfavourable, with the Catholic hierarchy, led by Dr MacHale, Archbishop of Tuam in Galway, strenuously opposed to the measure. Eventually three bishops consented to act, and the board came into operation in August 1844. Both Peel and Heytesbury regarded this as a substantial victory for the process of conciliation.

The second measure in Peel's policy of conciliation was to increase substantially the financial grant to Maynooth College, which was in serious financial difficulties and for which the Catholic bishops had privately appealed for help to the government. The Maynooth Act of 1845 increased the annual grant from £9,000 to £26,000 and decreed that this grant was to be drawn in future from the consolidated fund, which meant that it was no longer necessary to vote on it annually. In addition, a capital grant of £30,000 was provided for the enlargement of the college.[14] The act caused considerable political furore in the course of its passage through Parliament, leading to, among other things, Gladstone's resignation from the cabinet. In Ireland, the passing of the act, though popular, evoked little by way of change in attitude to the government on the part of the Catholic population, though arguably the act was most effective in removing Maynooth as a source of friction in the Irish university question for the rest of the century.

As the Maynooth grant was being debated, Peel and his home secretary, Sir James Graham, were devising a scheme of immense importance for the future of higher education in Ireland. This scheme was to provide Ireland with a system of university education which would be acceptable to all the major religious groups in the country, Catholics, Presbyterians, and Anglicans. Initially, the possibility of making Catholics eligible for scholarships in Trinity College, or of founding new colleges in the University of Dublin, was investigated, but was quickly abandoned given the hostility of the Anglican Church in Ireland. Consequently, it was decided to leave Trinity College untouched and to establish three new colleges, to be located at Cork and Galway, intended mainly for Catholics, and at Belfast, primarily for Presbyterians. The first reading of the bill to enact this development was introduced by Graham on 9 May 1845. The second reading was carried by a large majority on 30 May and, after a number of amendments at the committee stage, the bill was passed in the House of Commons on 10 July 1845. The bill passed through all its stages without a division in the House of Lords, and received the royal assent on 31 July as the Colleges (Ireland) Act.[15]

The act, Graham explained, was to improve the social conditions of Ireland by providing the benefits of higher education, particularly to 'the middle and higher classes of society'.[16] The problem of educational reform as perceived by the administration centred on the fact that the legally-established religion was not that of the majority of the people. A similar problem had been encountered and overcome at the primary school level through the provision of a system of national schools based on the principle of mixed secular education, and separate religious instruction, for the children of all denominations. The working of that system was deemed sufficiently satisfactory, in the peculiar circumstances, to justify its extension into higher education. In addition to this source of support for their scheme, the administration pointed to the experience of the Scottish universities, and to University College London. Therefore, the new colleges, which were incorporated in December 1845, were to be undenominational and free from all religious tests. In addition, they were forbidden to use their endowments from public sources to fund theological teaching. Private endowment for theological teaching on a voluntary basis was permitted, however. As in the Scottish universities, the new colleges were to be non-residential, and all teaching in the colleges was to be conducted by professors. The professors were to be appointed and dismissed by the crown.[17] To complete the scheme, the granting of university degrees to the students of the colleges had to be considered. The 1845 Act did not in fact address this issue, and considerable discussion ensued in an attempt to find an acceptable solution.

The Queen's Colleges scheme was completed in 1850 by the establishment of a new university, the Queen's University in Ireland. After Peel and Graham had abandoned their idea of linking the new colleges to the existing University of Dublin they looked to the University of London as a suitable model, so that the new university would be primarily an examining body with a number of affiliated institutions. Under this arrangement, they envisaged students from Maynooth competing with Presbyterians from Belfast and with Catholics and Anglicans from Cork and Galway. Under the new administration, now in office, the example of the autonomous Scottish universities, was canvassed by the prime minister, Lord John Russell. But Lord Clarendon, the Irish viceroy, argued against both options as being unsuitable for Ireland. He considered that, if applied to Ireland, the London University structure would lead to a lowering of standards and would merely facilitate the Catholic hierarchy in their demand for a Catholic university. Clarendon's thinking prevailed, and the Queen's University was established within a federal structure and designated as a teaching university in that only students educated in one of its three colleges could obtain its degrees. The Queen's University was empowered to prescribe all courses for the award of degrees and diplomas and to direct all examinations. It exercised a powerful control over the colleges and maintained a high and consistent standard of instruction.

Outside Parliament the passing of the Ireland (Colleges) Act received a very mixed reception, extending from enthusiastic support to relentless hostility. This scheme, which Peel intended as a measure of conciliation, became a source of bitter controversy and contention. It is virtually impossible to understand the history of the Queen's Colleges, their acceptability in Irish society, or their role in the dissemination of certain disciplines, particularly political economy, without an appreciation of the reactions of the different groups to the founding of the colleges. In Britain, in contrast to the passing of the Maynooth Act, the college scheme provoked little reaction. In Ireland opinions differed sharply. Those who supported the principle of mixed education, mainly non-subscribing Presbyterians, enthusiastically supported the measure. Nationalist opinion was divided. Representing one section, Daniel O'Connell condemned the measure vehemently when he spoke of the 'godless colleges', echoing the idiom of the militant Tory, Sir Robert Inglis, who had earlier denounced the bill as 'a gigantic scheme of godless education'.[18] In contrast, the Young Ireland movement welcomed the colleges. They viewed them as promoting and facilitating two of their most desired objectives, an educated and independent-minded laity and union between Irishmen of different religions. The Catholic hierarchy was also divided. One section, a minority, led by the primate, Dr Murray of

Dublin, was prepared to give the colleges a fair chance. The other section, led by Archbishop MacHale of Tuam, was utterly opposed to the scheme. It was under the influence of MacHale that the hierarchy, withholding their outright condemnation at the beginning, insisted that certain amendments be made to the scheme if their co-operation was to be secured. These included: that a fair proportion of the professors and other officers would be Catholics and approved by the bishops; that all officers should be appointed by a board of trustees, which should include the Catholic prelates of the province, and should have the power to dismiss any officer convicted of undermining the faith or morals of students; and that Catholic chaplains should be appointed at suitable salaries to supervise the religious and moral instruction of Catholic students.[19]

These demands would have effectively undermined the scheme of mixed education, and were rejected by Peel. A protracted struggle ensued between the hierarchy and the administration, which involved missions to Rome by both sides. The hierarchy, under MacHale's leadership, triumphed and three papal rescripts in 1847, 1848, and 1850 (the latter coinciding with a national episcopal synod held in Thurles), formally condemned the Queen's Colleges, and warned the laity to avoid the colleges as subversive to their faith and morals.[20] Thereafter the hierarchy acted in unison against the colleges and set about establishing a university of their own, which emerged in 1854 as the Catholic University, with John Henry Newman as its first rector. The bishops' hostility to the Queen's Colleges had a blighting effect on their development, particularly in Cork and Galway, and these colleges, while far from being failures, nevertheless did not succeed in realising their potential or the purpose of their foundation.

In Belfast the position was radically different, but even there the creation of alternative institutions to the Queen's College was not avoided. The essential difference between Belfast and the rest of the country was that the population from which potential university students could be drawn was almost totally Protestant, and the Presbyterian Church, which was comparable in influence to the Catholic Church in the rest of the country, saw its way to co-operate with the new Queen's College in Belfast. However, the Presbyterian general assembly, whose main concern was the education of its clergy, did not present a totally unified front on the question. Notwithstanding the establishment of a Presbyterian theological college at Belfast in 1853, which worked in harmony with the Queen's college, a minority in the general assembly insisted on establishing a completely independent college in Ulster to provide instruction in arts and theology and to be totally under their control. This they did in 1865 at Derry, with the help of a sizeable bequest from a Mrs Magee, when they established a college named in her honour.[21] Queen's College Belfast, in contrast to those at Cork and Galway, and in the different circumstances of Ulster, was immediately successful and shortly after its opening had as many students as Cork and Galway combined. It was in these circumstances that the Queen's Colleges were launched. The next fifty years were to prove just as turbulent as the years of their launching, and the 'Irish university question' was to remain a continuing source of grievance to Roman Catholics and an unsettling issue for successive British administrations.

The structure of teaching within the Queen's Colleges was centred on the three major faculties of arts, law, and medicine. Of these, the arts faculty was deemed the most important from the viewpoint of providing a general education, in contrast with the professional orientation of the law and medical faculties. Shortly after the passing of the Queen's Colleges Act in 1845 a board, consisting of the newly-appointed presidents and vice-presidents of the three colleges, was appointed. Over the next four years, from 1846 to 1849, it was the board, under the direction of the government, which grappled with the problems of organisation, curricula, and appointments for the new colleges. In their first documents, produced at the end of January 1846, the new board drew up a detailed course of studies in arts. The arts course was to be of three years' duration, with the academic year consisting of three terms, each averaging three months in length. According to its charter each college was allocated twelve professorships, and these were divided equally between a department of science which contained professorships in mathematics, natural philosophy, chemistry, anatomy and zoology, botany and rural economy, geology and physical geography, and a department of literature consisting of chairs in Latin, Greek, English, German, and cognate subjects, French and Italian, logic and mental philosophy. In addition, the entrance requirements were specified and the course of studies to be pursued in each year was also formulated. At this stage no mention was made for the provision of political economy in the arts faculty. In terms of the rigour of the entry requirements and the extensiveness of the subjects included for study, the course differed from most of the contemporary models available including those of Trinity College Dublin, the Scottish universities, and Oxford and Cambridge. It approximated most closely to the arrangement of London University. One evaluator of the proposed course of studies in arts summarised it as follows: 'In general that scheme was most closely akin to the London curriculum in its range of subjects and to the Dublin arts course in its orderly sequence of studies: in all respects it stood at the opposite extreme to the undergraduates of Oxford and Cambridge...'.[22]

During the remainder of 1846 and into 1847 a number of events conspired to interrupt the work of the board. These included a change of administration in England, the continuing battle in Parliament over the Corn Laws, and, in Ireland, the trauma of the Famine. However, in October 1847 the board reassembled to revise their earlier work on study courses and statutes and in addition to draft courses in law and medicine. Several changes were introduced in the board's work during 1847–8. Firstly, the number of professorships was increased from twelve to twenty for each college, of which thirteen were now to be located in the faculty of arts, five in medicine, and two in law. Secondly, a number of changes in the original professorial arrangements were implemented. The chair of English became history and English literature, the two modern language chairs were replaced by one chair in modern languages and one in Celtic languages, zoology and anatomy were amalgamated into a chair in natural history, botany and rural economy were replaced by a chair in agriculture, while geology and physical geography were reorganised into a chair in minerology and geology. In addition a chair in civil engineering was established within the faculty of arts.[23] Thirdly, the arts faculty was divided into a literary division and a scientific division. The former contained the chairs of Greek, Latin, history and English literature, modern languages, and Celtic languages, while the latter included the chairs of natural philosophy, chemistry, natural history, mathematics, logic and metaphysics, minerology and geology, civil enginering, and agriculture. Finally, changes were made in the number of subjects to be studied over the course of the three years and it was under this revised plan that political economy was included for the first time in the course of studies in the faculty of arts.

The chair of political economy was located not in the faculty of arts but in law. The board's decision to locate political economy in the faculty of law was largely influenced by the recommendations of a committee of the House of Commons which had addressed the issues of legal education.[24] This committee had been established in April 1846 and had reported by August of that year.[25] The committee commented on the fact that the charter of the Queen's Colleges envisaged the establishment of professorships of law, and pointed to the opportunity that this afforded for the introduction of courses in law, which the committee felt the existing universities had failed to supply. However, the committee also felt that the demand for these courses would perhaps be meagre, and consequently that the professor of jurisprudence should also incorporate in his brief responsibility for political economy. As a result, one of the two chairs in the faculty of law was to be in jurisprudence and political economy, the other in English law.

In the faculty of arts the principal courses prescribed were the degrees of Bachelor of Arts and Master in Arts, along with diplomas in civil engineering and agriculture. Candidates for the BA were required to attend lectures in one of the three colleges for a minimum period of two full terms in each of the three sessions, had to pass the requisite college examinations, and had to be recommended by the president of the college to enter for the degree examination. The three-year course consisted in the first year of English language, classics, a modern language, and mathematics. The second year courses included logic, chemistry, zoology, botany, and either classics or higher mathematics. The final-year courses contained physics, history and English literature, geography, and either metaphysics or jurisprudence and political economy. After graduation, Bachelors in Arts of the Queen's University could proceed to the degree of MA by examination in any one of the three groups of subjects: languages; history, metaphysics and jurisprudence; and mathematics and physical science. In the faculty of law the prescribed courses were for the diploma in elementary law and the degree of Bachelor in Laws. The diploma was a three-year course, in the first year of which property, conveyancing, and jurisprudence were studied. In the second year equity, bankruptcy, and civil law were covered, and in the final year common and criminal law. On completion of this course students were admitted to the diploma examinations. If successful at the diploma, and having obtained the degree of BA, students were entitled to proceed to the LL B examination, which was taken after a further year of study in any one of the three colleges. Likewise, Bachelors in Laws, after a period of three years, could proceed to the degree of Doctor in Laws by examination.

It was within this organisational framework that political economy evolved in the newly-established Queen's Colleges, and this structure remained largely intact during the course of the nineteenth century. In Queen's College Belfast, William Neilson Hancock was appointed the first Professor of Jurisprudence and Political Economy in 1849 while still Whately Professor at Trinity College Dublin, and retained the post until 1853. The number of students taking jurisprudence and political economy during Hancock's term of office fluctuated from a high of twelve during 1851-2 to a low of two in the academic year 1852-3. His prescribed reading for the academic year 1850-1 included Whately's *Lectures*, Smith's *Wealth of Nations*, Senior's *Political Economy*, and Burton's *Social and Political Economy*.[26] In 1853 Cliffe Leslie was appointed to the chair in succession to Hancock, and held it until 1882. In the early years of Leslie's term of office political economy was clearly subservient within the prescribed course structure to jurisprudence. This is evident from his entry in the President's Report for the academic year 1856-7:

> The subjects which a course of lectures on Political Economy must embrace are fewer and more definite than those classed under the less advanced and more complicated science of jurisprudence. It is the Professor's endeavour to illustrate the principles of Economic Science by the help of these applications which will be most interesting and useful in a large commercial town.[27]

That this was a view Leslie retained, can be seen from his various contributions to the annual Presidential Reports, over most of his term of office. After 1862-3 the number of students recorded as taking political economy increased relative to previous years, and by 1871-2 the extra work load which this entailed is reflected in the entry under Political Economy in the President's Report for that year:

> The Professor of Jurisprudence and Political Economy (Mr T.E. Cliffe Leslie) fills in reality two distinct and important

chairs, in the two distinct Faculties of Law and Arts. As Professor of Jurisprudence, he lectures, teaches, and examines in the general philosophy and history of law, in Roman Law, and in Constitutional Law and International Law. As Professor of Political Economy, he lectures, teaches, and examines Arts Students in that great subject. His instruction in Jurisprudence has the twofold purpose and result of teaching legal philosophy and history, both as a branch of higher University Education, and as a preparation for the legal profession; and the duties of the Professor in this Department, discharged as they are by Professor Leslie, would be sufficiently arduous if he had not also to fill the Chair of Political Economy, to which he devotes as much time and labour as though he had not other collegiate duties. The stipend and emoluments attached to this double chair are altogether disproportionate to the abilities, attainments, and exertions it demands on the part of the Professor.[28]

This was not a new theme as far as Leslie was concerned. As early as 1858, when Leslie provided evidence to the Queen's Colleges Commission[29] of that year, he argued for substantial organisational changes in the teaching of jurisprudence and political economy. His principal recommendations to the Commission focused on the need to reduce the volume of material to be provided by the Professor of Jurisprudence and Political Economy.

Leslie's objections to the work of the incumbent of this chair were based on the following considerations:

1   The provision of a suitable course of instructions on such a wide spectrum of subjects was not within the capacity of any one professor, particularly as the 'present emoluments of the Chair were settled upon the supposition that its occupants would always be a practising barrister'.[30] This interesting observation would perhaps largely account for the fact that all of the professors of political economy in both the Queen's Colleges and Trinity College in the nineteenth century were graduates in law.

2   The course in law was oppressive and militated, in Leslie's view, against the law student. Civil law and colonial law were particularly troublesome, as was the absence of

adequate textbooks on the general principles of jurisprudence.

3 The inclusion of Roman law as part of scientific jurisprudence, however valuable for purposes of comprehensiveness in a student's legal education, was unlikely to be either 'useful or interesting' to potential students of law at the Queen's Colleges.

4 The present arrangement, in Leslie's view, seriously impeded the incumbent of the chair from devoting adequate time to economical science, 'which is capable of being so treated as to prove a useful and profitable study, even in a commercial respect, in such a town as Belfast'.[31]

Leslie's recommendations, in the light of his foregoing criticism of the existing arrangements, sought the omission of both civil and colonial law from the course. In fact at an earlier stage in his submission Leslie felt that jurisprudence in total should be abandoned and that the duties and titles of the chair should be confined to political economy. However, he later argued that the total abandonment of 'the original design, as far as jurisprudence is concerned, would be for many reasons, to be deplored', and settled for a modification to the existing arrangements. His second main recommendation concerned the course available in arts in the Queen's Colleges. These, he argued, were also excessive in the range of subjects offered, and called for an alternative rearrangement of subjects into more orderly and logical groups. Specifically he recommended that political economy, logic, and metaphysics should be located in the same group, since they belonged to the moral sciences and in his view 'Economic studies furnish the most rigorous exercises in logical reasoning and the detection of fallacies'. Associated with this recommendation was his call for the creation of special degrees in mental and political sciences, along with special diplomas for industrial knowledge.

This latter proposal had been canvassed by Leslie at some length in earlier evidence to the Commission. Here Leslie argued the case for what he called another 'kind of education' which was predicated on the necessity of introducing the physical sciences into the practical operations of life. In reply to a question before the Commission as to the 'subjects which you would comprise in your commercial and mercantile education', Leslie singled out as the 'most necessary part of it', instruction in the 'Physical and Mathematical Sciences'. He went on to cite the arrangements at the Trade Institute of Berlin, which represented for him something of a prototype model.[32] Later Leslie developed this theme at more length when he submitted a supplementary statement to the Commission entitled 'The Demand for Scientific Industrial Instruction in the Queen's College, Belfast'.[33] In this contribution Leslie wished to argue in defence of two propositions. Firstly, that there was a demand for this kind of education which the Queen's Colleges were not supplying, and, secondly, that there existed ample evidence from continental countries of the kind of institutions which represented 'nearly complete models of the kind of additional instruction wanted'. In defence of these propositions Leslie offered a number of arguments, including his concern at the fact that not only the Queen's Colleges in Ireland but 'Universities and Colleges generally throughout the kingdom' provided education primarily for the middle classes, though there 'was no proportionate increase in the aggregate number of students'. This was, for Leslie, due to the fact that, increasingly, the middle classes, and particularly the merchant and commercial classes, perceived the poor remuneration from the 'learned professions' relative to the rewards from commercial activities, for which the available education provided no particular training. In addition to this line of argument, Leslie appealed to the evidence of the productive superiority of the continental countries relative to that of England, and cited at length the French example of the creation of centralised schools for the training of civil engineers. For Leslie all wealth was 'the result of a knowledge of the laws of nature, and that where this kind of knowledge is stationary, the modes of production must remain unimproved'.[34] In response to this situation Leslie recommended the establishment of an industrial school and outlined what he considered to be a suitable curriculum. Political economy would be a significant part of that curriculum, taking its place among such subjects as mathematics, descriptive geometry, linear drawing, chemistry, experimental physics, mechanics applied to arts, botany and modern languages. His defence for the inclusion of political economy is an interesting account of how, on the basis of a judicious selection of topics, it could be made to serve the mercantile and commercial interests of society. According to Leslie:

The importance of Economical Science, as a part of Industrial Education, may not at once appear obvious, and it has been overlooked in the Continental Institutions. It is sufficient, on this head, to observe that a knowledge of the causes on which the rate of profit, the present and future prices of labour, raw materials, manufactures, and the precious metals depend, and of the kinds of enterprises suited and unsuited to large partnership and not joint-stock companies, together with an acquaintance with the theories of banking, currency, the foreign exchanges, and taxation, must be of immense value to the heads or managers of factories and commercial establishments. Many of the most disastrous failures in business have occurred from an ignorance of the operation of those laws with which the Economist must be conversant, and could not have occurred under the direction of a person uniting this kind of knowledge to the other requisite qualification.[35]

Arguably Leslie's concerns with these issues of merging political economy with the interests of commercial society must have been largely influenced by his location in Belfast, which, at this time, was the undisputed industrial capital of Ireland. Outside of the north-east region of Ireland, centred on Belfast, economic activity was that of a largely underdeveloped agrarian economy.

The concerns expressed by Leslie with respect to political economy were not paralleled by the evidence available from the other Queen's Colleges at Cork and Galway. In Queen's College Cork, Richard Horner Mills was appointed Professor of Jurisprudence and Political Economy in 1849, a position he held until his death in 1893. The position of political economy within the BA degree structure was similar in all of the Queen's Colleges, with political economy and jurisprudence constituting a third arts optional course to metaphysics. In Cork and Galway the number of students attending courses in law in general and jurisprudence and political economy was particularly small compared with Queen's College Belfast. Apart from the opposition of the Catholic hierarchy to the Queen's Colleges, a more mundane set of reasons for this state of affairs was advanced by the professors of jurisprudence and political economy at both Cork and Galway in evidence to the Queen's Colleges Commission in 1858. Both acknowledged that since candidates aspiring to the Bar had in any event to attend either the Benchers' own law school in Dublin or the law school in Trinity College Dublin, the provision of legal education in the provincial cities was of little use to them. Neither did the other branch of the legal profession – the attorneys – appreciate the value of the law faculties in the Queen's Colleges. Consequently the only potential clientele were the apprentices to attorneys who were located in Cork or Galway, and even their attendance was not a necessary requirement. Therefore, both professors argued that the small numbers studying in their respective faculties was a function of the number of attorneys practising in their respective cities. This prompted Professor Mills to recommend to the Commissioners that the law faculty in Queen's College Cork should be abolished, but that legal instruction should be retained on a more modest scale.[36] D.C. Heron from Queen's College Galway could not agree with this suggestion, and expressed surprise at why either Belfast or Cork, given their relative sizes compared with Galway, should have experienced difficulty in acquiring students.[37] Mills was also of the opinion that political economy suffered greatly by virtue of its association with jurisprudence, combined as they were in the one chair. Indeed, part of his motivation for seeking the abolition of the faculty of law would appear to be his concern to develop the teaching of political economy. For Mills, 'the time allotted to the study of Political Economy is entirely too small for its due cultivation. It appears to me to constitute one of the most important branches of education.'[38] Heron proposed, in the course of providing evidence to the same Commission, a somewhat similar view to Cliffe Leslie in Belfast, that a number of new diplomas should be established in Galway, of which one should be a diploma of commerce. This was to meet the educational needs, as Heron envisaged the plan in operation, of the personnel from the various branch banks throughout the country. But he quickly conceded that this suggestion 'would be more useful in Cork and Belfast than Galway – especially in Belfast, because the system of banking is more extended in the North of Ireland than in any other part of Ireland'.[39] As suggested earlier, in relation to Leslie's envisaged role for political economy, the effects of location were not inconsiderable in their influence on the place and function of political economy in relation to the wider society.

The contents of the political economy courses as taught in the

Queen's Colleges were broadly similar. In Galway, Heron's course in political economy consisted of a series of topics which included history of political economy, elements of political economy, taxation, capital, labour, pauperism, and colonisation. The required reading material included Smith's *Wealth of Nations*, Senior's *Political Economy*, Burton's *Political and Social Economy*, Heron's *Lectures on Taxation*, and Bastiat's *Popular Fallacies*.[40] In Queen's College Cork, Mills's course in political economy included such topics as the nature and distribution of wealth; the principles which regulate rents, profits and wages; the principles of commerce, taxation, and the funding system; the principles of currency and banking. The reading material for this course included Smith's *Wealth of Nations*, Senior's *Political Economy*, Longfield's *Political Economy*, Longfield's *Lectures on Commerce*, Huskisson's *Questions Stated*, and John Stuart Mill's *Principles of Political Economy*.[41] The course, as in the other Queen's Colleges, consisted of twenty-four lectures, which were delivered during the months of December, February, and March of each session. By 1866–7 Mills had added to the reading lists Fawcett's *Manual of Political Economy*, McCulloch's *Taxation and Funding*, and Goschen's *Foreign Exchanges*. In the same year the reading material in Queen's College Galway centred on the work of Smith and John Stuart Mill, and by 1871–2 this was extended to include Ricardo's *Principles of Political Economy*, Cairnes's *Logical Method of Political Economy*, Goschen's *Foreign Exchanges*, and Price's *Currency*.[42] Over the period from the 1840s to the turn of the century no major changes in the position and status of political economy within the Queen's Colleges can be discerned. The changes that occurred were marginal; substantial changes were not introduced until the early part of the twentieth century.

In this chapter we have outlined the historical background to the foundation of the Queen's Colleges and traced in some detail the difficulties which attended their inception and evolution. These difficulties were to a large extent inevitable, given the complex political and religious circumstances within which the Queen's Colleges were viewed as a pivotal instrument in the administration's negotiation of, and solution to, these very difficulties. To have anticipated a successful outcome for the new colleges would have been unduly optimistic. That the Queen's Colleges never reached their full potential, with possibly the exception of Queen's College Belfast, should come as no great surprise. Neither, however, could it be argued that the Queen's Colleges were a failure. From their inception in 1849 they attracted very distinguished scholars, and, as reflected in the evidence to the Queen's Colleges Commission in 1885, their graduates compared very favourably with, and on occasion surpassed, their counterparts from universities in Great Britain. The Queen's Colleges undoubtedly represented the 'establishment view' as far as the majority of the population was concerned. Their foundation not only failed to solve Peel's problem of providing higher education for the Catholic majority, but in fact stimulated the establishment of the Catholic University in 1854, largely to counteract their influence.

The decision to establish a Catholic University emerged from the National Synod of Thurles in 1850. Acting on the advice of Rome, it decreed to found a Catholic university in Ireland. There were to be five faculties: theology, law, medicine, philosophy and letters, and science.[43] The philosophy and letters faculty included as subjects classical literature and languages, ancient and modern history and geography, English literature, modern languages, logic, metaphysics, ethics, Irish language, archaeology, and political economy.[44] The fact that political economy was on the syllabus marked an advance for Catholic higher education. It was to take a further 130 years or so for the first chair of economics to be established in Maynooth. But, in fact, very little political economy appears to have been taught at the Catholic University of Ireland. Indeed, its first rector, John Henry Newman, discoursing before it on *The Idea of a University*, described political economy as 'a science at the same time dangerous and leading to occasions of sin'.[45] No doubt this secular science, with its morals of the market-place, mocked spirituality, and propagated values unbecoming a gentleman. It is potently symbolic that the old Oxford friends, Newman and Whately, never met during the four years in which Newman lived in Dublin.[46]

In October 1854 the provisional appointment of a 'Lecturer in Political Economy' was announced.[47] The following year the appointee, John O'Hagan, was made professor of political economy.[48] In the *Calendar* of 1857 O'Hagan was still listed as professor, but by 1869 there was no incumbent. From 1897 to 1900 W.P. Coyne was lecturer in political economy, and from 1900 to 1930 the Jesuit T.A. Finlay was professor of political economy at what had become in 1908, University College Dublin, a constituent college of the National University of Ireland, including the former Queen's Colleges of Cork and Galway. But the actual teaching of political economy at the Catholic University seems to have been minimal. O'Hagan pursued a successful legal career, becoming eventually a Justice of the High Court. It is possible that occasional series of lectures were delivered in the university by guest lecturers. Frank Hugh O'Donnell, for instance, a former student of Cairnes at Galway and later to become a Parnellite MP, delivered a series of three lectures, 'On economic science' to the Catholic University.[49]

In November 1873, *A Memorial Addressed by the Students and Ex-Students of the Catholic University of Ireland to the Episcopal Board of the University* was published. *Inter alia*, it regretted the neglect of the teaching of science, the lack of a proper scientific library and also of exhibitions and prizes in science. There was, the *Memorial* claimed, too much emphasis on classics, whereas the 'distinguishing mark of this age is its ardor for science'. The bishops were informed that the 'absence of Political Economy from the course of studies in the University' had 'excited many unfavourable comments'.[50] One of the signatories, William Dillon, a son of the MP John Blake Dillon, was later to write a Ruskinian critique of political economy, called *The Dismal Science* (1882).

Viewed from the narrower institutional perspective of providing instruction in political economy, the Queen's Colleges were greatly impeded, as the discussion earlier in this chapter demonstrates, as a result of combining political economy with jurisprudence. This development, together with the explicit assumption that the holder of the chair would be a practising barrister, acted as a major constraint on the expansion of instruction in political economy within the Queen's Colleges. This contrasted with the Whately Chair in political economy at Trinity College Dublin, where no corresponding constraints operated. On the other hand there was considerable mobility between the holders of the Whately Chair at Trinity College Dublin, and the chairs of Jurisprudence and Political Economy at the Queen's Colleges. Hancock, Cairnes, and Bastable held chairs in both institutions at various stages in their careers. In addition, most of the incumbents of the chairs in the Queen's Colleges were graduates of Trinity College. This mobility ensured at least a certain homogeneity in course content and reading material within political economy between the two universities, but it also arguably contributed to the widely-held view on the part of the Catholic majority that political economy was primarily the intellectual preserve of the 'establishment' class, a view that was to evoke a hostile indigenous response from different sources in Ireland during the course of the troubled nineteenth century.

4

EASY LESSONS ON MONEY MATTERS

Political economy in the national schools

The dissemination of political economy in Ireland during the nineteenth century was not entrusted solely to the formal institutions of higher education such as the universities. At the other end of the educational spectrum, the elementary school system was, after the establishment of the Board of National Education in 1831, to become the unlikely location of one of the most elaborate experiments in the spreading of political economy among the 'lower classes', first of Ireland and later of Great Britain and its other colonies. This development was launched by Archbishop Richard Whately, whose formidable presence as the effective chairman of the National Board after 1832 provided him with an ideal platform. More specifically, the national system of education, under the control of the National Board, facilitated the introduction of Whately's *Easy Lessons on Money Matters: For the Use of Young People* (based on his Oxford *Introductory Lectures on Political Economy*) into the curriculum. The *Third Book of Lessons* and the *Fourth Book of Lessons*, which were prescribed reading for the pupils, contained the first four and the last six sections respectively of *Easy Lessons*. As a result Whately became 'for a time ... nothing less than the head schoolmaster of the Irish people'.[1]

A comprehensive examination of the philosophical basis of Whately's commitment to political economy is beyond the scope of this chapter. Nevertheless, for Whately political economy was neither a fortuitous choice of subject nor did it operate within an intellectual vacuum. On the contrary, it emerged from a theological and philosophical framework more cohesive than has been acknowledged by historians of ideas.[2] It is, for instance, only against the background of this larger framework that it can be demonstrated that Whately's political economy was designed to show that inequality was a 'natural' state of society and was, in fact, the basis for the organisation of efficient human communities based on the principle of the division of labour. Similarly, it is only from the perspective of his overall ideological framework that his concern with university and popular education can be adequately comprehended. His aim was to uphold on the social level the inequalities which it was no longer possible to maintain at the political level by the use of repressive legislation or physical coercion.[3] For Whately, increasing industrial and urban concentration was conducive to increasing the capacity of the masses to reflect critically on their political and social status. Confronted with this situation the 'higher classes' needed to re-establish their intellectual hegemony, to become the 'proprietors' of the educational system. The question for Whately, as he pointed out in a sermon delivered in 1830, was not whether the working classes should or should not be educated, but by whom and for what purposes.[4] Whately felt that the educational system was in danger of falling into the hands of middle-class radicals who would quickly replace the 'higher orders' within British society. Whately was motivated by his desire to recapture the educational system through the promotion of the teaching of science, including political economy, and through the use of the universities in performing the critical function of 'ideological supervision' within society,[5] while the extension of popular education was to recolonise and reshape the intellectual landscape of the masses.

By the early 1830s, when Whately arrived in Ireland, the process of popularising political economy was well established in Great Britain. The principal social groups at which these efforts were directed included the adult working classes for whom, according to the Scottish political economist J.R. McCulloch, instruction in the economic principles 'that must determine their condition in life' was absolutely imperative, as well as those of school-going age.[6] A number of powerful intellectual and religious currents of thought combined in identifying the newly established science of political economy as an essential instrument of social reform. At this time the prestige of the physical sciences was such that it was confidently assumed that their methodology could be applied to other branches of learning where it would be equally productive of exact and universal laws, especially in the elucidation and explanation of social phenomena. Political economy, as a newly emergent science, was clearly viewed in these terms and did not disappoint, by producing an array of 'natural laws' through the work of Smith, Ricardo, and Malthus. A textbook published in Edinburgh, itself a centre for the popularisation of political economy because of the pioneering efforts of McCulloch, spoke of political economy as providing 'an explanation of the operation of certain natural laws ... a knowledge of which is of the greatest importance and utility'.[7] Viewed from this perspective, political economy was an indispensable source of social enlightenment, and the need to instruct the mass of the population in its principles became a social imperative. The *Westminster Review*, in 1825, described, with no apparent irony, the evangelical mission of political economy:

> The principal difficulty is overcome – the road to happiness is discovered – no groping, no perplexing research, no hopeless, thankless toil is required – all that remains to be done is, to remove the obstacles which conceal that road from the view of those who are less fortunate than ourselves.[8]

This secular gospel received powerful religious support from Thomas Chalmers and Whately, who argued that orthodox economic doctrines were compatible with Christian belief.[9] An intellectual discipline which combined the apparently universal and incontrovertible authority of physical law with the moral prestige of Christianity was twice-blessed. It became the sovereign social discourse in the nineteenth century and was assured a central role in education reform.

As the nineteenth century progressed, a third justification for a popular education where political economy played a pivotal role was provided by what might be called the ideology of social control or social containment.[10] Increasingly educationalists and leaders of public opinion came to perceive education as a crucial instrument for avoiding social strife and facilitating the peaceful transition to an industrial and urbanised society. The educational movements of the nineteenth century have been described as 'a battle of ideas ... on which the future of society, of capitalism itself, seemed to depend'.[11] Other commentators have argued that 'in the 1830s and later ... it was the education-as-insurance, rescuing-from-revolution, schools-rather-than-prisons that was the most representative'.[12] A variation on this theme, albeit more restrained in tone, has been put forward by Harrison who has argued that 'the development of a literate section of the working classes opened the way to the spread of radical and unorthodox opinions, and a good deal of adult educational effort stemmed from the middle-class desire to check this'.[13] This was the central ideological position of leading Whig spokesmen of the time, whose commitment was to a philosophy of gradualist adjustment to rapidly-changing social circumstances. These spokesmen shared with radicals a vigorous commitment to popular education, and particularly political economy, not as an instrument of social critique, but as the blueprint of a correct code of ideas to contain the aspirations of the emerging working class.

The work of popularising political economy, which, it has been argued, 'was, with the fierce debate which accompanied the publication of Darwin's *Origin of Species*, perhaps the most deeply contested development in nineteenth century intellectual history',[14] proceeded apace during the first half of the century. This task was undertaken by two distinct groups. The first consisted of 'economists of the second rank'[15] who were active in the educational field, such as J.R. McCulloch and James Mill. The second consisted of a group of individual writers who undertook the task of translating the complexities of the 'natural laws' of political economy into a form suitable for intellectual digestion by schoolchildren.[16] One of the most celebrated examples of the latter genre was Mrs Marcet's *Conversations on Political Economy* in which the essentials of the discipline were explained in a manner suitable for the edification of the young. Originally published in 1816, it was reprinted five times by 1824. Other works in this tradition included J. MacVickar's *First Lessons in Political Economy for the Use of Elementary Schools*, which was based on the alleged axiom that the 'first principles of Political Economy are mere truisms which children might well understand, and which they ought to be taught'.[17] Harriet Martineau, influenced by Marcet's book, wrote her political economy series between 1832 and 1834 using the familiar pedagogical device of relating tales to provide moral, religious, and economic lessons. By the 1830s the tradition of popularising political economy for both adults and schoolchildren was well established in Britain.[18] It is ironic that the person who was to exert the most profound influence in the popular dissemination of political economy, Richard Whately, did so not from his influential chair in that subject at Oxford, but from his archiepiscopal seat in Dublin, to which he was appointed in 1831.

Whately's arrival in Ireland coincided with the introduction of what was to be a major experiment in a state-supported system of non-denominational 'national' education.[19] Forty years were to elapse before a similar system was established in Britain. Whately was appointed a commissioner of national education and he became the *de facto* chairman of the Board. While this of itself was immensely significant, the administrative structure of the new system greatly facilitated Whately in exerting a profound influence. Administratively, the Irish national system of education 'assumed not the shape of the traditional bureaucratic pyramid, but of a misshapen hourglass'.[20] At the lower level the local people, mainly clerics, organised the routine management of the schools. At the highest level the commissioners of national education formulated policy and took the major administrative decisions. Between these two levels there existed only a thinly-dispersed inspectorate, along with a small complement of civil servants. Consequently the commissioners, of whom Whately was undoubtedly the most important, exerted a major direct influence on the local schools. They dictated activities within the schools, since they possessed the power to direct government financial aid only to those schools which adhered to their regulations. In addition, they produced a set of textbooks at a reduced price for the schools, the prototype for similar experiments in Britain.[21]

The rationale for establishing the national system of education, the principles on which it was managed, and the organisational structure adopted were influenced by three major considerations: the changed political circumstances of the late eighteenth and early nineteenth centuries, the need to secure the agreement of the major religious denominations in Ireland, and the contribution of key individuals at crucial stages in the educational debate. Politically the central consideration in the late eighteenth century was undoubtedly the perceived threat of radical ideas emerging from the French Revolution. For different reasons the British administration and the Irish Catholic Church were apprehensive that these ideas might foment large-scale popular unrest in Ireland. Just as the administration had met the demands of the Catholic hierarchy to establish a national seminary at Maynooth in

1795, so a similar ideological accommodation was required if the lower classes were to be protected from the influences of revolutionary propaganda. In short, the successful implementation of any scheme of popular education required the support of the Catholic hierarchy.[22]

With the exception of that strenuous critic of British policy in Ireland, John MacHale, Archbishop of Tuam, the co-operation of the Catholic hierarchy was forthcoming for a number of reasons.[23] This agreement was secured notwithstanding the fact that the new system of national education was to be state financed and non-denominational in character. At first sight this may appear paradoxical coming from the Catholic hierarchy who had traditionally insisted on a denominational education system under the control of their clergy. This anomalous behaviour is, however, readily comprehensible viewed from the perspective of the forms of mass education available up to the 1830s.

The first, dating from the 1530s, resulted in the establishment of formal educational systems consisting of parish, diocesan, royal, and later charter schools. The second centred on the activities of the proselytising societies of the late eighteenth and early nineteenth centuries. The development of the formal schooling system correlated closely with the sequence of systematic colonisations which commenced in the sixteenth century. In the area of Irish educational policy the state pursued an active policy of intervention long before the nineteenth century, and at a much earlier date than in Britain.[24] The use of public education became an integral part of the state's ideological armoury to achieve cohesion and impose political and social control. It is against this tradition of extensive state intervention in Irish education that the establishment of the national system in 1831 must be viewed. It was the culmination of a protracted process, albeit now on the basis of a non-denominational charter.

The non-denominational character of the national system was to undermine what had been the second major historical line of development in Irish education – Protestant voluntary education societies committed to proselytisation. While largely unsuccessful in their primary objective, they served the critical if unintended function of stimulating and later consolidating Catholic opinion, both lay and clerical, in seeking and supporting a state-financed non-denominational system of education. They thereby contributed in a crucial way to the incorporation of Catholic opinion into the emerging consensus on education that was evident by the end of the 1820s. The institutional expression of this consensus was the national system of education, under the control of the National Board which was comprised of the powerful and influential commissioners of national education. The Catholic hierarchy supported the new system, not because it was ideal from its viewpoint, but because it was less unpalatable than maintaining the status quo. In like fashion, the hostility of the established and the Presbyterian Churches to the national system was motivated by the perceived loss of their hegemonic power in the educational arena.[25]

As with university education, the reactions of the various churches to new developments in the elementary sector were of crucial importance. The hope was that the national system would alleviate sectarian divisions, principally between the established or Anglican Church and the Roman Catholic and Presbyterian Churches. But in the words of the leading historian of Irish education, these divisions jeopardised the very operations of the national system itself, losing a 'singular opportunity of binding the sectarian wounds of Irish society'.[26] The response of the established Church to the national system of education was one of hostility. The majority of its bishops and clergy expressed opposition to the new system, and in particular to Whately's involvement in it. This response can be largely explained by political and ideological considerations. Politically the established Church in Ireland was overwhelmingly dominated by conservatives who had actively opposed Catholic emancipation and disapproved of Whig reforms in general but in particular those relating to tithe laws and church temporalities.[27] Being a Whig creation, the national system was, from the outset, treated with deep suspicion. More fundamental than these considerations was the opposition of the clergy of the established Church to the perceived loss of their control over the educational system. A widely-held belief among the clergy defended the right of the established Church to maintain control over any system of education that the state might provide. A less extreme version of this proposition argued that while the state had the right to intervene in the education of Catholics and Presbyterians, it had no such rights with respect to Anglicans. Following the setting up of the national system, members of the established Church campaigned against it, vigorously, both inside and outside

Parliament. The most important positive achievement of the established Church was the creation of the Church Education Society in 1839, to rival the national system. Under the direction of Archbishop Beresford, and organised along diocesan lines, the society at one stage of its operation had enrolments which exceeded those of the national system.[28] By the late 1850s, however, the society was in serious financial trouble, and in 1860 Beresford publicly recommended that the established Church schools be placed under the control of the commissioners of national education.

In contrast to the established Church, the response of the Catholic Church to the national system of education was one of general support during the 1830s and 1840s.[29] After 1850, however, this was withdrawn and pressure for a Catholic denominational school system intensified. Initially, however, the Catholic population was the major source of strength for the national system. This resulted from the positive disposition of a number of leading figures within the Catholic hierarchy, especially Daniel Murray, the Archbishop of Dublin, William Crolly, Bishop of Down and Connor, and James Doyle, Bishop of Kildare and Leighlin. John MacHale, Archbishop of Tuam, dissented from this view and from 1838 engaged in public dispute with Murray. This dispute was eventually referred to Rome for arbitration, but no definitive judgement was forthcoming. The matter was therefore left to the discretion of individual bishops, who, apart from MacHale, generally encouraged the Catholic schools in their dioceses to join the national system. On the positive side, for Catholics, the new system was preferable to the only alternative available prior to 1831, government-financed Protestant Society Schools. It was only after the Great Famine, when the political influence of the Catholic Church was greatly enhanced under the leadership of a new and less accommodating hierarchy, that the demand for an alternative to mixed national education was articulated and pursued. This alternative was to take the form of separate Catholic denominational schools financed largely from government funds.[30]

The initial Presbyterian response was similar to that of the established Church; they too were extremely suspicious of the national school system primarily because of its creation by a Whig administration. They too were hostile to the idea of sharing control of the education of their children with other denominations. In contrast to the established Church they did not attempt to provide an alternative schooling system of their own. They pursued what amounted to a campaign of violence and intimidation which achieved considerable concessions from the commissioners of national education as early as 1840.[31]

It is against this background of the different denominational responses to the national system of education that the complex web of Whately's relations to the various religious groupings must be viewed. It explains why, within the established Church, Whately was regarded with suspicion and even outright hostility for his contribution to the work of the Board. Similarly, the response of the Catholic hierarchy, especially in the 1830s and 1840s, to national education helps to explain the extent to which Whately could work with considerable ease and success with Daniel Murray. It has been argued that the 'Whately–Murray axis was the foundation stone of the Irish national education system, and without their cordial understanding it is possible that opposition Protestant forces would have destroyed the system'.[32] Throughout the period of his involvement with the national system Whately remained committed to the principle of non-denominational schooling, even when it entailed the risk of estrangement from his co-religionists.

The reason for Whately's commitment to a system of non-denominational education deserves further examination. His response to the Dean and chapter of St Patrick's, Dublin in January 1832 provides us with some insight into his thinking on this issue.[33] What separated Whately from most of his fellow clergy was his view that the provision of education was essentially a civil responsibility which should be administered by the government and not be dominated or controlled by any one religious denomination. He returned to and expanded on this theme later in the same year. He argued that while a number of serious questions could be raised with respect to the national system, it was still the best that could be devised in the difficult Irish circumstances. Whately's view that any solution to the problem of popular education in Ireland had to be acceptable to the major denominations, including the Catholic Church, alienated him from most of his co-religionists.[34]

In the troubled sectarian circumstances of Ireland, Whately saw a mixed education system as having a positive unifying role. He returned to this theme on numerous occasions. In conversation with Nassau Senior, in the early 1850s, he argued that the educational system 'prevents the diffusion of an amount of superstition, bigotry, intolerance, and religious animosity'.[35] Whately actively opposed any system of education which would allow the schools to act as denominational institutions, and in the 1840s, when a Tory government considered the adoption of a denominational system, he threatened to resign as commissioner.[36] But Whately's commitment to the success of the Irish national education system was also influenced by religious considerations. He believed that Catholicism, in contrast to Protestantism, was irrational and that mass education would effectively subvert its potent superstitions. He also subscribed to the view that the reading of Scripture in the schools would undermine the dogmatic influence of the Catholic Church. This was ironic, as the scriptural extracts chosen by Whately for use in the schools had been approved by Archbishop Murray. Both agreed on the principle of using such extracts, but differed in their estimation of the likely effects.[37] Despite the theological differences between them, Whately was convinced that the schools should impart the rudiments of elementary morality which, he believed, were common to both religions. On this issue, as on others, Whately was negotiating the difficult terrain of extracting from scriptural sources the elements of a moral instruction which offended neither Catholic nor Protestant. The syntax and vocabulary of this moral language were, of necessity, scriptural, thereby risking the charge of proselytisation. Consequently, the search for a secular language for moral and ideological instruction was of immense significance in the circumstances of the sectarian divisions and tensions in Ireland. Whately's response to this challenge was to prove extremely effective, enabling him to exert enormous influence on popular education not only in Ireland but also in Britain. This he did through his extraordinarily deep and extensive involvement in the provision of school textbooks, as author, editor, ubiquitous reviser, as influential policy-maker and as administrator of the system which published, distributed, and, through its inspectorate, supervised the use of these books.

The commissioners published a series of textbooks, each volume of which was designed to provide material for a year's instruction. In addition, a number of supplementary volumes, on more advanced topics, were also produced. A major distinguishing characteristic of these textbooks, in contrast with the existing alternatives, was the graduated nature of the course of instructions which they contained. The use of these particular texts was not compulsory; school managers could, with the approval of the commissioners, substitute alternative texts, so long as these were deemed to be non-sectarian.[38] The textbooks produced by the commissioners were quickly adopted throughout the national school system, notwithstanding that teachers were given this concession to choose alternatives.[39]

The high regard in which the Irish-produced textbooks were held was reflected in the rapid expansion of demand for their use in schools not only in Ireland but in a number of countries, including England and Scotland. In response to these external demands the commissioners felt it necessary, in 1836, to appoint agents in London and Edinburgh to oversee the supply and sales of their textbooks. During the 1850s the Irish textbooks were unquestionably the most popular and widely-used set of schoolbooks, not only in Ireland but in England and a number of other countries. In 1851 about 100,000 of these were sold on the English market.[40] The popularity of the Irish books provoked the anger of English publishers, and in 1849 Longman and John Murray wrote to Lord John Russell, charging unfair competition on the part of the Irish commissioners of national education. Invoking the principles of free trade, the English publishers sought to curtail the Irish commissioners selling their books directly to the British public or to British schools at reduced prices. Their efforts were successful and, in November 1852, the treasury withdrew this right.[41] Notwithstanding this development, Irish school-books had become, by the mid-nineteenth century, the most extensively used and influential set of basic textbooks in the history of popular education.

Whately's contribution to the basic lesson-books began in 1844 when he produced a *Sequel to Second Book of Lessons*. This arose from the fact that the movement from the second to the third books was considered too difficult for most children to negotiate with ease. The purpose of Whately's *Sequel* was to ease this transition. Two years later, Whately undertook a complete revision of the *Third Book of Lessons*, originally written by William McDermott, and in the same year he also produced a *Supplement to the Fourth Book*. It might be noted that Whately's interest in pedagogic literature for children dated back to a lengthy article of his in the *London Review* of 1829 on the 'Juvenile Library'.[42] Whately's contributions to the textbooks of the commissioners of national education were extensively used until at least the mid-1860s in both Ireland and England.[43] In these books Whately adopted a high moral tone and, despite the apparently rigid demarcation between the secular and the sacred, did not feel he had transgressed either letter or spirit by including strategically-placed accounts of biblical history in 'secular' texts. Nevertheless, he made every attempt to achieve a scrupulous neutrality in interpretation with respect to the major religious denominations. Notwithstanding the good intention of the authors, the inclusion of moral and biblical anecdotes facilitated covert sectarianism, a charge which was made with increasing frequency against the books of the commissioners of national education. This was inevitable in that the provision of a purely secular education, uncontaminated by religious considerations, was unacceptable to the general ethos of the major religious groups in Ireland. The dilemma was how to maintain a strictly non-denominational system of education while, at the same time, seeking to impart a denominationally-neutral form of religious and moral instruction. The achievement of this aim was fraught with danger. However, Whately enlisted the assistance of the most powerful secular discourse of the nineteenth century, political economy, a discipline claiming scientific neutrality while being both overtly and covertly ideological.

Whately's involvement in the popular teaching of political economy came about through an initiative of the Society for Promoting Christian Knowledge.[44] In 1832 the Society set up a committee to produce a series of publications for popular consumption. The publications were, in general, consistent with the aims of the Society in promulgating Christian principles, but were not exclusively religious. Their initial aim was to produce publications for adults, but soon they focused their attention on the provision of cheap textbooks for schools. This concentration on school-books was largely motivated by the perceived success of the Society for the Diffusion of Useful Knowledge, a rival organisation held in deep suspicion by the major religious groups involved in education.[45] In 1833 Whately proposed to the Society for Promoting Christian Knowledge that a text on political economy be produced for use in the schools. His original proposal was that a simplified version of his *Introductory Lectures* on *Political Economy* be published. The Society tentatively agreed, insisting that extracts should first be published in the *Saturday Magazine*. Satisfied with the reaction, the Society agreed that the work should be published in book form, under the title *Easy Lessons on Money Matters: For the Use of Young People*, as a private venture on the part of their official publisher, Parker.[46]

Easy Lessons on Money Matters was from the outset a popular text. Anthony Richard Blake, a Catholic commissioner of the Board of National Education, told the Select Committee of the House of Commons (17 August 1835) that the book was 'valued very highly', and was 'much sought for, not only at home but abroad'.[47] By 1862 the English language edition reached its sixteenth impression. Certainly Whately himself was pleased with its reception. By 1835 an Irish translation had been published and there was also a French edition. Writing to Thomas Arnold in 1835, Whately pointed out that *Easy Lessons* had even been translated into Maori and 'proved *Easy Lessons* highly acceptable to the natives'.[48] While the response to the book was very satisfactory, its audience was largely middle-class, not the working-class as Whately had intended. 'The lower orders', he wrote in 1833, 'would not ... be, as now, liable to the misleading of every designing demagogue ... if they were well grounded in the outlines of the science, it would go further towards rendering them provident, than any other scheme that could be devised'.[49] Using his very considerable influence as a commissioner he had *Easy Lessons* incorporated into the *Book of Lessons* series. The original edition of *Easy Lessons* was divided into ten sections, of which four were included in the *Third Book of Lessons* and the remaining six in the *Fourth Book*.

It was the inclusion of *Easy Lessons* in the lesson-books that provided Whately with his most extensive readership. A Royal Commission on primary education in 1851 established that in that same year the commissioners sold approximately 300,000 of their textbooks to Irish schools and disbursed another 100,000.[50] Of this total, almost 50,000 consisted of the advanced readers, namely the *Third*, *Fourth* and *Fifth* lesson books.[51] By 1865 almost 140,000 Irish children were studying the *Third* and *Fourth* books.[52] Whately's theories of political economy were reaching enormous numbers of the school-going population in Ireland.

The success of the Irish textbook (with Whately as the central figure) not only in Ireland but also in Britain, is a significant example of the colonial periphery, its dependent status notwithstanding, exerting influence over the metropolitan centre. By the 1850s the Irish commissioners were supplying schools in more than a dozen countries, including England and Scotland.[53] In 1851 about 100,000 books were sold in the English market, and by 1859 this number had trebled. On the basis of a conservative estimate, Goldstrom claims that nearly one million Irish school-books were in use in England in 1859.[54] If we assume, at a minimum, that one-fifth of this total comprised the *Third* and *Fourth* lesson books, then at least 200,000 children, primarily from the working classes, were nurtured in Whately's theories of political economy.

Whately's influence was not confined to either the direct use of *Easy Lessons* or of the *Third* and *Fourth* lesson books. The immense appeal of the Irish school-books ensured that they were widely imitated. In 1840 the British and Foreign School Society produced its first set of school-books containing non-religious material. Modelled closely on the Irish originals, the contents of their *Daily Lesson Book, III*, included ten lessons on political economy, a number of which were made up of extracts from Whately. Later in the 1840s, the Society for Promoting Christian Knowledge reprinted the *Irish Fourth Book of Lessons* which, of course, included the final six sections of Whately's *Easy Lessons*, and also decided to publish a separate version of Whately's text. In the 1850s the Society produced its own readers which included extracts from *Easy Lessons*, while, in the following decade, the National Society also produced its own advanced readers which again included extracts from Whately. From the 1830s to the 1880s, as Goldstrom observes, no school reader published by religious societies concerned with popular education was without its quota of Whately, either in direct form or indirectly through adaptation.[55] By 1860, it has been estimated, the Irish school texts had about half the market in England, a fact commented on by the Newcastle Commission on the state of popular education in England which published its findings in 1861.[56] This implies that about one million Irish school-books were in use in England, with the corollary that a further million texts were in circulation, many of which contained extracts from Whately. From the 1830s to the 1860s, the numbers of Irish and English schoolchildren who encountered the principles of political economy, whether directly or indirectly, through Whately's *Easy Lessons*, could be numbered not in their thousands, or even hundreds of thousands, but in their millions. It is difficult to dispute the conclusion that, in his time, Whately was 'the most widely published of economists'[57] and, by implication, perhaps, the most influential.

What, one might ask, did Whately attempt to teach his vast audience of Irish (and other) schoolchildren? In what does Whatelian political economy, as presented in *Easy Lessons*, consist? The first four sections, which were produced in the *Third Book of Lessons*, presented a brief and elementary exposition of the following topics: money, exchange, commerce, and coin. In these early sections, Whately attempted to seamlessly combine the positive and normative, the apparently neutrally descriptive with the morally prescriptive. For instance, having extolled the virtues of money as a medium of exchange in facilitating the smooth operation of trade, Whately quickly modulated to the moral and religious discursive mode:

> We are cautioned in Scripture against the love of money. It is indeed, a foolish and wicked thing to set your heart on money, or on *any* thing in this present world. ... But we ought to be thankful for all the good things which Providence gives us, and to be careful to make a right use of them. The best use of wealth, and what gives most delight to a true Christian, is to relieve good people when they are in want.[58]

This was followed by an ingenious description of how money not only facilitated exchange for goods and services, but also facilitated the efficient administration of charity:

> For this purpose, money is of the greatest use; for a poor man may chance to be in want of something which I may not have to spare. But if I give him money, he can get just what he wants for that; whether bread, or clothes, or coals, or books.[59]

The lesson on 'Exchange' provided a simple account, in the tradition of Adam Smith, of the division of labour and the advantages that accrued from it. The lack of this practice 'in some rude nations' was highlighted and the consequences starkly summarised: 'Where everyman does everything for himself, everything is badly done; and a few hundreds of these savages will be half-starved, in a country that would maintain as many thousands of us in much greater comfort'.[60] Lesson III on 'Commerce' extended the discussion of the benefits of the division of labour and exchange to the international domain, again in the Smithian tradition. The lesson ended with the characteristic moral note:

What a folly it is, as well as a sin, for different nations to be jealous of each other, and to go to war, instead of trading together peaceably; by which both parties would be the richer and the better off. But the best gifts of God are given in vain to those who are perverse.[61]

The fourth lesson, on 'Coin', provided a simple and lucid account of the characteristics which made coin, derived from precious metals, acceptable as a medium of exchange.

The content of Lesson V and of subsequent lessons (all of which were included in the more advanced *Fourth Book of Lessons*) was more extended and the analysis considerably more sophisticated than is the case in the earlier material. The first edition of the *Fourth Book* contained six lessons, but this was increased to seven in later editions. The topics dealt with included 'Value', 'Wages', 'Rich and Poor', 'Capital', 'Taxes', 'Letting and Hiring', and, in later editions, 'Interference With Men's Dealings With Each Other'. These lessons reveal the explicit ideological commitment to the defence of the status quo and the maintenance of the existing social order. Extracts from these lessons were reproduced extensively in other school readers, and so reached a vast audience of schoolchildren in Ireland and abroad. Lesson V, 'On Value', was one of the most interesting sections in *Easy Lessons* and was, in itself, a convincing refutation of Goldstrom's view that this work is 'a simple, orthodox exposition of classical theories'.[62] Whately clearly did not subscribe to the conventional classical theories of value either in the 'cost-of-production' tradition of Adam Smith or in the 'labour theory of value' tradition of David Ricardo. Whately was concerned to establish the determining factors of exchange value, which was value 'in the proper sense of that word; that, no one will give anything in *exchange* for them; because he can have them without'.[63] He distinguished three contributing causes that conferred value on products. The first, after alluding to the difference between value and usefulness, was scarcity. 'In some places', Whately argued water is scarce; and then people are glad to buy it ... But water is not more *useful* in those places where people are glad to buy it, than it is here, where, by the bounty of Providence, it is plentiful. It is the scarcity that gives it value. And where iron is scarce, that is of great value.[64]

But scarcity was not sufficient to explain value on its own. The product had to be desired: 'scarcity alone, however, would not make a thing valuable, if there were no reason why any one should *desire* to possess it'.[65] There was, finally, a third characteristic required to complete the necessary and sufficient conditions to establish the exchange value of a product: it had to be transferable. Whately stated that

> besides being desirable, and being scarce, there is one point more required, for a thing to have value; or (in other words) to be such, that something else may be had in exchange for it. It must be something that you can *part with* to another person.[66]

This view of value was practically identical with that held by Whately's friend and predecessor at Oxford, Nassau Senior.[67] It was firmly based on a theory of supply and demand as the determinants of value, and resembled, in structure, Alfred Marshall's treatment of the same topic later in the century.[68]

In the second part of the same lesson Whately refuted the labour theory of value. The flavour of his reasoning is best conveyed in his own words:

> When anything that is desirable is to be had by labour, and is not to be had *without* labour, of course we find men labouring to obtain it; and things that are of very great value will usually be found to have cost very great labour. This has led some persons to suppose that it is the labour which has been bestowed on anything that *gives* it value. But this is quite a mistake. It is not the labour which anything has cost that causes it to sell for a high price; but, on the contrary, it is its selling for a high price that *causes* men to labour in procuring it.[69]

Whately had recourse to theology to explain what 'causes men to labour'. 'It is not', said Whately repeating his refutation of the labour theory of value, labour that makes things valuable, but their being valuable that makes them worth labouring for. And God, having judged in his wisdom that it is not good for man to be idle, has so appointed things by his Providence, that few of the things that are most desirable can be obtained without labour.[70]

In speculating, as historians of economic thought have done, on why at Trinity College Dublin a 'school' of thought devoted to a subjective theory of value, clearly at odds with the then predominant classical theories, should emerge in the 1830s, one must necessarily pay close attention to the doctrinal position of the founder of that chair.[71] Whately's influence, whether directly or indirectly exercised, on the education system was such that from the age of eight up to university level, Irish students were left in no doubt about the analytical and ideological errors of classical cost-of-production and, more especially, the labour theories of value.

The determination of wages, dealt with at length in Lesson VI, was an area of central concern for Whately. In these matters Whately shared the general anxiety of his class generated by developments during the 1820s and 1830s.[72] His immediate aim was to establish why some 'labourers are paid higher than others' and he established early on in this lesson that 'the rate of wages does not depend on the hardness of the labour, but on the *value* of the work done'.[73] On what, asked Whately, 'does the value of the work depend?' His answer was unequivocal: the value of each kind of work 'is like the value of anything else; it is greater or less, according to the *limitation of its supply*; that is, the difficulty of procuring it'.[74] The 'limitation of its supply' was in turn influenced by three contributing factors. Firstly, the costs of additional education acted as a barrier to entry, which in turn restricted the supply, thereby leading to higher wages for those occupations requiring extended education. Secondly, a restricted supply of 'natural genius' in an occupation had the same effect, Whately argued, of pushing up the wage-rate as in the case of extended educational requirements. Finally, any 'occupation that is *unhealthy*, or *dangerous*, or *disagreeable*, is paid the higher on that account; because people would not otherwise engage in it'.[75] What Whately provided here was a detailed but succinct account of the supply-side of the labour market.

While allocating considerable space to considerations of factors that influenced the wage-rate based on the supply-side, Whately was emphatic that wage-rates were determined by the free interplay of supply and demand, and vigorously defended this proposition. 'The best way', he stated, was 'to leave all labourers and employers, as well as all other sellers and buyers, free, to ask and to offer what they think fit; and to make their own bargain together, if they can agree, or to break it off, if they cannot'.[76] This followed (in part II of Lesson VI) his defence of the proposition that fixing the wages of labour was intrinsically harmful, claiming that, in general, 'laws of this kind come to nothing'. He also rejected the view that 'the rising and falling of wages depend on the price of provision', a proposition which may have appeared intuitively obvious to a young mind. But Whately skilfully used the logic of market supply and demand to demonstrate the 'error' of this line of reasoning.[77] Whately bestowed no sympathy on those labourers who 'often suffer great hardships, from which they might save themselves by looking forward beyond the present day'. If when a man, insisted Whately,

> is earning good wages, he spends all, as fast as he gets it, in thoughtless intemperance, instead of laying by something against hard times, he may afterwards have to suffer great want when he is out of work, or when wages are lower. But then he must not blame others for this, but his own improvidence.[78]

Closely related to Whately's analysis of wage-determination was Lesson XI entitled 'Interference with Men's Dealings with Each Other' which was not included in the original edition of *Easy Lessons*. This lesson was, in effect, an attack on all kinds of interference in the labour market on the part of government. 'It may be said', Whately argued, 'that more harm than good is likely to be done, by almost any interference of Government with men's money transactions'.[79] But his most vituperative criticism was directed at trade unions, which for its intensity and unrelenting hostility deserves quotation at length:

> Most of the people of this kingdom reckon themselves freemen, and boast of their liberty, and profess to be ready to fight and to die, rather than submit to slavery. They look

down with pity and contempt on the Russian bond-men [or serfs] and the negro-slaves, and on the subjects of the despotic governments of Turkey or Persia. And yet many of these people choose to subject themselves to a tyranny more arbitrary and more cruel than that of the worst Government in the world. They submit to be ruled by tyrants who do not allow them to choose how they shall employ their time, or their skill, or their strength. Their tyrants dictate to them what masters they shall work for, what work they shall do, what machines they shall use, and what wages they shall earn. Sometimes these tyrants order them not to earn more than a certain amount; sometimes not to earn less; and sometimes to refuse all work, and see their families starve. They are heavily taxed for the support of their tyrants; and if they disobey, they are punished without trial, by cruel beatings, by having their limbs broken, or their eyes put out with vitriol, and by death.

These unhappy persons are those who have anything to do with *Trades-Unions and Combinations*.[80]

The remainder of this lesson was devoted to a more systematic examination and critique of the behaviour of combinations, with particular reference to the effects of strikes. Whately drew heavily on Irish experience to highlight his central points and, at one stage, he could be credited with discovering yet another theory for explaining Ireland's economic underdevelopment and social unrest: 'In Ireland', Whately argued,

> Combinations have driven away most of the manufacturers and commerce: so that *all* the people are forced to seek employment on the land. And as there is not land enough for all, there is a continual struggle to obtain land and to keep it, which often leads to outrages and murders.[81]

It is likely that Whately's implacable hostility towards trade unions owed a great deal to the influence of his friend, Nassau Senior. According to Marian Bowley, 'Senior looks to Whately for help with questions of logic, and vice versa in regard to economic theory proper'.[82] Senior's involvement with the issue of trade unions went back to 1830, when he was asked by the Melbourne Government to undertake an examination of the law on trade combinations and to make proposals for reform. Senior was deeply disturbed by the sometimes violent events which followed the repeal of the Combination Laws in 1824: the strikes for higher wages, the widespread riots, and the sporadic destruction of machinery which paralysed a number of industries.[83] The report which Senior (assisted by Thomas Tomlinson) submitted to Lord Melbourne, in August 1832, contained 'the most intolerant measures which, if they had been enforced, and provided they had not provoked a revolution, would have effectively hampered the Trade Union Movement'.[84]

The draconian measures[85] urged against trade unions, their members and supporters, proved politically unfeasible for the Melbourne administration and Senior's Report was, in effect, ignored, which was a source of major disappointment to him.[86] Notwithstanding its official reception, Senior's Report contained interesting material which he later included in the *Report of the Royal Commission on the Condition of the Hand-Loom Weavers* published in 1841.[87] By 1841 Senior's views on trade unions had mellowed somewhat, his main concern now being with their economic effects, especially on the mobility and freedom of labour. But in the 1830–2 period he was clearly so alarmed by events that his proposed stringent measures were, in his view, warranted; which, had they been implemented, 'would have undone the work of the Philosophical Radicals in achieving the repeal of the Combination Laws in 1824–5'.[88] Notwithstanding this critical assessment, there is no evidence that Senior ever advocated or desired a return to the pre-1824 state of the Combination Laws. He later characterised the old laws as demoralising, and argued that their administration had been 'partial and oppressive'.[89] He later conceded his 'limited knowledge of the facts' and his 'incompetence to report fully on the amendments necessary in the existing law'.[90] It is also to Senior's credit that, on further consideration and in response to criticism, he was prepared to abandon many of the original proposals. While in the 1832 Report he defended the state of common law concerning combinations, he later insisted that modifications of that law were 'required both by expediency and by justice'.[91] Like most nineteenth-century liberals, Senior felt that trade unions were inimical to the freedom of the individual and he remained ideologically hostile to them.[92]

Senior's influence on Whately in Lesson XI of *Easy Lessons* is clearly discernible. What the schoolchildren of Ireland and elsewhere were exposed to in *Easy Lessons* was a deep-seated hostility to trade combinations, which was not, in general, representative of the response of the classical economists to the trade union movement, nor did it reflect the part they played in the repeal of the Combination Laws in 1824.[93] Whately's stance on trade unions (as represented in *Easy Lessons*) was far from being 'a simple, orthodox exposition of classical theories',[94] its dogmatism and unqualified ideological hostility being uncharacteristic of classical political economy. Whately's views, unlike those of Senior, were never modified. It came as some comfort, Whately mused, 'to reflect that the people have it in their own power to remedy the worst evils which they are liable to. Whenever they come to understand their own true interests, they will agree to resist all illegal combinations.'[95] Properly taught, with the aid of such a powerful instrument of ideological instruction as *Easy Lessons*, future generations of Irish citizens could no doubt, in Whately's view, be relied on to identify correctly 'their own true interests', thereby ensuring economic and social harmony.

It was in Lesson VII, entitled 'Rich and Poor' that Whately was, arguably, at his most ingenious. It was logically appealing that this lesson should follow on from the lesson on wages where Whately had established the 'laws' of differential wage determination. In Lesson VII the propertied classes were introduced. 'Besides those' the lesson began 'who work for their living, some at a higher rate, and some at a lower, there are others who do not live on their labour at all, but are rich enough to subsist on what they, or their fathers, have laid up'.[96] Lest the impression be given that life among the men of property was one of agreeable idleness, it was quickly pointed out that 'many of these rich men ... do hold laborious offices; as magistrates, and members of parliament'; and that their motives were most laudable in that 'this is at their own choice. They do not labour for their subsistence, but live on their property'.[97]

The introduction of this social class inevitably meant that the questions as to how property was acquired and its rights established would have to be addressed. This topic was introduced with the salutary reminder that there 'can be but few of such persons compared with those who are obliged to work for their living'.[98] The analysis of the means of acquiring property followed Senior's theory of profits based on his celebrated theory of abstinence.[99] 'Young people', Whately promised, who make good use of their time, and who are quick at learning, and grow up industrious and steady, may, perhaps, be able to earn more than enough for their support; and so have the satisfaction of leaving some property to their children. And if these again, should, instead of spending this property, increase it by honest diligence, prudence, and frugality, they may, in time, raise themselves to wealth.[100]

Such was the glittering prize that Whately offered his audience of pauper children in nineteenth-century Ireland. Lest expectations be unduly raised, that the diligent pursuit of Whately's own recommendations would result in widespread upward social mobility, a cautionary note was sounded. 'It is, of course', Whately warned, 'not to be expected that many *poor* men should become rich; nor ought any man to set his heart on being so'. But by way of consolation 'it is an allowable and a cheering thought, that no one is shut out from the hope of bettering his condition'.[101] The rights of property and the security of property were justified by Whately within a developmental perspective. Whately repeated on numerous occasions throughout *Easy Lessons* that 'in any country in which property is secure, and the people industrious, the wealth of that country will increase'.[102] By inverting this argument, Whately proposed a 'theory' of underdevelopment. It was the case

in some countries; where property is so ill-secured, that a man is liable to have all his savings forced from him, or seized upon at his death. And there all the people are miserably poor; because no one thinks it worth his while to attempt saving anything.[103]

The second part of Lesson VII addressed the crucial problem of distribution within society. 'Can it be supposed', Whately asked, 'that the poor would be better off if all the property of the rich were taken away and divided among the poor, and so allowed to become rich for the future?'[104] Whately was quite emphatic in his position on this question. A number of lines of argument were brought forward to sustain his verdict that, in these circumstances, the 'poor would then be much worse off than they are now'.[105] The high point of his argument was surely reached when, as a result of the hypothetical redistributive process, the rich 'would have become poor; but the poor, instead of

improving their condition, would be much worse off than before.
All would soon be as miserably poor as the most destitute
beggars are now. Indeed, so far worse, *there would be nobody to
beg of*.[106] Even to eight-year olds, for whom Whately felt *Easy
Lessons* was appropriate, his conclusion, after that graphic piece
of deduction, must have sounded reasonable. It was

best for all parties, the rich, the poor, and the middling, that
property should be secure, and that every one should be
allowed to possess what is his own, and to gain whatever
he can by honest means, and to keep it or spend it, as he
thinks fit, – provided he does no one any injury.[107]

Having established the unacceptability and unviability of
redistribution, Whately proceeded to demonstrate that the rich, in
disposing of their income, produced an acceptable and efficient
means of distribution which, echoing Adam Smith, was achieved
notwithstanding the fact that the rich man might be 'a selfish
man', who cared 'nothing for the maintaining of all these
families', though he still maintained them.[108] Summarising his
position, Whately concluded that

the rich man, therefore though he appears to have so much
larger a share allotted to him, does not really consume it;
but is only the channel through which it flows to others.
And it is by this means much better distributed than it could
have been otherwise.[109]

This lesson ended, as did so many in *Easy Lessons*, with scripture
being cited to buttress the fundamental 'laws' of Whatelian
political economy. 'It is plain', Whately wrote, 'from this, and
from many other such injunctions of the Apostles, that they did
not intend to destroy, among Christians, the security of property
which leads to the distinction between the rich and the poor'.
Scripture forbade us to 'covet our neighbour's goods', not
because 'he makes a right use of them, but because they are
his'.[110] This was the characteristic mode of Whately's presentation
in *Easy Lessons*; as preacher, ideologue, and teacher he conveyed
the principles of political economy as incontrovertible 'laws'.

Easy Lessons in Money Matters was among those school-books
which were not published by the commissioners of national
education, but sanctioned by them and supplied to national
schools at reduced prices. It was available to the public for one

shilling, to national schools for threepence, and to 'poor schools' for sixpence.[111] It was also among the 'gratuitous stock' given to schools when they were taken into the national system and which was renewed at the end of every four years. This consisted in one specimen copy of each book which had to be kept in the classroom.[112] *Easy Lessons* was also the text used in teacher training and as a basis for both annual and general examinations of teachers for classification and promotion. In 1835 the commissioners of national education proposed to establish five professorships in their Central Training Institution and Central Model Schools in Marlborough Street, Dublin, including one in 'Composition, English literature, history, geography, and political economy'.[113] The professor appointed was Robert Joseph Sullivan who lectured on, among many other subjects, 'The *Elements of Political Economy*, taking Archbishop Whateley's [sic] "Easy Lessons on Money Matters", as the basis; and touching only on those topics which are *plain, practical,* and *corrective* of *popular prejudices*'.[114] By 1855 Sullivan was assisted in his labours by John Rintoul.[115] In 1870 Rintoul was giving 'special instruction' in the English Department in the '*Elements of Political Economy*', using *Easy Lessons* and the 'lessons in the national school books on the same subject' and still touching 'only on those topics which are *plain, practical,* and *corrective* of *popular prejudices*'.[116]

Political economy was also taught at the Albert National Agricultural Training Institution at Glasnevin, Dublin.[117] In 1879 'literary instruction' was given by D.P. Downing, which included a course in the 'elements of political economy'.[118] Writing in 1853, J. Macdonnell, a teacher in Larne Model Agricultural National School, stated that political economy had 'always formed a part of the education of the boys here, but more especially during the past year have I felt myself called on to devote more than ordinary attention to it'.[119] It seems quite certain that other agricultural schools also provided instruction on the subject. Political economy was also studied by pupil teachers in the District National Model Schools who were required to master the complete text of *Easy Lessons on Money Matters*.[120] To judge by the evidence of Ballymena and Coleraine District Model Schools, one hour per week was devoted to the combined study of *Easy Lessons on Reasoning* and *Easy Lessons on Money Matters*.[121] In competitive examinations for inspectorships political economy was an obligatory subject. As well as *Easy Lessons*, Books I and II of Adam Smith's *Wealth of Nations* were also prescribed. There was also a more advanced optional course in the subject which required potential school inspectors to study, in addition to the basic course, Books III and V of *Wealth of Nations*, Malthus's *Essay on Population*, Senior, and Books I, II, III and V of John Stuart Mill's *Principles of Political Economy*.[122] There is some evidence that political economy was taught in elementary schools outside the national system, for example in the schools of the Church Education Society. This Society was founded in Dublin in 1839 by clergy and laity of the established Church 'united in conscientious objection to the recently established system of National Education in Ireland'.[123] *Easy Lessons* was available (for ninepence) in the lists of books recommended for use in its schools.[124] It was also used for instruction at the Society's Training School, Kildare Place, Dublin.[125]

National teachers were appointed by local patrons and school committees but the commissioners had to be satisfied as to their moral and intellectual fitness. Teachers were categorised as first, second, and third class (with 'divisions' within the first class) as well as 'probationers'. Some teaching was also done by monitors and by pupil-teachers in the model schools. Teachers had to have been instructed at the 'normal establishment' or Central Training Institution in Marlborough Street, Dublin 'or shall have been pronounced duly qualified by the superintendent of the district in which the school is situated'.[126] The salary received by teachers depended on their classification, 'regard being had to their qualifications, the *average number* of children in attendance, the state of the school' and the 'extent of instruction afforded in it'.[127] Women teachers were graded in the same way as men but were paid less in every class. There was an obligatory classification every five years and an annual optional examination for classification and promotion (or, in some cases, demotion). The first general classification for male teachers took place in 1848 and for female teachers in 1849. These examinations were both written and oral, the written usually preceding the oral by five to six months. The written examinations were usually held on the same day throughout Ireland, were corrected by the district inspectors and the results forwarded to the head inspectors. Failure at the written meant disqualification from the oral examination.[128]

In their first general examination, held in 1848, male teachers were examined in a wide range of subjects, including political economy. The questions were based on *Easy Lessons* and the standard of answering was, in general, considered by the head inspectors as reasonably satisfactory. According to Edward Butler, head inspector, the answering appeared 'to have been of a fair average character, and such as would lead us to infer that the lessons are taught in the school with care and judgement'.[129] He stated that 47 per cent of the teachers examined in his jurisdiction answered in this manner, and 21 per cent 'acquitted themselves in a very creditable manner', while 32 per cent performed unsatisfactorily. He concluded that 'much yet remains to be done'.[130] William McCreedy reported as follows: 'The answering of above a half was satisfactory, and of these a large number showed a thorough comprehension of the entire subject, and expressed themselves well in their replies; not seldom, indeed, in a masterly manner, and with great precision and neatness'.[131] James W. Kavanagh reported that, in general, 'all the teachers who are upwards of a year in office showed some, and the trained teachers, and such as had been taught in National Schools, showed a very general and accurate knowledge of the substance of the lessons'. The oral answering on the subject was far better than the written, but very many teachers 'appeared not to have studied the little treatise itself – the extent of their knowledge being confined to the chapters contained in the class books'.[132] James Patten, head inspector for the north west district, found the teachers ill-prepared for the examination in political economy and disappointing in their answering. The teachers expressed regret at having 'omitted to make themselves more familiar with the principles treated of' in *Easy Lessons* and promised to amend their ways.

In the following year, 1849, James Patten found the answering again unsatisfactory. Only 13 per cent of those examined in his area reached the highest standard; he received no answers from 31 per cent of the candidates. He graded 26 per cent of the teachers as 'middling' and 30 per cent as 'defective'.[133] Matters improved in 1850, however, with Patten reporting that the satisfactory marks of 'good' and 'pretty fair' had risen to 47.5 per cent and the proportion of candidates not submitting answers had declined dramatically to 7.3 per cent.[134] The 'satisfactory' ratings in Patten's area improved again in 1852 to 54 per cent, and to a remarkable 84.5 per cent in 1853, moving down marginally to 82 per cent in 1855. The lowest grading of 'very bad' improved to

6 per cent in 1852, and reached zero in both 1853 and 1855. The number of candidates whose answering was 'very superior' was zero in 1850, but rose to 0.68 per cent, 1 per cent, and 9 per cent respectively in 1852, 1853, and 1855.[135] In his 1850 report, William McCreedy also noted that teachers had improved in their answering in political economy on their 1848 performance.[136] The 'satisfactory' ratings for McCreedy for the years 1850, 1851, and 1852 were 67 per cent, 47.5 per cent, and 63 per cent respectively, while his 'very bad' category was 10 per cent in 1850 and 8 per cent in 1852, having climbed dramatically to 28 per cent in 1851. His 'very superior' category was vacant in 1850 but stood at 3 per cent and 2.5 per cent respectively in 1851 and 1852.[137]

The results of the written examination for teachers seem to have been reproduced even less frequently than for the oral ones in the various Reports of the Commissioners of National Education, though the actual examination questions in the various subjects were frequently printed. The accounts of the written examinations give details of the number of teachers examined, the number of questions in each subject, the total number of answers possible, the number of *satisfactory* answers, the number of *imperfect* answers, and the percentage of questions attempted. There were three categories of examination papers, A, B, and C which were set for first-class, second-class and third-class teachers (including probationers) respectively. Given the limited information available it is impossible to draw any firm conclusions concerning the standard of performance. However, from a truly homoeopathic sample it seems as if, in general, the amount of 'satisfactory' answering compared quite favourably with that marked 'imperfect'. For example, the ratio of 'satisfactory' to 'imperfect' answering for William McCreedy's area in 1851 was 0:60, 16.7:61.1, and 23.8:30.4, 31.8:36.4, and 15.7:34.5. The equivalent figures from James Patten's returns for 1852 were 16.7:41.7, 32.8:18, and 10.1:19.7.[138]

The annual reports contained occasional accounts of examinations in various subjects (including political economy) for pupil teachers, paid monitresses, agricultural pupils, and regular national school pupils. For example, the returns from Bailieborough District Model School in 1851 gave details of the performance in political economy of four pupil-teachers (three Bs and one C), two agricultural pupils (one B and one C), and four paid monitresses (three Bs and one C), where A, B, C, D, and E stood for 'very good', 'good', 'middling', 'bad', and 'very bad'.[139] The report from the Trim District Model School for the same year informed us that the five (named) pupil-teachers answered two questions satisfactorily, nine questions imperfectly, and one question wrongly.[140] In Coleraine District Model Schools six candidates were adjudged to have been 'very good' (two), 'good' (one), 'tolerable' (one), and 'poor' (two).[141] In the District Model Schools in Ballymena there were seven pupil-teachers presenting for examination and they were marked 'excellent' (three), 'very good' (two), 'good' (one), and 'poor' (one)[142]

There were a number of accounts in the reports of the annual public examinations of schoolchildren in the District Model Schools. For example, in October 1851 the boys of Bailieborough District Model School were examined in several subjects, including political economy, by Inspectors James Patten and Eugene A. Conwell, 'in the presence of many respectable residents in the town and neighbourhood'.[143] The Newry District Model School's examination of the same year (which also included political economy, for boys only) was conducted by Inspectors James Patten and Edward Butler, 'in the presence of a large and representative audience'.[144] In 1853 this public examination of the pupils in Newry was conducted by the head teachers, pupil-teachers, and monitresses and it included several questions in political economy, again only for boys.[145]

The examination questions set for teachers were frequently reproduced in the Reports of the Commissioners, but those for other groups were rarely published. An exception was the very comprehensive Powis Report which contained the papers in political economy set by the civil service commissioners for the competitive examinations for inspectors of national schools, held in December 1869 and February 1870.[146] The annual Report for 1851 contained an example of an examination for pupil-teachers given by Edward Butler at Trim District Model School.[147] He asked students to give an 'abstract of the lesson on *rent*' and to 'write out the heads of a lesson on *value*, for Fourth Class boys'.[148]

In the examinations for teachers, questions were asked on such topics as the division of labour, fixed and circulating capital, rent, wages, interest, taxation, money, and the national debt. But the topic which recurred most frequently was the theory of value. The questions leave us in no doubt that cost-of-production and especially labour theories of value were not only unscientific, but also wicked. Teachers were asked, for instance, to show that 'it is not the labour employed in producing any thing that makes it valuable',[149] and the following question was put in 1850: 'To suppose that it is the labour which has been bestowed on any thing that *gives* it value, is quite a mistake'.[150] Even when questions were couched in neutral terms, there was little doubt as to what answer was required.

The first general examination for male teachers was held in the revolutionary year of 1848 and the examination papers, which were reproduced *in toto* in the Report for that year, reflected the ideological anxieties of the upper orders in Irish society, as indeed did the papers for subsequent years. Several questions reflected the fear that anarchy was about to be loosed upon the country. There was even a hint of desperation about a question in 1848: 'Why is even a bad government *better* than no government? Why *cheaper*?'[151] In 1856 candidates were asked to prove that 'anarchy is more prejudicial to a country than tyranny'.[152] According to the ruling ideology, the main function of the state was to provide the conditions necessary to enable the market to function efficiently, the *sine qua non* of which was the guaranteeing of security of persons and property. The state was strictly precluded from having a determining role *within* the market system. State intervention, usually pejoratively described as 'interference', was held to be, at best pointless, and, at worst, positively pernicious. 'How do you show', candidates were asked in 1855, 'that all attempts of government to regulate *by law* the rate of wages must be useless and mischievous?'[153]

Security of property was a ubiquitous theme in the examination questions of the late 1840s and throughout the 1850s. According to Nassau Senior, writing in 1843, the reason British capital did not flow to Ireland was because of the chief 'moral evil' of that country – 'the insecurity of persons and of property' arising from the 'tendency to violence and resistance to law which is the most prominent, as well as the most mischievous, part of the Irish character'.[154] This insecurity of property put capital, notorious for its timidity, to flight. It was accepted, in the words of an examination question in 1848, that 'inequality of fortunes must necessarily arise with security of property'.[155] This individualist, libertarian ideology bought liberty at the expense of equality, but this inequality was twice blessed as it enabled not only liberty but also the Christian duty of charity. If the poor did not exist then the propensity of the rich towards being charitable would have remained unexercised. Charity benefited the poor materially and the rich spiritually and, as a bonus, helped to counteract communism.[156] In 1848 teachers were asked to show that 'security of property is essential to the exercise of charity as recommended by the Apostles'.[157] Egalitarian ideas were condemned as uneconomic, morally and politically dangerous, and unscriptural.

A few examples of questions on these related themes should suffice: 'Is security of property necessary to the growth of wealth?',[158] 'Illustrate, by historical examples, the evils arising from insecurity of property',[159] 'Would the spoliation of the property of a rich man ... and its division among the people, prove beneficial to the labouring population of a country? Show why not',[160] 'Relate the fable by which the mistake that the existence of the rich causes the poor to be worse off, is exposed'.[161] All of these examples come from 1848. In 1849 a whole paper was devoted to the section 'Rich and Poor' in Easy Lessons on Money Matters. Candidates were asked to develop such points as to the 'Injurious effects of laws that would, with regard to amount of property, place all persons, and oblige them to remain, upon the same footing', the 'Advantages resulting to all the inhabitants of a country from security of property', 'The rich cannot but benefit the country', and 'The Apostles did not intend that the distinction between rich and poor should be abolished among Christians'.[162]

Examination questions leave us in no doubt as to the pernicious nature of trade unions and strikes. In one examination teachers were asked to 'State the evils resulting from Trades' Unions and Strikes',[163] and in another, in the same year, were asked to 'Give a brief account of an unsuccessful Strike'.[164] In the following year candidates were asked to 'Enumerate the several ways in which labour and the employment of capital have been sometimes interfered with, by what are called Combinations and Trade Unions'.[165] In 1852 a question was asked as to whether a successful or an unsuccessful strike was likely to prove 'more hurtful to the workman' and this was followed by the question: 'In what way can the teacher exert himself with a view to prevent the lamentable consequences of such unions or combinations of the employed against the employer?'[166] In the same year teachers were asked 'To what departments of trade in Dublin have Trades' Unions proved injurious?'[167]

It is interesting to note that in the years immediately following the Great Famine, the activities of corn dealers were felt to be in need of justification. 'What is the illustration made use of', began a question in 1848, 'to show the beneficial action of the corn dealer upon the market of provisions, in times of scarcity?'[168] In another examination, in the same year, candidates were asked to show 'in what way the business of the *Corn Dealer* ministers to the public services', meaning the common good.[169] The question was rephrased the following year: 'How is it shown that the interest of the Corn Dealer coincides with that of the public?'[170]

Although the scientific nature of the discourse of political economy was much trumpeted, where necessary it was supplemented (and perhaps eventually subverted) by the more traditional and more ideologically-potent discourses of morality and religion. To give a small example, candidates were asked in the examination to prove that, with respect to interest, it was not only reasonable but 'just' to be 'required to pay for a loan of money, as for the loan of any thing else'.[171] In like fashion, when the redistribution of wealth is described as 'robbery' and 'spoliation' it is difficult not to conclude that this activity is morally disapproved of. We have already seen that 'spoliation' of the property of the rich was not considered to be beneficial to the labouring poor. 'Would the robbery of the rich', candidates were asked in 1848, 'and the equal distribution of the wealth among the poor, prove beneficial to the people?'[172] On the crucial questions concerning security of property and the distinction between rich and poor, the authority of the Apostles was sometimes invoked. We have already noted that the Apostles taught that security of property was 'necessary to the exercise of charity', and that they did not intend abolishing the distinction between rich and poor among Christians. In 1856 the following question was asked: 'Passages from the New Testament are often quoted to prove that the security of property was not recognised by the Apostles; show that this opinion is exactly the reverse of the fact'.[173]

The not-so-hidden agenda of the examination questions was to undermine the cost-of-production and especially the labour theory of value, and to deny the state any function in the redistribution of wealth. The questions were clearly intended to justify the ways of landlords and capitalists to tenants and wage-earners, and of the owners of the means of production to the consumers. Rent was justified on the basis that it was not responsible for the high price of agricultural produce and, in like fashion, the cost of provisions was held not to determine the rate of wages. In general, the coincidence of the individual and the common good was assumed and harmony was seen to exist (where the market was allowed its uninhibited course) between labour and capital, tenant and landlord, poor and rich, and also between nations. Inequalities were justified on economic, moral, and theological terms, but these imbalances of power were not held to vitiate the notion that all exchanges were mutually enriching, that, as one question put it, 'what the people receive in exchange is, on the whole, a fair equivalent'.[174]

When Whately commented, 'I am a very unpretending writer, for my best works are the little ones', he had in mind, no doubt, the school textbooks he had produced. Of these *Easy Lessons* and the extracts from it which were reproduced in school readers throughout the nineteenth century were the most widely disseminated and influential of Whately's writings. *Easy Lessons* was one of the pivotal texts in the popularisation of political economy among the children of the working classes from the 1830s to the 1880s. Whately's role as an evangelist for political economy was pervasive in the formal educational system. He was the *de facto* head of the Board of National Education (1832–53) and he founded and funded the Whately Chair of Political Economy at Trinity College Dublin and took a close interest in its progress. Outside the confines of schools and universities, he exerted considerable influence through his enthusiastic involvment in the Dublin Statistical Society, of which he became the first president (1847–63), an office he held until his death. It is to this Society (later to become the Statistical and Social Inquiry Society of Ireland) that we turn in our next chapter in order to examine its significant role, in association with the Barrington lectures, which it administered, in spreading the gospel of political economy.

5

'TO THE POOR THE GOSPEL IS PREACHED'
The Dublin Statistical Society and the Barrington Lectures

When John Barrington (1800–36), a merchant of the city of Dublin and a member of the Society of Friends, discovered a combination of workmen against the firm of which he was a member, he was struck with the 'ignorance of their own true interests which the workmen displayed, and he thought if they had been better informed they would not have entered into unwise Combinations to regulate Wages'.[1] As a result, he bequeathed, on 14 July 1834, a sum of £3,000 in trust to Edward and Richard Barrington 'to be invested in public securities; the interest arising from which to be applied to the payment of a fit and proper person or persons, duly qualified to give lectures on Political Economy in its most extended and useful sense, "but particularly as relates to the conduct and duty of people to one another"'.[2]

In 1849 the trustees of the Barrington bequest offered the council of the Dublin Statistical Society the administration of its endowment for promoting its lectures in political economy, an arrangement which endures to this day.[3] The trustees authorised the council to appoint one or more lecturers, to be called 'Barrington Lecturers on Political Economy', to hold their appointments for a period of one year. John Barrington directed that the lectures should be given 'in the various towns and villages of Ireland, without distinction, and as often as might be'. Applications from towns for courses of lectures were sent to the Statistical Society each year in the month of March. According to the 'Regulations Respecting the Barrington Lecturers on Political Economy', applications emanating from 'literary and scientific societies, or from municipal bodies, are more favourably entertained than those coming from persons in their private capacity'.[4] Such organisations were expected to provide local arrangements and to pay for the lecture room and for advertising. A small charge for admission might be made, though care had to be taken that the 'working classes have an opportunity of attending in some part of the room at a charge not exceeding one shilling for the entire course'.[5]

In 1860, the trustees decided to change the method of selecting Barrington lecturers with a view to having only one lecturer, to be appointed by competition, and to hold office for a period of three years, with an annual income of £120, less income tax. Previous incumbents were chosen by the council on the basis of holding university positions in political economy, of having performed well in the competition for the Whately chair in Trinity College Dublin or as undergraduates, or on the basis of testimonials. Now each candidate had to read a lecture of his own composition before the trustees and members of the council, and also to give an unwritten lecture on a subject chosen by council at one day's notice. The successful candidate had to give four courses of public lectures each year, three in provincial towns, and one in Dublin.[6] The first contest was held in the Dublin Athenaeum in May, 1861 and the winner was Andrew M. Porter, a barrister and graduate of Queen's College Belfast.[7] When Porter completed his three-year stint, advertisements for candidates were placed in the leading Irish and English papers. The extempore lecture was replaced by an oral examination, 'to be conducted by three members of Council, being professors or ex-professors of political economy in the University of Dublin'.[8] The examiners were Longfield, Cairnes, and the current Whately Professor, Arthur Houston. Six of the candidates passed 'a highly satisfactory examination in economic science, and subsequently delivered lectures of no ordinary merit' before the council,' on topics chosen by themselves.[9] The appointment went to John Monroe, a barrister and graduate of Queen's College Galway, where he had been a student of Cairnes. He graduated in 1857 and was a Senior Scholar in Metaphysical and Economic Science (1858–9). He later became Solicitor-General for Ireland and a judge of the High Court.

During the twenty-third session of the Society (1869–70), the council 'entered into a new and permanent arrangement' with the Barrington trustees and 'resolved to enlarge the subject of the lectures' by adopting the name 'Lectures on Social Science', which, they felt, was the modern equivalent of the testator's intention. They also reverted to the original mode of selecting lecturers: instead of electing one lecturer for three years, they decided to elect two or more lecturers for one year only.[10] Under the new arrangements Robert Donnell, later to become Whately Professor (1872–7), and Professor of Jurisprudence and Political Economy at Queen's College Galway (1876–83), and William Mulholland were the selected candidates. They were reappointed the following year. However, in the twenty-fifth session (1871–2) an earlier arrangement, whereby four lecturers were selected, each responsible for one course, was resorted to.

Because of a decline in demand for the Barrington lectures by local societies in the 1872–3 session, the council appointed a committee to consider the matter, under the chairmanship of John Kells Ingram and including William Neilson Hancock. Having consulted with Edward, Richard, and Arthur Barrington, trustees of the fund, the committee decided to substitute 'teaching lectures' for the existing prelections, 'with local committees to superintend and give prizes, and local lecturers to be selected'.[11] However, those lecturers had to be approved by the lecture committee of the council. They were divided into two classes: those who obtained university prizes in political economy, and schoolmasters who had passed an examination set by the Barrington lecture committee and obtained a certificate of qualification to teach political economy. Of the first class, two lecturers were selected in the twenty-seventh session (1873–4), Revd Samuel Prenter, on the recommendation of a Political Economy Class Committee of Belfast,[12] and William H. Dodd, on the recommendation of the committee of the Church of Ireland Young Men's Christian Association. The Belfast class numbered fifty-five, of whom eighteen passed the examination while eleven of the eighteen participants succeeded in Dublin. Prizes were awarded to successful students from funds collected locally. Sixteen schoolmasters presented themselves for the certificate examination, having been recommended by local committees. Eleven succeeded and eight of these were appointed Barrington lecturers.[13] This scheme remained in operation for the next twenty years though with declining success. In the 1894–5 session the trustees reverted to the old system of appointing a single Barrington lecturer. There were about seventy candidates in all and the victor was Charles Hubert Oldham, who continued in office until 1901.

Like the holders of the Whately chair at Trinity College Dublin, many of the Barrington lecturers were young men who distinguished themselves in various occupations in later life. James Anthony Lawson, who held the Whately chair from 1841 to 1846, was 'requested' to be one of the first four Barrington lecturers 'on account of his distinguished position as a Political Economist'.[14] The other three, Moffett, Heron, and Hearn, were selected from a list of candidates 'who had all distinguished themselves at the professors' examinations in the University'.[15] Lawson, who was, for a short time, an MP, became Solicitor-General, Attorney-General, and finally a judge. Thomas William Moffett became Professor of Logic and Metaphysics (and later of History, English Literature and Mental Science), Registrar, and finally President of Queen's College Galway. Denis Caulfield Heron became Professor of Jurisprudence and Political Economy at Queen's College Galway, was, for a brief period, an MP, and had a distinguished legal career. William Edward Hearn was the first Professor of Greek in Galway; he emigrated to Australia where he was one of the original professors in the University of Melbourne, becoming, for a time, its Chancellor. Apart from Lawson, three other Whately Professors had been Barrington lecturers: Richard Hussey Walsh, John Elliot Cairnes, and Robert Cather Donnell. Cairnes and Donnell also became professors at Queen's College Galway, while Cliffe Leslie became Professor of Jurisprudence and Political Economy at Queen's College Belfast, and Charles Hubert Oldham went on to hold the Chair of Commerce at University College Dublin. James H. Mussen Campbell became Lord Chancellor of Ireland. Like John Monroe, Thomas Busteed also went on to become a judge. Andrew Marshall Porter had a successful legal career culminating in the office of Attorney-General.

Barrington lecturers were required to give 'at least eight lectures in Dublin, and at least twenty-four lectures in not less than four other towns or villages in Ireland'.[16] These lectures were organised locally, especially by mechanics' institutes and various literary, scientific, and philosophical societies. In the session 1849–50, for instance, lectures were delivered to the Working Classes Association, Belfast (by Lawson), to the Mechanics' Institute at Clonmel (by Moffett), to the Mechanics' Institute at Waterford (by Heron), to the Mechanics' Institute at Dundalk (by Hearn), to the Dublin Mechanics' Institute (by

Lawson, Heron, and Hearn), and to the Mutual Improvement Association in Dublin (by Moffett). Additional voluntary courses were delivered at Galway (by Moffett) and at Belturbet (by Hearn). As might be expected, mechanics' institutes were very active in the organisation of Barrington lectures, not only in Dublin, Dundalk, Clonmel, and Waterford as already mentioned, but also in Ardee, Portaferry, Wexford, Carlow, Navan, Lurgan, and Drogheda. Lectures were also held in Coleraine and Downpatrick and, as both towns had Mechanics' Institutes which were Corresponding Societies with the Statistical Society, it is almost certain that they organised the lectures.[17] Barrington lectures were held in the Literary Societies of Tuam and Lurgan and, presumably, at those of Kilrea, Lisburn, and Enniskillen, all of which were Corresponding Societies. The Literary and Scientific Societies of Limerick, Belturbet, Garvagh, and Cork held lecture-courses, as, most likely, did Belturbet which was a Corresponding Society. There were Mutual Improvement Societies in Waterford and Limavaddy and a Mutual Instruction Society in Mountmellick; all were Corresponding Societies and were, presumably, hosts to the Barrington lectures. Certainly the Mutual Improvement Association of Dublin was exposed to political economy on more than one occasion. Series of lectures were organised by an extraordinarily varied array of societies: Dublin Church of Ireland Young Men's Christian Association, Dublin Presbyterian Association, Dublin Mercantile Clerks' Association, Dublin Working Men's Committee, Kilkenny Literary and Scientific Institution, Belfast Working Classes Association, Cork Catholic Young Men's Society, Dundalk Free Public Library, Enniskillen Committee for Promoting Exhibitions of Manufactures, Armagh Natural History and Philosophical Society, Dungannon Society for Promoting Science, Literature, and the Arts, and the Friends' Institute, Dublin. Again, it is highly probable that the Barrington lectures held at various times in Newry, Banbridge, Galway, and Limerick were organised by the Newry Institute, the Banbridge Literary Institute, the Royal Galway Institution, and the Limerick Social Inquiry Society, respectively, all of which were Corresponding Societies with the Statistical Society. Sometimes local societies were especially set up to avail of the Barrington scheme, and on a few occasions public bodies such as the Commissioners of the Boroughs of Trim and Clonakilty and the 'Mayor and inhabitants of Belfast' took the initiative.

As we have noted, eight Barrington lecturers were appointed from the ranks of schoolmasters in the session 1873–4. They were: Andrew Clements (Anahilt Endowed School, Co. Down), D. Campbell (Blackwater Town National School, Co. Tyrone), Michael Mulhern (Caddlebrook, Co. Roscommon), C. McDermott (Corraclare Science School, Co. Clare), Edward Reynolds (Dunmanway Model School, Co. Cork), John Lyons (Drumcoe National School, Co. Donegal), J. Moylan (Limerick Model School), John Magennis (Lisded National School, Co. Fermanagh). These seem to have been the only venues at which political economy was taught under this particular scheme.

The Barrington lectures were most in demand between 1850 and 1872, and the scheme was reasonably satisfactory in the 1870s. However, in the 1880s and 1890s it went into serious decline. It is worth analysing the twenty-two year span between 1849–50 and 1871–2 (there was no Report for the session 1869–70) when the lectures were at the height of their popularity. A total of 113 courses (there were usually six lectures in a course) were given in political economy, at some fifty locations throughout Ireland, giving an average of five per session over the twenty-two year period . The busiest session was 1853–4 when courses were provided at a total of eleven different locations, followed by 1871–2 with nine, and 1870–1 with eight. On the other hand, only two courses were given in 1866–7, and three in 1863–4 and 1868–9. In this period twelve courses were conducted in Dublin, followed by Cork with six and, curiously enough, Armagh, also with six. Belfast and Clonmel organised five courses each, followed by Waterford, Dundalk, Limerick, Derry, and Lurgan with four, Galway, Coleraine, Kilkenny, Drogheda, and Enniskillen with three, Belturbet, Lisburn, Holywood, Downpatrick, Portaferry, Kilrea, Limavaddy, Newry, and Ballymena with two, while the remaining twenty-six locations had one series of lectures each. The popularity of the Barrington lectures was greatest in Ulster, where almost half of the entire series of courses was given. It accounted for 46.9 per cent of all Barrington lectures, followed by Leinster with 28.32 per cent, Munster with 20.35 per cent, and Connacht with a mere 4.42 per cent (a grand total of five courses).

In 1850, at the end of the first year of its stewardship of the Barrington lectures, the council of the Statistical Society declared that it had 'much reason to be satisfied with the manner in which the lecturers discharged their duties' and that the trustees of the bequest were happy with the new arrangements.[18] The following year the council reported that it had received communications indicating 'how completely the lectures have fulfilled the intention of the founder'.[19] At Tuam, the Report went on,

> we learn that the numbers attending the lectures were very large, considering the size of the town; that 100 attended the first lecture, and at each succeeding lecture the numbers attending increased, so that 1,100 and upwards enjoyed the benefit of the lectures; and the committee describe the lectures of Dr Lawson as calculated to advance the knowledge of economic science, and win attention to its principles.[20]

The directors of the Dublin Mechanics' Institute stated that the attendance was '400 at each lecture', adding that 'lectures on political economy had been heretofore viewed by the class who frequent the Mechanics' Institute as adverse to the interests of the working man', but that Professor Moffett, in his recent course, 'had invested the subject with a charm that would, on a future occasion, insure it a more favourable, perhaps, they might say a more just reception and hearing, than it has hitherto been wont to meet with'.[21]

According to the council, the 1851–2 session was also very successful. Lawson's lectures at the Royal Dublin Society 'were very numerously attended, and great interest was taken in them', while there were 'most favourable accounts of the effects produced by the lectures in carrying out the objects of the founder'.[22] In 1853 both Moffett's and Cliffe Leslie's courses in Dublin 'proved extremely successful', and Moffett's lectures at Derry, Downpatrick, Coleraine, Holywood, and Portaferry were 'attended with the most marked success, – a result, we believe, which that extremely efficient lecturer never fails to produce'.[23] The 1853–4 results were again successful, and 'most satisfactory accounts' were received from the various bodies under whose auspices the lectures were given.[24] 'We can refer with pleasure', stated the council in its Report for the following year,

> to the accounts received from several of the provincial towns of the lectures, lecturers, and attendance. Even in the small town of Trim, the numbers attending exceeded, on an average, one hundred, and on occasion were so high as one

hundred and sixty. The audience, we are informed, were highly gratified with the course of lectures, and expressed a hope that on a future occasion they might be favoured with another. This growing taste for economic science must be very pleasing to all who are interested in the successful working of the Barrington bequest, and the best results may be anticipated to flow from the diffusion of sound principles in this department of knowledge among the rural population and the poorer classes of our towns and cities.[25]

According to the Report of 1855–6, Professor Moffett's (and political economy's) success continued. The return forwarded by the secretary of the Dundalk Mechanics' Institute disclosed the 'gratifying fact, that the attendance was nearly double at the last lecture what it was at the first, and that it increased progressively between the two extremes, – a sure indication of efficiency on the part of the lecturer, and of appreciation of his efforts by the audience'.[26] The council also reported favourably for the following two years. In 1861–2, the council 'received the most satisfactory assurances of the pleasure and profit' that Andrew Porter, the first lecturer to be appointed under the new system, 'gave to the audiences who attended the lectures'.[27] At the end of his three-year stint the council expressed their 'entire satisfaction with the manner in which that gentleman discharged his duties, and also their belief that through his able agency sound views of economic science have been very widely diffused'.[28]

The first clear indication that there was a decline in the support of the Barrington lectures occurred in the 1864–5 session, when John Monroe, Porter's successor, began his three-year incumbancy. He reported that the attendance at Banbridge, Armagh, and Kilkenny 'was in general fair', while in Dublin such lectures did not seem 'to prove as attractive as their value to the working classes, for whom they are intended, unquestionably deserves'.[29] The following year Monroe delivered courses in Cork and Lurgan, both of which were successful, especially in Cork where the audiences 'were never less than one thousand, and on one occasion exceeded twelve hundred', if we are to believe the lecturer. The audiences in Lurgan were not numbered but they were 'large and attentive' and they 'manifested their interest in the subjects discussed by asking a variety of questions at the close of the course'.[30] The Report for the year 1866–7 session pointed out that in recent years lectures in the provinces had been attended by 'large audiences, who evinced considerable interest in the subjects brought under their notice', whereas in Dublin applications for courses were now seldom made and there was sometimes 'much difficulty in procuring an opportunity for the delivery of these lectures'.[31] The council's Report for the following year revealed that no application had been received by them for lectures in Dublin, nor had any room been placed at their disposal for the delivery of lectures. In Dublin alone, the council felt, there was 'an apparent apathy and indifference among the classes whose benefit was especially contemplated in the establishment of these lectures'.[32] In an attempt to counteract the declining interest in political economy, especially in Dublin, in the session 1869–70 the council decided to enlarge the subject of the lectures by adopting the name of 'Lectures on Social Science' and to revert to their original mode of selecting lecturers.[33]

These measures did not manage to halt the decline in interest in political economy in Dublin, a decline which soon extended to the rest of the country. This state of affairs was blamed on the 'number of Societies formed for the purpose of giving lectures',[34] presumably without recourse to the Barrington fund. The council appointed a committee, with Ingram as chairman, 'to consider the best mode of conducting the Barrington Lectures'.[35] The operation of the plans devised by this committee was pronounced 'so far successful' in the Report for the session 1873–4,[36] and as 'working satisfactorily' in the year 1875–6.[37] We are informed that the Council had 'three classes in successful operation in Dublin' in the session 1878–9.[38] Throughout the 1880s and in the early 1890s there were either no reports on the Barrington lectures, or more often a perfunctory statement of the fact that the report of the examiners for the Barrington lectures was read and prizes and certificates distributed to the candidates. According to the Report for 1893–4, there were 'no lectures under the Barrington Trust delivered' and the lectures had not been 'during the last few years, as successful as the trustees could desire'.[39] Another new scheme was adopted, and the lectures of 1895 were pronounced 'a most complete success'.[40] The lecturer was C.H. Oldham, who had been chosen from as many as seventy candidates.[41] He held office until 1901, but nothing further of his labours was reported by the council of the Statistical Society. Apart from intermittent lecturing in the 1920s, the first three decades of the twentieth century saw the virtual total collapse of the Barrington scheme. In 1919 S. Shannon Millin stated that the Barrington fund 'had lain dormant for 12 years in consequence of the difficulty of finding suitable persons who would administer a trust which involved very considerable care and judgement'.[42] But there was also an all-too-visible deficiency in demand for political economy in Ireland, beginning in the mid-1860s and continuing relentlessly (despite occasional outbursts of enthusiasm for economic knowledge) for the rest of the century and well into the succeeding one. The scheme for schoolmaster-lecturers seems to have been no more successful than the others. When it was inaugurated in the session 1873–4, eight lecturers were selected. By 1875–6 only four schools were providing Barrington lectures: Limerick Model School, Dunmanway Model School, Blackwatertown National School, and Anahilt Endowed School. By the following year Blackwatertown was no longer providing classes, and a year later Edward Reynolds ceased lectures at Dunmanway. By 1880 only Limerick and Anahilt schools were in operation and the scheme seems to have failed, as there is no further reference to it in the council's Report.

Given the circumstances which led John Barrington to endow the teaching of political economy, there is no doubt that his intended audience was the working classes. Furthermore, the 'Regulations Respecting the Barrington Lecturers on Political Economy' specified that the charge levied for each course should not exceed one shilling for members of the lower orders seeking economic enlightenment.[43] A number of the council's annual Reports refer specifically to the fact that the Barrington lectures were primarily intended for the working classes.[44] Lectures were given to various working-class groups such as the Working Classes Association of Belfast and, in 1876–7, to a 'class of working men in Bolton-street under the auspices of a working men's committee'.[45] In 1878–9 and in the following year courses were given to Working Men's Clubs in Christchurch Place and in York Street, Dublin. The council's Report for 1879–80 proudly noted that 'Mr Murphy, the Dublin working-man who was selected to preside at the recent Trades Union Congress', had 'obtained a certificate for proficiency in Political Economy' at an examination following one of these courses in a Working Men's Club.[46] John Monroe's extraordinarily successful course of lectures in Cork in 1865–6 was arranged by a committee consisting of the 'foremen of the principal shipbuilding and mercantile establishments in that city' and the audiences were 'composed principally of large numbers of intelligent artisans'.[47]

Barrington lectures were organised by eleven mechanics' institutes, but it is highly probable that a large majority of the approximately twenty-six institutes in the country were also involved. In Great Britain, most mechanics' institutes had their origins in the 1820s, began to decline in the 1830s and had, more or less, collapsed by 1850. Several mechanics' institutes were founded in Ireland in the 1820s – such as Cork, Ennis, Galway, Limerick, and Waterford. However, they were most active in the years 1840 to 1855, rather later than in Britain.[48] It is generally held that in Britain the movement as a whole was a failure because it did not teach operatives work-related skills, and was soon taken over by the middle classes. In Ireland, it is probably true to say that while in the early days the 'rough but intelligent sons of industry'[49] were well represented in the institutes, in later years few mechanics were to be found within their walls. According to Cliffe Leslie, in a two-part paper which he delivered to the Statistical Society in February and June 1852, there was a 'universal complaint, that mechanics' institutes are attended by persons of a higher grade than that for which they were designed; and the same observation applies to the athenaeums and literary societies'.[50] While this evinced 'on the part of the higher classes, a willingness to associate themselves both in name and fact with their humbler brethren',[51] it also meant that the classes for whom these institutes were intended were largely excluded from them. Significantly, Leslie dealt with both mechanics' and literary institutions, observing that 'Mechanics' Institutions, Athenaeums, and Literary Societies are, for the most part, names for associations of the same character, composition, and objects',[52] which 'in their full development exhibit so close a resemblance, both as to their arrangements and the classes by which they are supported, that they may be considered and treated of together by the social inquirer'.[53]

Leslie relied heavily on J.W. Hudson's *History of Adult Education* but found it seriously lacking in authority in regard to Ireland. Leslie disputed Hudson's claim that mechanics' institutes 'never prospered in Ireland for any lengthened period' and that the literary and philosophical societies presented the 'same state of inactivity and uselessness' that characterised similar institutions in

Great Britain.[54] Leslie conducted a limited survey of Irish institutions to discover what services they provided and, more importantly for our purpose, the social composition of their membership. Thirty-five such societies had come under his notice and he received replies with regard to twenty-seven of them. Only four of these existed prior to 1840, and thirteen had come into existence since the commencement of 1848. Leslie had no exact knowledge of the number of members 'belonging to different ranks and occupations', but his impression was that about 50 per cent of the total number were shopkeepers, shopkeepers' assistants, and clerks, 25 per cent had trades (carpenters, masons, and so forth) or were 'workmen or mechanics', 20 per cent were professional men or merchants, and the remaining 5 per cent were designated 'members of the higher class'.[55] Leslie emphasised that this was a mere impression, but it gives us some idea of the social composition of the likely audiences for the Barrington lectures in mid nineteenth-century Ireland.

According to the Regulations, Barrington lecturers had to be 'duly qualified to give lectures on Political Economy in its most extended and useful sense, "but particularly as relates to the conduct and duty of people to one another"',[56] a formulation frequently reiterated in the annual Reports of the council of the Statistical Society. Each lecturer was required to 'furnish an abstract of all his proposed lectures to the Council, to be submitted by the Council to the trustees for their approval', and lecturers were forbidden to deliver any lecture the abstract of which had been 'disapproved of by the Council or by the trustees'.[57] On completion of the course, each lecturer had to make a statement that all his lectures had been 'in conformity with the terms of the bequest, and the regulations of the Council on the subject'.[58] There was a strict instruction that every lecturer should 'abstain in his lectures from all allusions to party politics or religious polemics'.[59]

It was not until May 1859 that a specific letter of instruction was addressed to Barrington lecturers. It was issued by the honorary secretaries of the Statistical Society, W. Neilson Hancock, J.E. Cairnes, and Henry Dix Hutton, to inform lecturers what procedures the council wished them to adopt in their courses. It reminded lecturers of the circumstances which had led John Barrington to set up the fund, and was, in essence, a vindication of his purpose: if workers were better informed (through the good offices of political economy) then they would not enter into 'unwise Combinations to regulate Wages' or to oppose machinery.[60] Paragraph two of the letter made reference to recent disturbances in Ireland: 'The Council observe that recently there have been in Ireland several cases of Combinations against machinery; for example, that of the agricultural labourers against reaping machines in the County of Kilkenny, of the shoe-makers and tailors against sewing machines, and of the small against the large shopkeepers in Dublin, and of the weavers against power looms at Lurgan'.[61] It is worth noting that in the published Report of the council for that year, no reference was made to these events; the 'expediency' of dealing with the topic of combinations was justified on the basis of 'recent strikes in London' and 'similar movements of a less formidable kind in other parts of the country'.[62]

In view of the circumstances of the foundation of the Barrington lectures and of the intention of the founder, the council urged each lecturer 'to devote one lecture at least to the subject of combinations amongst workmen – the Lecture to be based on ascertained facts and applications of principle to them'. The lecturer should consider 'not only the conduct of the workmen, but also the means by which the partial suffering incidental to industrial progress' might be diminished.[63] With respect to the other lectures, the council thought it desirable that the lecturer should 'select practical questions in illustration of general principle rather than treat of the principles of Political Economy in the abstract'. Such questions as emigration and the effects of the discovery of gold, the letter went on, as well as 'the Ship-owners' complaints as to Navigation Laws, the Paper Duties, and other unwise modes of raising a revenue, would afford opportunities of illustrating some of the chief principles of Political Economy'. Such illustrations, it concluded, would 'in the opinion of the Council, be more attractive than abstract expositions of the elementary parts of the Science'.[64]

Only on a few occasions did the Reports of the council on the Barrington lectures give any indication of the actual topics dealt with by the lecturers. The most detailed account of the content of lectures was published in the Report for the year 1862–3:

The law of free trade in relation to commerce and to labour;
– the nature of money, and the effect of modern gold dis-

coveries; – the conditions of national prosperity in relation to Population; – Emigration; – Taxation; – the Galway Contract; – our Postal System; – Public Subsidies; – Work and Wages, with special reference to Irish Industry; – Results of Co-operative Organisation; – Schemes for providing Employment for Women; – the Irish Land Question Stated; – Tenant Right; – the Irish Poor Law; – Public Charities; – the Social Condition of Ireland, as evidenced by recent Statistics of Population and of Agriculture.[65]

In the session 1864–5, John Monroe lectured on 'Free Trade and Protection; on Trades' Unions and Strikes; on the Economic Aspects of Slavery; on Emigration; on our Fiscal System &c'.[66] In the following year, Monroe delivered his enormously successful lectures in Cork and Lurgan on the subjects of 'Co-operation, its rise and progress – Post Office savings banks, Friendly Societies, Government Annuities, and Free Trade'.[67] When, in 1869–70, the council decided to enlarge the scope of the Barrington lectures by replacing the term 'political economy' with that of 'social science', there was, in consequence, a more extensive range of topics available to the lecturers. The council decided 'to propose as a guide to the lecturers, that they should enter upon any subjects discussed at the meetings of the Social Science Congress'.[68] This was the name commonly given to the National Association for the Promotion of Social Science founded in Birmingham by Lord Brougham in 1856, an organisation whose interests were wide-ranging, extending far beyond the confines of even a generously-defined political economy. Occasionally, cards were issued announcing a series of Barrington lectures, and one of these which survives informed the public that C.H. Oldham, (who held office between 1895 and 1901) would be lecturing on the following topics: 'The Sources of Wealth in Ireland', 'British Supremacy in Foreign Trade', 'The Currency Question in Europe and America', 'The Present Position of the Working Classes', 'The Work of Business Management in Industrial Progress', and 'The Eight Hour Day and the Comparative Efficiency of Labour'.[69]

Though it was not part of the original plan of the Dublin Statistical Society to engage in the popular broadcasting of political economy through lectures and teaching, when asked to do so by the Barrington trust it gladly accepted. Thereafter the Society saw the organising of these lectures as one of its most significant functions. According to Captain (later Sir) Thomas Larcom, a vice-president of the Statistical Society, the Barrington lecturers fulfilled 'an important part in our general objects', carrying 'to all parts of the country sound information on important points' and diffusing 'insensibly an appetite for the information they convey'. In return the Society would receive 'local support and local collection of facts' to place the Society's researches 'on a wider and firmer basis'.[70] Sir Robert Kane, a vice-president of the Society and author of the celebrated *Industrial Resources of Ireland*, praising the liberality of the donor and the 'admirable efficiency' of the lecturers, remarked on 'how great a scale the benevolent intentions of the founder of that liberal endowment' had been carried out.[71] According to Jonathan Pim, who became president of the Society (1875–7), the study of economic questions in Ireland received its first impetus with the founding of the Whately chair, was added to through the efforts of its various holders and through the lectures and publications of the Statistical Society, 'but yet more by the lectures which, under the Barrington trust, have been delivered in various parts of Ireland, diffusing widely a knowledge of these subjects, and popularizing the abstract principles of statistical science'.[72]

In his address delivered at the opening of the eleventh session of the Society, James A. Lawson spoke of the Barrington lectures as having given to the Society 'a very extended sphere of usefulness'. The lectures had been 'attended with very marked success' and their benefit had been twofold:

> First, in the diffusion of sound economic knowledge; and secondly, it has been the means of training up for us in this city a class of young, educated, able men, fresh from our universities, who are induced to devote their special attention to the subject of political economy, and who then propose themselves to us to be sent out as lecturers for the purpose of carrying out the administration of this trust.

The council had never encountered any difficulty in finding lecturers and, in eight years, they had never received a complaint from the public,[73] sentiments Lawson repeated in his address in November 1862.[74] In his obituary notice of the Archbishop, Hancock stated that Whately's funding of the Trinity chair and Barrington's bequest were the 'two endowments to which our country has been so much indebted for a diffusion of the knowledge of social science'.[75] Finally, both Lord O'Hagan, president of the Statistical Society from 1867–70, and William Huston Dodd, president from 1894–6, were agreed on the success of the evangelists the Statistical Society, on behalf of the Barrington trust, had sent out to preach the gospel of political economy to the plain people of Ireland.[76]

6

'NEXT TO GODLINESS'
Political economy, Ireland, and ideology

'Absolute authority', wrote J.E. Bicheno, the philosophical tourist who visited Ireland in 1829, 'is never exercised by brute force alone. It obtains its ascendancy by appeals to antiquity, established institutions, the social affections, honour, glory, the weaknesses and infirmities of our nature, and everything which influences the imagination'.[1] He distinguished between the government of people through their 'affections' and 'understanding', claiming that authority was best exercised over Roman Catholics and the Irish by appealing to their affections and imagination. However, within three years of Bicheno's visit a state-sponsored system of elementary education was established in Ireland with the firm purpose of enlightening the darkened intellects of the Irish masses. Education was to play a crucial role in the pacification of Ireland and in combating Irish disaffection in the nineteenth century. Education, formal and informal, set out not only to augment the meagre store of Irish knowledge and to deplete the impressively abundant holdings of Irish ignorance and error, but, in effect, to change what was perceived as the Irish 'character', to substitute ordered, rational discourse (hence the teaching of logic in the national schools) for rhetorical excess, thereby promoting affection for England and the established Church. W.E. Hearn described protectionism as a 'killing kindness', a phrase which could also be applied to national education in the opinion of many Irish people. It was perceived as a Greek gift, being at once an instrument of national advancement and an organ of empire. Controversial topics were more-or-less excluded from the curriculum of the national schools (as indeed from the fare on offer from the Queen's Colleges, the Statistical Society, the Barrington lectures, mechanics' institutes, and all such improving

116

bodies) but the feeling of establishment figures, such as Whately, was that the ideological ends of education were achievable by formal means, by the inculcation of habits of disciplined and orderly thought. Central to this rational education was the new science of political economy, the dominant mode of English political discourse.

Political economy claimed ideological neutrality and the universal validity of its laws; modestly descriptive, it saw itself as superseding previous prescriptive moral and religious discursive modes. Here, at last, there seemed to be a form of incontrovertible, value-free knowledge which could adjudicate impartially between all conflicting social claims, an unprecedented boon to a society so spectacularly divided as Ireland. Here, at last, was solid, uncontested ground. In like manner, utilitarianism had attempted to reduce morality to a descriptive, scientific calculation of utility, without prescriptive content. In a truly Copernican revolution in morality, individual hedonism was miraculously transformed into social utility. The general good was achieved by the principle of *laissez-faire*, whereby each individual pursued his self-interest. In general, it was held that the new science of political economy had proved beyond doubt the coincidence of individual and general interests. Individual and social utility were to be achieved through the operation of *laissez-faire*, and the interests of classes, peoples, and nations pleasingly coincided. There is an important sense in which it was only when *laissez-faire* was seriously challenged that it became central to economic discussion. Arthur J. Taylor remarks that, unlike his predecessors 'for whom the question of *laissez-faire* had been at best incidental to the general discussion of economic principles, Mill set the role of government in the forefront of his argument'.[2] We would argue that the efficacy of *laissez-faire*, and by extension political economy, of which it was seen to form an intrinsic part, was most searchingly and most dramatically questioned as a result of the Great Famine of 1846–7. It is a considerable irony that the repeal of the Corn Laws and the first concentrated attack on *laissez-faire* happened simultaneously.

During the Famine and for the following decade or so, almost all Irish political economists defended *laissez-faire*. But by the end of the 1850s moral attacks on political economy were being heard more frequently, even from economists themselves. There was increasing opposition to the commodification of, for example, education, land, and labour. The absolute dominion of political economy was called into question and there was increasing emphasis on what Cliffe Leslie called the 'imperious conditions of time and place'. Methodologically there was a new tendency towards the historical and comparative and the Irish economists Leslie and Ingram were pioneers of historical economics in the English-speaking world. Many writers distinguished Irish conditions from English, so that economic policies appropriate to one country were not necessarily appropriate to the other. For some this was a powerful argument for a repeal of the Union and for various forms of home rule and self-determination; for others, such as Mathew Arnold, Ireland's difference made up for deficiencies in the English character, so that the 'marriage' of male John Bull and female Hibernia formed a perfect union.

Though most commentators, including, for instance, Hancock, Hearn, and Moffett, denied that the Irish character and the Catholic religion were among the causes of Irish economic backwardness, it was widely held that, in the words of Sydney Smith, the Irish character contributed 'something to retard the improvements of that country'.[3] The general feeling was that Irishness and Catholicism, especially when combined, were seriously lacking in economic virtue. Unfortunately the good qualities of the Irish, such as hospitality and open-handedness, were wasteful ones which militated against prudence and self-interest, the economic values *par excellence*. In 1820 Smith, a generally friendly observer, wrote that the Irishman had many good qualities:

> he is brave, witty, generous, eloquent, hospitable, and
> open-hearted; but he is vain, ostentatious, extravagant, and
> fond of display – light in council – deficient in perseverance
> – without skill in private or public economy – an enjoyer,
> not an acquirer – one who despises the slow and patient
> virtues – who wants the superstructure without the
> foundation – the result without the previous operation – the
> oak without the acorn and the three hundred years of
> expectation. The Irish are irascible, prone to debt, and to
> fight, and very impatient of the restraints of law. Such a
> people are not likely to keep their eyes steadily upon the
> main chance, like the Scotch or the Dutch.[4]

If these stereotypes were accepted, clearly the Irish, in Bicheno's terms, should be governed through their 'affections' rather than their 'understanding', and the English establishment and their intellectual garrison in Ireland made the serious mistake of applying to Ireland a system which was English, Protestant, individualistic and utilitarian. In Bicheno's words, the 'principle which governs mankind by reason, is of more modern date, and has grown out of the improvement of the human race. It relies for its success upon individual conviction, and appeals to utility, self-love, interest, profit, abstract truth'. Limited monarchies, he added, and 'modern republics, the Protestant religion, govern principally through the influence upon the understanding. Science, and all inductive philosophy, mechanics' institutions, and popular education, rely for their success upon this foundation'. However, the system of authority through affections was 'oldest and most universal':

> [It] has developed the character of man in its noblest of aspects: it has carried the social virtues to the highest pitch of perfection, and has crushed the selfish vices: it has nourished honourable feelings, generosity to the oppressed, charity to the poor, protection to the weaker sex, and has enabled man to exercise the most extraordinary self-denial.

The Catholic religion was a 'striking illustration of the government of men by their affections', for it appealed to their 'imaginations, by insisting on divine succession, by its splendid hierarchy, its architectural magnificence, shows, processions, music, pictures, images, dresses, and ornaments of the church'. Its services were almost altogether 'devotional' and its liturgy 'animating and impassioned'. Its pulpit addresses and manuals were not 'critical or argumentative, but the preachers and writers aim at the heart, and wing their arrows with all the sympathies and excitements their imaginations can supply'.[5]

Next to religion, Bicheno saw schools as 'one of the most powerful levers by which the mass of society in modern times is moved forward and directed'. Protestant education ministered to the understanding and had a tendency to 'magnify self-importance' and to withdraw the child 'from the influence of social sympathies and affections'. It gave 'vigour to a particular class of virtues, those which conduce especially to his prosperity, and which are well suited for a commercial and enterprising life'. The Catholic system, on the other hand, had 'a tendency to foster virtues of another kind, – generosity, social affections, fidelity, honour'. English and Protestant virtues were more appropriate to

119

a mercantile and industrial society, while those of the Irish and Catholics were more fitted for a feudal or clan social order. Political economy was the self-knowledge of bourgeois society, with its rational appeal to the understanding and with its presuppositions of personal conduct guided by individual self-interest. Bicheno condemned the narrowness and immorality of this approach: 'To paralyse the noble virtue of charity by the calculations of prudential reason, or the statistics of political economy, can never be the wish of any wise or good man'. In terms of political economy, Bicheno wrote, absenteeism might not have been injurious to Ireland, but the real evil was that the landlord was encouraged to treat land as merchandise, and to regard the relation between himself and his tenantry as 'little more than that between a buyer and a seller. The old connection was of a more social nature, and brought with it a most beneficial influence on all parties'. The old philanthropy and charity were gone and political economy had contributed 'very materially to this great and irreparable mischief '.[6]

It is potently symbolic that the two erstwhile friends, Richard Whately and John Henry Newman, never met in the four years (1852–6) Newman spent in Dublin as Rector of the Catholic University. Whately, a distinguished exponent of liberal Christianity, was the great evangelist of rational education and political economy in Ireland, while Newman, a convert to Catholicism, despised the 'cold doctrines of Natural Religion',[7] and described political economy as a discipline 'at once dangerous and leading to occasions of sin'.[8] In 'The Tamworth Reading Room', Newman denounced the view that scientific and secular knowledge had a considerable effect in promoting religious truth. He wrote:

> This is why Science has so little of a religious tendency; deductions have no power of persuasion. The heart is commonly reached, not through the reason, but through the imagination, by means of direct impressions, by the testimony of facts and events, by history, by description. Persons influence us, voices melt us, looks subdue us, deeds influence us. Many a man will live and die upon a dogma: no man will be a martyr for a conclusion.[9]

It is worth noting that the object of Newman's scorn was Sir Robert Peel, who, in a few brief years, was to again become

Prime Minister and to set up the 'godless' Queen's Colleges in Ireland, in opposition to which the Catholic University was established, with Newman at its head. It is significant that little political economy was taught at the Catholic University.

In his book *Irish Ideas*, published in 1893, William O'Brien stated tersely a commonly held perception: 'Sir R. Peel relied on two instruments to denationalize Ireland – the policeman and the schoolmaster'.[10] But a series of three articles in the *United Irishman* in April 1848, significantly entitled 'Educational Police', described national education bluntly as a 'police system', the school-room as the 'cunning focus of surveillance over the country round about', with school inspectors being used as 'spies', reporting to the 'police office' in Marlborough Street, under the direction of Whately, the 'principal agent in the perversion and corruption of this "national system"'. Whately had converted the national schools into an instrument for inculcating the 'doctrines of English imperialism' and the 'Gospel of Mammon' into schoolchildren,[11] and for teaching them the 'folly and vice of nationality'.[12] But it was not only radical nationalists who saw teachers as part of what Louis Althusser called the 'repressive state apparatus'. Anthony Richard Blake, a Commissioner of National Education, was asked the following question when he appeared before a Select Committee of the House of Commons on Education in Ireland on 17 August 1835: 'Do you see any objections, on constitutional grounds, to placing at the disposition of a Board, acting under the Government, the power of sending throughout the country an army of intelligent men disciplined by them, and to a great extent under their control?' Blake, a Roman Catholic, had no problems with seeing the body of national teachers as an 'army'. He could conceive nothing

> in our constitution to prevent so great an improvement, as I think would be affected by sending forth, through the National Board, teachers to every part of Ireland; on the contrary, I consider that the true constitutional principle to be that rather moral than physical power should be the means of government, and that this principle would be best called into effect through a good system of national education, conducted through well-educated and well-disposed teachers; they would be a moral Police, as useful, I should hope, as the existing constabulary force.

Blake's description of national teachers as a 'moral Police' force is obviously the source of the term 'Educational Police' in the *United Irishman*. Blake believed 'the more the influence of the teachers is exercised in support of lawful authority, in promoting constitutional obedience to constitutional power, the better'.[13] The general aim of the Commissioners was to train 'a new class of schoolmasters ... whose conduct and influence would be highly beneficial in promoting morality, harmony, and a good order, in the country parts of Ireland'. These teachers would be in friendly contact with the people and 'identified in interest with the State and therefore anxious to promote a spirit of obedience to lawful authority'.[14] According to the Commissioners, a national teacher should be

> a person of Christian sentiment, of calm temper and discretion; he should be imbued with a spirit of peace, of obedience to the law, and loyalty to his Sovereign; he should not only possess the art of communicating knowledge, but be capable of moulding the mind of youth, and of giving the power which education confers a useful direction.[15]

Next to the church, the school was seen as the most powerful social institution for the dissemination of 'correct' ideas. In the words of one head inspector, the school was the 'vestibule to the temple'.[16] Education acted as a 'preventive to intemperance',[17] not only in the consumption of drink but in conduct in general and in language, a necessary prophylactic against Irish violence, lawlessness, indiscipline, imaginative extravagance, rhetoric; in brief, an imperial measure against Irish colonial 'excess'. Properly functioning schools were seen as allaying 'social hostilities between class and class, and sectarian prejudices and antipathies between creed and creed'. In a country where poverty was 'arrayed against property, employed against employer, land against trade, creed against creed', all of these differences were 'blended' in well-run schools.[18] The general feeling was that this blending was best achieved by excluding controversial subjects and by teaching the others in a dispassionate and rational manner. Hence the frequent complaints about the celebrated 'dryness' of Irish national school books and the relatively austere character of primary education. Even singing was treated as a means of learning the 'most ennobling, moral, and religious truths', in the words of Head Inspector W.H. Newell. 'I canot help thinking', he added,

POLITICAL ECONOMY, IRELAND, AND IDEOLOGY

that if vocal music were generally taught in the National Schools, the songs learned would supersede those that the humble classes now generally sing, which are for the most part vicious trash, hawked about by itinerant ballad-singers; in times of political excitement too often seditious, and frequently obscene and demoralizing.[19]

According to another authority, music could be made more 'useful if the children were taught by it a lesson of self-restraint and subordination'.[20] A price, however, had to be paid for this utilitarian disparagement of the aesthetic. Writing in 1850, William McCreedy hoped that the Book of Poetry would 'inoculate' the children 'with a taste for the polite and more humanising parts of our literature, from which hitherto, unfortunately, many of them have either been entirely shut out, or so precluded from cultivating as to leave them unimproved by their softening influences'.[21] The problem was that this softening and humanising, this concern for the allegedly feminine aesthetic and moral spheres, unfitted people for the public, competitive, self-interested, male sphere of the market-place. Wishing to contain the excesses of the Irish character by inculcating rational knowledge, the establishment was also faced with a severe dilemma, for it would have been self-contradictory for it to achieve its ends by rhetorical or aesthetic strategies, but could well be self-defeating for it to attempt to achieve it by dry, rational means.

By and large the official view was that, in contrast with 'hedge schoolmasters', national teachers were moral, and politically loyal. The books used in hedge-schools were seen as inculcating disloyalty and irreverence for the law, consisting, according to various reports, of tales of rogues, robbers, rapparees, and loose romances. Glorifying outlawry they scarcely fostered 'habits of regularity and discipline which are yet more valuable than mere learning'.[22] The Commissioners of National Education produced their own textbooks and distributed them *gratis* or sold them cheaply, thereby introducing conformity throughout the system and encouraging loyalty and respect for the law.[23] The monopoly enjoyed by the Commissioners in the supply of books was objected to on *laissez-faire* grounds by the publishers Longman and Murray, while critics like Myles O'Reilly MP considered this 'virtual imposition' as exerting 'an evil political influence upon the people',[24] and Canon Toole, an English witness before the 1870

Royal Commission, spoke of it as 'limiting intellect'.[25] This glozing over of differences, at once utilitarian and imperial, led Patrick Pearse to denounce the intermediate education system introduced in 1879 as the 'murder machine' which 'took absolutely no cognisance of the differences between localities, of the differences between urban and rural communities, of the differences springing from a different ancestry, Gaelic or Anglo-Saxon'.[26] Paramount among all of the differences that were denied by the system of national education was that of nationality; Ireland was identified with England, and the coincidence of their interests assumed.

With reference to the national school-books, Assistant Commissioner Coward reported that

> it was of their un-Irish character that I heard most complaint made. The absence of any mention of Irish history in books intended to teach the inhabitants of Ireland was regarded as an attempt to destroy the feeling of nationality, and was the only feature which provoked much resentment.[27]

There was controversy from time to time over a song, 'The English Child', in *Hullah's Manual* which was provided to teachers who were qualified to teach singing. The opening stanza was as follows:

> I thank the goodness and the grace
> That on my birth have smiled,
> And made me, in these Christian days,
> A happy English child.[28]

From an Irish perspective the shortcomings of the system were best recorded by perhaps the most able Inspector of all, P.J. Keenan, in his invaluable *General Report* for 1855. 'We are', he wrote, 'quietly but certainly destroying the national legend, national music, and national language of the country', and Irish history was all but 'entirely neglected'.[29] The *Second Book of Lessons* unproblematically informed children that Ireland and England were 'called one nation'.[30] Indeed Whately himself and his family had an extraordinary input into the composition and revision of the *Reading Books*,[31] and the contents reproduced his assimilationist views. 'I have', said Whately, 'always looked upon Ireland as a part of my own country'; he wanted Ireland to become 'a really valuable portion of the British Empire, instead of a sort of morbid excrescence'.[32] According to the entry on Whately in Webb's *Compendium of Irish Biography*, he was 'thorough' in his opposition to 'Repeal and in the advocacy of centralization. He favoured the abolition of the Viceroyalty, of the Irish office, and of everything that tended to perpetuate a feeling of distinct nationality in Ireland.'[33] No wonder Whately regarded his 'small and unpretending' publications as of 'more real importance than his larger works'.[34]

Assimilation for Whately had also a religious dimension. In a famously controversial statement, reported by Nassau Senior, Whately said that

> mixed education is gradually enlightening the mass of the people ... if we give it up, we give up the only hope of weaning the Irish from the abuses of Popery. I cannot openly support the Education Board as an instrument of conversion. I have to fight its battles with one hand, and that my best, tied behind me.[35]

That the desire for religious assimilation might conflict with other forms of assimilation is best illustrated by the case of the establishment of a Professorship of Irish at Trinity College Dublin in 1835. A majority of the Board, 'under certain Limitations', approved of its foundation in order to 'promote the Civilization of the Irish Peasantry, and facilitate the preaching of the established Religion'. However, Dr Robert Phipps opposed the measure chiefly because 'the difference of Language is one of the chief Distinctions between the English & Irish Nations, whereas to identify them as far as possible is most desirable'.[36]

The Irish educational system, formal and informal, sought to exclude religious proselytism and political controversy. There is no doubt that the 'civilization' of various classes of Irish people was thereby promoted but the ideological price to be paid (sometimes willingly) for the interdiction on controversial subjects was a defence of the *status quo*, making it unquestioned and unquestionable. Dryness was ideologically conservative. But people like Whately felt that their ideological projects would best be achieved by making the Irish more *rational*, thus counteracting superstition in religion and the innate tendency of the Irish to lawlessness and violence and fortifying them against the rhetoric of agitators. In the economic sphere rationality consisted in behaving in an individualist, self-interested way. Hence logical thought and rational behaviour combined to change the character of the Irish: stern English logic was to repress Irish rhetoric and the manly ethic of strenuous competition was to replace a morally admirable (in traditional terms) but economically unproductive ethic of self-abnegation and altruism. Celebrated Irish economic improvidence was paralleled in discursive areas by a similar lack of foresight, where, to quote a distinguished schools inspector's characterisation of a certain widespread 'incidental mode of teaching', there was no '*predestined march*' chalked out but rather movement 'without goal or starting point' in a 'sort of zig-zag, winding, and uncertain route'. Such 'flexibility and quickness of association', though 'very valuable mental habits', were inferior to 'solidity and coherence of thought' and could degenerate into 'giddiness of mind' or a 'wandering wit'.[37] Disturbed by the perceived indirection and want of linearity of the Irish, Whately's mission was to make these crooked ways straight and rough ways smooth.

In the Royal Commission of Inquiry into Primary Education in Ireland in 1870 some commissioners, especially William Brooke, found excessive emphasis on the wickedness of the English, not only in Ireland but also in North America and India, in the textbooks of the Christian Brothers.[38] These school-books were also found wanting for insufficiently adverting to the 'blessings, the advantages of the British Constitution' and for the 'constant praises of insurrection against power'.[39] Lord Erskine's speech in defence of John Stockdale, for example, was seen by Brooke as politically tendentious, but Brother John Augustin Grace, the head of the Richmond Street School, who was being examined, denied political intent and defended its inclusion on *aesthetic* grounds. 'I think the passage is magnificent', stated Grace. It had, added Grace, been selected 'not to impress the minds of the pupils with any political idea, but for the same reason that all literary class-books have such selections, namely, for the purpose of teaching elocution'.[40] Brooke saw that the power of such passages politically lay in their ability to 'stimulate the feelings'.[41] He had no doubt about the effect of the 'most eloquent passages of the most eloquent men', the 'highly eloquent language', the 'very beautiful poetry', on impressionable children, and he was especially obsessed by the frequent repetition of such passages, as the pupils of the Christian Brothers often learned them 'off by heart'.[42] These passages, Grace replied, 'are of great literary merit, and as such have been selected as models of style for our literary class-book'.[43] Brooke noted that moral lessons in the school-books were usually culled from religious, political, and forensic advocacy, where cases were being argued and passions appealed to and were thus, in his view, inappropriate sources of history. Whereas the national school-books were largely dry and non-controversial, Brooke and others found those of the Christian Brothers, in terms of their content, inflammatory. In general terms national school-books were seen as ministering to the understanding, those of the Christian Brothers to the affections. No wonder Anthony Blake thought the mode of teaching of the Brothers not 'sufficiently scientific', as it did not 'work the mind sufficiently'.[44] In the matter of 'scientific' education, Cardinal Cullen agreed with Newman in rejecting mechanics' institutes as 'nothing but schools of infidelity', though they were encouraged by the government.[45] In like manner Hayes, in his introduction to the *Ballads of Ireland,* lamented the change from the days when the 'rustic Schoolmaster' was chosen 'more for his skill in the muses than for his acquaintance with the doctrines of Political Economy'.[46] And Patrick Pearse's dismissal of political economy as rational, calculating, and English is in this tradition: 'Ye men and peoples burn your books of rent theories and land values and go back to your sagas'.[47] In Bicheno's terms, the practice of the Christian Brothers, the preferences of Hayes and Pearse, as well as, for example, the Young Ireland project of a ballad history of Ireland, testify to an acceptance of the view that the Irish were best governed according to their affections.

Several commentators, including people within the system, saw the limitations of the abstract universalism which informed national education in Ireland, as entailing a denial of Irish difference, whether political, social, economic, or cultural. In concrete terms this involved the effacement of the 'history of the people', their 'poetry, habits, and manners' and their 'individuality as a nation of ancient race'.[48] Keenan, in particular, regretted the virtual absence of music, especially Irish music, in the schools. Hullah's system of music had no 'national character'. There must be, continued Keenan,

> a homeliness in tunes as well as in words, if they are to touch the heart; and we are abandoning a great humanizing power we have at our command, when we disregard the

natural homeliness of the strains hummed by a mother over the cradle and substitute in their stead tunes that are foreign to all sympathy, that belong to no country, that are sung in no home, that are inelegant in their style, and cheerless in their effects upon the ear.[49]

Here national music is seen as the bearer of humane, family, specifically female values of the home. It was appropriate that Keenan should single out music in his critique of the curriculum, as music has traditionally been regarded as having little or no conceptual content but as wielding powerful influence over the affections. For similar reasons Keenan regretted the lack of the Irish language and of Irish history in the national school curriculum.[50] He wanted a system of elementary education that appealed both to the understanding and to the affections.

Whately remarked, conventionally, in his *Rhetoric* that the 'language of savages', among whom he would include most of the native Irish, was 'highly metaphorical'.[51] A major part of Whately's project was to curb this linguistic excess, to bring this affective language to heel in the name of intellect. He had, his first biographer tells us, a 'doric contempt for ornament', never appealing to the heart, whether addressing adults or children, for 'all his efforts aimed to convince the intellect'. With reference to the early education of children Whately had been heard to say: 'Speak to their reason; you can always make them comprehend what is fit for them to know; my children know nothing they do not understand'.[52] Predictably, he had a lower opinion of learning by heart, than had the Christian Brothers.[53] With reference to political economy, the rational science *par excellence*, he concluded that its principles 'could be explained even to the ploughmen and made clear to the comprehension of children', just like the gospel itself. No wonder Dublin Protestants 'would not, or could not appreciate him'.[54] It was a rhetorical commonplace that the human voice was far more persuasive than words upon a page, and the Irish were seen as pre-eminently an oral people. Indeed a main function of the national schools was to combat the effects of the rhetoric of agitators on the public. Significantly, inspectors of schools often reported that oral answering among teachers was markedly better than was the written.[55] Bicheno distinguished between Catholic preaching, which was 'striking and energetic' and the 'cold official reading of the established clergy'.[56] And Fitzpatrick found Whately's austere linguistic practices 'a great disadvantage in Ireland', for rhetoric was a 'particularly acceptable gift to the Irish, who are a speaking rather than a reading people'.[57]

Rhetoric, in the narrow sense, the art of persuading the will, was much practised in Ireland, but Whately saw the convincing of the understanding as an essential part of persuasion. It might be argued that the typical English view of language was as representational and reflectionist of the 'real', whereas the Irish sought in language a fullness not to be found in harsh Irish reality, and a realm of freedom and pleasure unjustified by existing Irish conditions. For the Irish, language did not merely obsequiously and oppressively reflect the real, it foreshadowed future plenitude. England, the possessors, needed only to understand the world; the Irish, dispossessed, needed urgently to change it. So the colonial relationship between the two countries had its linguistic correlative. Hence a main purpose of the educational system was to restrain this linguistic excess and to replace an allegedly primitive form of thought with a more rational and scientific mode. The assimilationist process was never fully realised. In William O'Brien's words, the 'policeman proved to be an efficient ally of England, but the schoolmaster did not turn out so satisfactorily, and the schoolmaster is the more potent man of the two when all is said and done'.[58] And Samuel Ferguson, author of 'Inheritor and Economist: A Poem', saw Whately as having been taught a not particularly easy lesson, not only in morality but in forms of knowledge in his 'Epitaph on Archbishop Whately':

> Here lie I, Richard Whately
> Archbishop of Dublin lately,
> Who, for the amelioration
>
> Of the ignorant Irish nation,
> Coming hither with much vain knowledge,
> Having learned in these poor people's college
> Some things that have been a boon to me.
>
> I taught quibble
> And I learnt the Bible;
> I brought ability
> And took away humility.[59]

According to a Royal Commission of 1861, next to religion, the 'knowledge most important to a labouring man' was political economy.[60] Whately himself had written in 1833 that if the 'lower orders' had been taught political economy, they would not be 'as now, liable to the misleading of every designing demagogue' and would also have been rendered more 'provident' in their ways.[61] In a letter to a friend in the same year he wrote that 'perhaps the sort of thing most wanted now for children and the poor, is some plain instructions in Political Economy'.[62] Such was Whately's belief in the efficacy of political economy that at a meeting of the Statistical Society held on 19 June 1848, 'a moment when all Ireland was drilling, and Dublin seemed like a slumbering volcano, the Archbishop propounded a panacea against the threatened siege'. That panacea was political economy, and he urged Young Ireland to study it.[63] At that meeting Whately spoke of political economy as the '*only* means which existed of rescuing the country from convulsion'. He then made the extraordinary statement, especially by an Archbishop, that in a crucial sense, political economy was *more* important than religion or morality:

> It was a mistake to suppose that religion or morals alone would be sufficient to save a people from revolution. No; they would not be sufficient, if a proper idea of Political Economy was not cultivated by that people. A man, even of the purest mind and most exalted feelings, without a knowledge of Political Economy, could not be secured from being made instrumental in forwarding most destructive and disastrous revolutions.

Though he claimed that next to 'sound religion, sound Political Economy was most essential to the well-being of society', he was only too aware of the social and political dangers of unfettered charity and benevolence.[64]

Even as early as 1833, Hugh Hamill, a schools' inspector from Cork, made a powerful plea for political economy as a tranquillising force in Ireland:

> One Subject more I beg leave to suggest to the Board, – Political Economy. I wish it were properly taught in every School in the Kingdom. The Title is a formidable one; nor should I wish it introduced under that Name; if so it probably would not succeed. I believe that, next to good Religious

Education, a sound Knowledge of Political Economy would tend as much to tranquillize this Country, if not more, than any other Branch of Knowledge that can be taught in Schools. Were a Knowledge of this Science more diffused I should not have heard such exciting or disquieting Doctrines as I did during the Summer, speciously supported too, as far as regards the Working and Middle Classes; the natural and inevitable Distinction of Ranks, – the Dependence of Classes and of Countries on each other.[65]

Hamill's views were shared by other inspectors. Patton wrote of the 'great prominence' he gave political economy and of the 'importance' he attached to a knowledge of its principles 'which appeared so important and necessary' for the children to know 'as occurring in some way or other in all the ordinary transactions of civilized life'.[66] It was generally agreed among educationalists that ignorance or error in political economy had social consequences much more serious than in other disciplines. At the training institution at Marlborough Street political economy was taught which was *plain, practical*, and *corrective* of *popular prejudices*.[67] According to McCreedy, among the truths revealed by political economy were 'the necessity that exists for security of individual property, and how thence there must necessarily spring up differences of wealth and rank', the folly as well as crime sometimes committed in interfering with the 'free employment' of capital. The 'correction and exposure of many pernicious *economic sophisms*' was a prime function of political economy. 'All these', concluded McCreedy,

> it must be acknowledged, are matters of the deepest interest, upon which it is most desirable all men should entertain correct views; for as misunderstanding and error in reference to them have often given rise to turbulence and confusion, so it may be expected the right apprehension of them, and the diffusion among a people of true ideas of their nature, may have a contrary effect, and tend powerfully to the preservation of security and order.[68]

The early writings on political economy in Ireland in the nineteenth century emphasised its strictly scientific credentials; it was, in Whately's words, a science of wealth, having no connection with 'virtue and happiness'.[69] Its laws were of universal applicability and did not respect mere political boundaries. Having 'a science of exchanges peculiar in Ireland, under the name of Irish Political Economy' was, in the words of Hancock, 'about as reasonable as proposing to have Irish mechanics, Irish mathematics, or Irish astronomy'.[70] Longfield defended political economy as a 'pure science', like trigonometry, having no political objectives or tendencies.[71] Its principles, maintained Pim, were 'natural laws which regulate the material interest of society' and which were therefore 'fixed and unchangeable as the principles of any other science'.[72] Numerous other examples could be given.

Many authors devoted considerable energy to defending the alleged fact that political economy was non-political. Politics was the place of turmoil, division, and of passion, whereas political economy was an oasis of calm rationality, a place of harmony rather than of conflict, and, in a frequently-used metaphor, an uncontested 'common ground'. Whately himself held that 'party politics' had about 'as much to do with Political Economy as they had with manufactures or agriculture'.[73] The Statistical Society frequently congratulated itself on replacing divisive political discourse with the healing discursive mode of political economy. In 1854 the Council of the Society reported that in the seven years of its existence there had been 'an increasing tendency in the public mind, to remove social questions from the domain of party politics to the more tranquil region of scientific research'.[74] The same year, Pim spoke approvingly of 'that alteration in public feeling which has disconnected political economy from party politics'.[75] A year later Longfield wrote that the continuing existence of the Society of itself afforded 'a sufficient proof of the possibility of uniting Irishmen of all creeds and parties in one common object'.[76] Lawson remarked that free trade would have been considered as a political question in 1847, but by 1858 its principles were not to be disputed, having now become the 'very alphabet of economic science'. The Statistical Society had 'supplied the wholesome food of rational discussion instead of the unwholesome diet of party politics'. It was 'a common ground upon which Irishmen of every sect, class, and creed can meet, to discuss those questions which bear upon the welfare of their fellow countrymen, in a spirit of amity, peace, and concord'.[77] This theme was frequently reiterated by members of the Society:

When our lot has been cast in a land so divided by party

132

and religious differences as Ireland, it is a matter of no sm
importance to have a Society where men of all parties ar
of various religious denominations can cordially wor
together in investigating and discussing important socia
questions.[78]

In Thomas O'Hagan's words, a 'spirit of rhetorical exaggeration',
inseparable from political discourse, was being replaced by the
'simplicity and directness of those who honestly seek to know
things as they are', those with 'an ever growing sense of the value
of economic truth'. The Society was not only 'a union of classes'
but also of 'creeds and parties', according to O'Hagan, and it had
'proved that, for Irishmen, there is common ground, in connexion
with questions of high public moment, on which they can stand
together, in perfect amity, whilst they hold firmly by the
antagonistic religious and political confessions to which they are
respectively attached'.[79] According to Sir Robert Kane, only by
degrees did the principles of political economy manage to
extricate themselves from the 'mire of political discussion' and be
considered 'upon purely scientific grounds'.[80] And, to give one
final example, Jonathan Pim, in his presidential address in 1876
said it had been the object of the Statistical Society 'to offer to
thinking men of all creeds and parties the opportunity for
discussing on common ground all questions relating to the well-
being of Ireland which are not governed by party or sectarian
considerations'.[81]

Political economy, as a form of irrefutable knowledge, imposed
intellectual consensus and, overwhelmingly, presented existing
social and economic relations in Ireland as harmonious and
beneficent. Arthur Houston held that it was the 'glory of Political
Economy to have shown that the true and ultimate interest of the
community' was ' inseparably bound up with that of the
individual'.[82] In like manner the interests of classes, such as those
of employers and employees, landlords and tenants, were seen to
coincide, as did the interests of nations, the ultimate basis for the
doctrine of free trade. Through the agency of competition,
individual, class, and national interests spontaneously coincided
with one another and with the general interest through the
automatic and dispassionate operation of the market mechanism,
through *laissez-faire*, rather than through regulative state agency.
Irish economists were particularly anxious to reject the class

133

conflict which was implicit in classical theory, and Ricardo was their *bête noire*. In the very first paper delivered to the Statistical Society, Lawson opposed the Ricardian analysis of wages and profits which represented the interests of the employer and labourer as 'diametrically opposed to each other', preferring Senior's view of the matter where wages and profits rose and fell together.[83] In the second paper to the Society, delivered on the same night as Lawson's (21 December), at the end of 'Black '47', when the Great Famine was at its height, Hancock argued that the interests of provision dealers and those of the community were 'identical'.[84] Though he was soon to change his views, in his first paper before the Society, Cliffe Leslie attacked Mill's view of the 'antagonism of the interests of capitalist and laborer', a view Leslie found 'unscientific as well as mischievous'.[85] Before the late 1850s and early 1860s almost all Irish economists would have agreed with Hearn that the 'principle of competition' was 'beneficent, just and equalizing'.[86] There was virtual consensus that the laws of political economy were universally valid and that a political economy appropriate to England applied with equal force to Ireland.

There was an opposing tradition in political economy, as in other discursive areas, that Ireland was different, that in a word frequently used by nineteenth-century observers, Ireland was an anomaly. Ireland seemed to confound all received (usually English) wisdom. We have already mentioned the widespread view that the laws of political economy did not apply to Ireland, a position which attracted many more adherents in the wake of the Great Famine. There was an increasing perception that the Irish economy and society differed from the English, leading to the conclusion that English economic theories and policies were not necessarily appropriate to Ireland. Political economy was regarded as of English origin, and its laws, increasingly, were seen as having English rather than universal applicability. In Cairnes's words, Great Britain, 'if not the birthplace of political economy, has at least been its early home, as well as the scene of the most signal triumphs of its manhood'.[87] Even the unimpeachably orthodox Hearn admitted that 'much of the opposition to political economy has been due to the very natural, or at least very British desire of some of its earlier teachers to generalize from British phenomena alone'.[88]

In more general terms, many commentators drew attention to anomalies in Irish conditions and Irish 'character'. Bicheno declared that he had

POLITICAL ECONOMY, IRELAND, AND IDEOLOGY

long harboured the desire of visiting a country, which
contradicted the received theory of population, and the
established doctrines of political economists; where,
contrary to experience, the higher and lower orders profess
different religions; and whence spring as Pliny says of Africa
in his time all the marvellous and unaccountable
contradictions of nature. Ireland is therefore, to the moral
and political philosopher what Australia is to the naturalist,
– a land of strange anomalies.[89]

In 1845 the Revd J. Godkin wrote of the 'anomalies of the social
condition of Ireland',[90] and a number of years later Harriet
Martineau referred to the 'anomalous condition of Ireland'.[91]
These, and many other writers, were usually drawing attention to
the contradiction between the rich natural endowments of Ireland
and the degradation, economic, moral, and intellectual of its
people, a matter that was sometimes explained by the presence
of, in the words of the Revd F.F. Trench, *something anomalous
in the Irish character*.[92] To an economist, to use Hancock's
words, the 'contrast between a destitute peasantry and prolific
resources suggests an investigation into the social arrangements
of the country, where such an anomaly prevails'. But such
inquiries vindicated the Irish from the charge of 'general
indolence' by 'showing that such anomalies arise from the social
arrangements transmitted from less enlightened ages' which were
at variance with the teachings of political economy.[93] Similarly,
Hearn rejected the idea that there was something 'inherent in the
Roman Catholic religion, and in the Celtic race' which presented
'an insuperable bar to industrial progress', though there were
people to be found

> who will gravely argue that the Irishman is an anomaly; that
> his case is utterly hopeless; that the laws which actuate all
> other men are not for him; that he does not care to gain the
> comforts of life; that he is lazy, improvident, and idle.[94]

Where it was accepted, as it increasingly was, that Irish conditions
were anomalous, this provided justification for differences in
legislation, especially with respect to the role of the state. As H. M.
Posnett put it, the 'peculiar conditions of Ireland have enabled
economists to treat State interference as purely exceptional'.[95] To
take one example, Professor William Nesbitt of Galway submitted

an article on education to the *Westminster Review*, the editor of which, John Chapman, wrote to Nesbitt's friend Cairnes, that the condition for acceptance of the article was:

> That state interference with education shall not be advocated as right in principle and shall only be justified in practice with reference to Ireland as an exceptional instance, the duty in this instance being alleged to rise out of the conditions resulting from the peculiar and exceptional relations of the Conquerors and Conquered.[96]

Indeed it was precisely this relationship that was at the heart of Ireland's anomalous position. Was Ireland a colony or an intrinsic part of the United Kingdom? With reference to Ireland, was England a 'mother country' or a 'sister kingdom'? Calling for the 'assimilation of the laws and institutions of the two countries', for the purpose of 'incorporating Ireland more thoroughly, more completely, into that glorious Empire', Henry L. Jephson wrote with some insight on Ireland's 'anomalous position'. Ireland occupied a 'perfectly unique position in the British Empire'. It was an 'incontrovertible fact' that

> amongst the numerous dependencies of the British crown there is not one that stands in the same relation to Great Britain as Ireland does. She is not a colony, for although she is governed by a governor-general, as they are, she has not her own houses of representatives as colonies have. She cannot be regarded as an integral part of the United Kingdom, for although she sends her representatives to the Imperial Parliament, she is not governed as the other parts of the United Kingdom are, but is governed by a deputy. Ireland hangs as it were between union and colonial independence; and this anomalous position lends on the one hand an aspect of intelligibility to the demands put forward for placing Ireland on the footing of a colony, and granting her a colonial constitution; whilst on the other hand it prevents the only conclusive answer being given to such demands – the answer that Ireland has been thoroughly and completely united to Great Britain, and that consequently no higher privileges remain to be granted to her.

There were, continued Jephson, such differences between English and Irish legislation and government 'that Ireland appears almost as if she were a separate country, and the practice of separate legislation is so uniform that one might almost believe that it is intended she shall remain a separate country', at a time when, 'in imperial interests, every effort should be made to draw the two countries closer to each other'.[97]

Many observers came to the conclusion that Ireland was not so much *anomalous*, as different from England in a wide range of areas and that the English economy and society did not necessarily constitute a universally valid model. It was increasingly felt that a political economy generated from English circumstances and ideas was quite inappropriate to Irish conditions. From the 1850s onwards there was increased emphasis on what Cliffe Leslie called, in 1852, the 'imperious conditions of time and place'.[98] Several authors emphasised the difference, in Kane's words, between the 'true abstract science of political economy' and the art of political economy, and that the application of the 'strict principles of science to real life' should be 'subject to modifications which local circumstances will always indicate'. Kane went on to speak of 'those local conditions, separating practice from theory' but he felt that with 'industrial and moral progress' these differences would disappear, bringing about an increasing harmony between 'practice and science'. But before such an eventuality, Kane condemned as 'utopian' the belief that 'we can at any time apply the rigorous dogmas of abstract political economy to human society, regardless of personal and local habits, and even prejudices'.[99] In 1865 Thomas O'Hagan argued against 'a too trenchant application of economic principle to the management of Ireland' because 'our circumstances are in many respects, abnormal. Our society is studded all over with anomalies'.[100] He was more positive than Kane in that he celebrated national differences and condemned the 'undistinguishing passion for assimilation which has possessed the minds of able men – sometimes, from the rigidity of theorists and the intolerance of doctrinaires'.[101] Even a thorough assimilationist like Jephson demurred at laying down 'an invariable rule that all legislation for Ireland should be absolutely identical with English legislation'.[102] By 1869 even the Lord Lieutenant, Lord Spencer, felt safe in saying to the Statistical Society with reference to political economy that

abstract theories are much dreaded by politicians. They do not like the application of mere abstract theories, and they are quite right to be afraid of their universal application, for I believe the principles of political economy can never be applied universally. You must consider the position of the country, the state and progress of the people, before you apply its principles.[103]

And, as we saw, even the conservative Hearn came to speak of the 'error' in political economy of generalising 'from British phenomena alone'.[104]

The most celebrated confrontation of the 'old' and 'new' versions of political economy took place in the House of Commons. The topic of debate was, significantly, Irish land. In the discussion of Maguire's Motion (10 March 1868), Mill clashed with Robert Lowe, a staunch defender of traditional political economy. Lowe held the view that political economy 'belongs to no nation; it is of no country'.[105] In reply to Lowe, Mill remarked that to his

> right hon. Friend's mind political economy appears to stand for a set of political maxims ... my right hon. Friend thinks that a maxim of political economy if good in England must be good in Ireland ... I am sure that no one is at all capable of determining what is the right political economy for any country until he knows the circumstances.[106]

The abstract and unhistorical nature of the subject came under increasing attack. What began as a polemical onslaught on political economy during the Famine was now becoming a theorised and systematic critique, which was soon to lead to a fundamental methodological challenge to classical orthodoxy. In and around 1847, charges of abstraction against the science were frequently made. In the words of one such critic, 'sciolists of political economy having got a conception of one or two abstract truths ... insist that they, and they only, are the fitting prescriptions for Ireland'.[107] By 1881 Gladstone was uttering what was then conventional wisdom when he condemned those who applied the 'principles of *abstract* political economy to the people and circumstances of Ireland' exactly as if they 'had been proposing to legislate for the inhabitants of Saturn and Jupiter'.[108] Even as early as 1870, and again with reference to Irish land, Lowe had relented on his universalism: 'the principles of political economy! Why, we violate them every day!'[109] Ingram excoriated the 'vicious abstraction' of political economy in his famous address to the British Association in 1878,[110] and his friend Cliffe Leslie had already claimed that its new philosophic method had to be historical. At least in the English-speaking world, Ireland was the first country where the universality of the laws of political economy was systematically challenged. Leslie and Ingram were the pioneers of historical economics in the English-speaking world, and the almost inextricable problems of Ireland and land were at its very source. As a modern scholar puts it, 'from the late 1850s until his premature death in 1882, T.E. Cliffe Leslie's efforts to solve the problems of Ireland produced a critique of political economy that laid the chief intellectual foundations for English historical economics'.[111] What is less well known is that Cairnes, from a very different standpoint, launched a devastating attack on the universalist pretensions of orthodox economics, in an analysis, both extensive and intensive, of Ireland and its tribulations, over-whelmingly the problem of land.

During and after the Famine the laws of political economy (by which was usually meant the policy of *laissez-faire*, seen as an intrinsic part of the science) were attacked for being abstract, unhistorical, and for being misapplied in Ireland,[112] and as not applying to Ireland's anomalous general condition or to the specific circumstances of the famine period. But almost all of the practitioners of political economy (with the partial exception of Butt) would have agreed with Hancock that there was 'no country in the world which affords a stronger proof of the disastrous consequences of neglecting the doctrine of *laissez-faire* as Ireland'.[113] Three years later, Edward Lysaght said that all economists of reputation, with the exception of Mill (who was at that time frequently criticised by Irish economists such as Hancock, Leslie, and Hearn) were agreed 'in attributing the wretched state of agriculture in Ireland to the absence, rather than to the excess of competition'. For the same reasons Lysaght castigated the Irish Tenant League for violating the 'principles of economic science'.[114] But by 1865 Hancock had relented on his doctrinaire views, referring to the 'rigid economists of the *laissez faire* school'.[115] So too did Lawson. Writing in 1872 he noted that *laissez-faire* 'was not very long ago the doctrine of the economists' but that the current had now 'set in the opposite direction'. He did not say that they had 'as yet advanced too far upon this road', though he advised caution.[116] Henry Dix Hutton wrote, in 1870, that the Irish land question had confirmed the 'impossibility, now recognized, of reforming the relation of landlord and tenant in Ireland by the English system, or economic *laissez-faire*.[117] Ingram found that existing economists of the English school isolated economics from other social studies, were excessively deductivist, abstract, and absolutist in their conclusions. The 'most marked example the economists have afforded of a too absolute conception and presentation of principle,' declared Ingram, 'both theoretic and practical, is found in the doctrine of *laissez-faire*.[118] Cairnes observed mordantly that political economy was commonly seen as 'a sort of scientific rendering' of the maxim *laissez-faire*, the 'one and sufficient solution of all industrial problems'. But he argued that *laissez-faire* had 'no scientific basis whatever' and was 'at best a mere handy rule of practice' which was 'totally destitute of all scientific authority'.[119] But the reputation of political economy itself declined concomitantly with that of *laissez-faire*. To take but one example, in a short paper which he presented to the Statistical Society in 1879, entitled 'Causes of slow progress of political economy', Samuel Haughton reported that the discipline had not of late 'made progress in public estimation, nor can it be placed in rank, by its most ardent admirers, as a science of which the laws – it may almost be said any one law – are undoubted or capable of positive proof'.[120] The widespread perception, and not only in Ireland, was that the 1870 Irish Land Act had begun and the 1881 Irish Land Act completed the violation of the laws of political economy, of *laissez-faire*, of contract, and of private property, especially in land.

Even when political economy was at its most flourishing in Ireland, there was occasional unease expressed at its 'narrowness' and at treating social phenomena exclusively in terms of its doctrines. In 1830 Bicheno warned against 'that narrow treatment' of the Irish question which regarded it 'as one of political economy', the theories of which were built on the 'narrow basis of national wealth' and so were of 'insignificant importance when applied practically to the actual circumstances of a country'.[121] Lawson pointed out to the Statistical Society in 1858 that before 1856 the 'Section of Statistical and Economic Science' of the British Association had been known as the 'Section of Statistics' and dedicated itself very much to the 'mere collection of facts', being consequently 'comparatively barren of useful results'. He pointed out proudly that their own Society had borne the new title for all of its ten years of existence.[122] Though named initially the Dublin Statistical Society, it was established for the purpose of 'promoting the study of Statistics and Economical Science'. Indeed the first paper read to the Society was by Lawson himself and was entitled 'On the connection between statistics and political economy'.[123] In 1855 the Society (founded in 1847) amalgamated with the Social Inquiry Society of Ireland, which it had set up in 1850 when, in Lawson's words, 'it was deemed that our Society had laid down limits too narrow for itself'.[124] In 1862 the Society became the Statistical and Social Inquiry Society of Ireland, extending its remit to include 'Jurisprudence and Amendment of the Law' and 'Public health and Sanitary reform', and 'Statistics and Economical Science' was broadened to become 'Social Science, including Education; and Political Economy, including the principles of trade and commerce'.[125] Indeed the council of the Society boasted in 1860 that they had the honour of being the 'earliest society in the empire formed for the cultivation of the entire range of Social Science'.[126] The Society could, according to Lawson, 'claim the credit of having been the first society established in these kingdoms for the cultivation of social science, and we had been at full work for many years when the National Association for the Promotion of Social Science was formed'. [127] John Barrington stipulated that the lectures which he endowed should be on 'political economy in its most extended and useful sense, but particularly as relates to the conduct and duty of people to one another'.[128] But in 1870 the council of the Statistical Society resolved 'to enlarge the subject of the lectures by adopting the name of "Lectures on Social Science", which at the present day corresponds with the intention of the testator'.[129] Clearly, the reduction of the curiously singular 'Irish Question' to the exclusively economic dimension, and the treatment of economic problems in isolation from their social, political, and cultural contexts, were, from the beginning, highly problematic strategies in Ireland.

In the proceedings of the Statistical Society itself speakers often dealt with the alleged 'narrowness' of political economy. In 1849 Longfield considered the objection that it had 'confined the attention of its votaries too exclusively to wealth, and that there was something dangerous in that narrowness of their views'. He conceded the position if such people devoted themselves solely to a study of the science.[130] In 1851 Kane objected strongly to the narrow conception of political economy 'having for its object a gross and mundane avarice, which would subordinate every consideration of country and of culture to the mere grovelling art of money getting'. But he was glad that the Statistical Society had adopted for its object the 'comprehensive definition of statistical and economical science'.[131] The once narrowly-focused Neilson Hancock claimed that Adam Smith's commitment to moral philosophy and jurisprudence in his *Wealth of Nations* added 'extraordinary value to his book', for he treated 'economic science always as a part, and not as the whole of the scientific considerations connected with human affairs'.[132] In like manner Ingram, the disciple of Comte, praised Smith for not separating politics, jurisprudence, and political economy; for being, in effect, a precursor of sociology.[133] And Samuel Haughton attributed the decline in status of political economy in the late 1870s to, in part, the 'over-estimate of many writers and advocates, who assume for this science a position of eminence or control over human affairs'. He concluded that political economy should properly be subservient to the emerging science of sociology.[134]

Objections to political economy, and especially to *laissez-faire*, were overwhelmingly *moral*. Whately defined the discipline as an enquiry into the 'nature, production, and distribution of wealth, not its connection with virtue and happiness', and this remained the view of Irish economists until the late 1850s.[135] They were frequently called upon to rebut the charge of 'hard-heartedness', which they usually did by pointing to the scientific status of political economy, a matter of hard-headedness, and not of the heart, whether hard or soft.[136] Economic laws were ineluctable laws of nature but, as a later critic put it, all 'laws of nature are cold, heartless, and cruel, if not properly bitted and bridled'.[137] In the late eighteenth and early nineteenth centuries the 'science' of political economy began to supersede the earlier moral discourse of what has been called civic humanism. Though political economy was avowedly descriptive, its laws, usually characterised as 'laws of nature' or 'natural laws', had powerful prescriptive force. Its scientific authority was frequently augmented by a judicious appeal to the humanistic perspectives of the earlier tradition, sometimes overtly, but usually covertly, where terms from the old discourse were surreptitiously imported into the new. Aimed simultaneously at convincing the intellect and persuading the will, their combined power was awesome and seemingly invincible. But, at least in Ireland, morality became a kind of Trojan horse in the very citadel of political economy. When the science was under siege during the Famine the authorities felt that it had to be defended morally as well as intellectually. To give one small example, in 1848, teachers were asked in an examination to define 'interest' and to 'prove that it is as reasonable and just to be required to pay for the loan of money, as for the loan of any thing else'.[138] The term 'just', in the context, is obviously a moral one and the term 'reasonable' is fruitfully and obfuscatingly ambiguous, eliding the difference between 'is' and 'ought', between description and prescription, between economics and ethics. As we saw, John Barrington defined political economy in an 'extended and useful sense' to include morality, the 'conduct and duty of people to one another'. By and large, writers saw no real conflict between economic interests and ethics. The council of the Statistical Society, for example, referring to James Houghton's paper on the subject, said his contention was that 'free labour is on the whole, and taking long periods, cheaper than slave, and that, therefore, slavery is not merely a crime, but an economical blunder',[139] a view developed more systematically by Cairnes in his celebrated *The Slave Power*. Within capitalism the doctrine of the communality of interests was held to ensure that ethics and economics were in harmony, that the pursuit of rational self-interest in the market-place not only solved the economic problem but, in effect, eliminated the moral one.

From the late 1850s there was increasing emphasis on areas where economics and ethics conflicted and on areas where economic values were held to be inappropriate. In a number of papers in the second half of the 1850s Hancock, the most conspicuous defender of rigid *laissez-faire* in the previous decade, attacked the workhouses and the Scottish bothy system for violating 'family principles'. The communality of interests notwithstanding, Hancock approvingly quoted Adam Smith that capitalists had 'generally an interest to deceive and even to oppress the public, and accordingly have on many occasions both deceived and oppressed it'.[140] Hancock added that the 'care of wealth has now, as ever, a tendency to hardness of heart, which moral discipline is necessary to control. It has, too, a tendency to generate strong selfishness and a want of consideration for others.' He was anxious to show that 'social science does not sanction any law of competition as a substitute for the important moral duties that devolve on every owner of wealth and every employer of labour'.[141] In another paper he condemned the 'materialism' where 'too little attention is paid to higher views, which make business subservient to man instead of man to business'.[142] For moral, religious, and 'family' reasons Hancock defended the journeymen bakers of Dublin in their demand for shorter working hours, despite *laissez-faire* principles.[143] On the same grounds he vigorously repudiated *laissez-faire* in the labour market in relation to the employment of women.[144]

In a paper 'On the use and abuse of apprenticeship', George F. Shaw declared that

[the] omission of moral considerations, by most of the writers who have given to political economy its form and impress at the present day ... inspires the bulk of society with a distrust of its conclusions so remarkably contrasted with the respect universally tendered to the conclusions of physical science.[145]

The following year Henry Dix Hutton, a follower of Comte, put forward what he called the 'sociological theory' of property which recognised not only its legal but also its moral aspect.[146] Ingram claimed that the 'egotistic spirit' was, in part, responsible for the growing distrust of political economy, and in his view that very spirit was 'closely connected with vicious method'.[147] According to Bicheno, writing as early as 1830, the 'cold and frigid philosophy' of political economy ill-suited a people governed by their affections, like the Irish.[148] Writing early this century 'Pat' (P.D. Kenny), in a volume aptly entitled *Economics for Irishmen*, maintained that defining political economy as a 'science of wealth' was inadequate, so he included an increased 'human and moral element' in his conception of the discipline, which would 'make the science less discordant to the Irish national psychology'. He added that

[it] ought to be of interest to Irishmen to know that the tendency of modern development in economic science is in what we may call the Irish direction, taking into account factors of feeling and moral impulse that were comparatively ignored by the explicit but rigid dogmatism of Stuart Mill and his co-creators of 'the economic man'.[149]

Early Irish political economists were frequently called upon to defend their science against the charge of irreligion. Whately had accepted the Drummond Chair at Oxford to prevent 'anti-Christians' who were 'striving hard to have the science to themselves' and he saw himself as 'making a sort of continuation of Paley's "Natural Theology", extending to the body-politic some such views as his respecting the natural'.[150] Hearn wrote in 1850 that research into social science must necessarily lead to the 'most powerful confirmation of religious truth', and it was 'a merciful arrangement that our real interest ever coincides with our duty'.[151] By 1866 Thomas O'Hagan could claim that the idea that political economy presented a 'formidable danger to morals or religion' had passed away, for 'it has been found that the revelation of God is not less consistent with that law which He has so marvellously established to make the free volition of His creatures work out unforeseen results, than with the constitution of His physical universe'.[152]

There was, however, a widespread feeling that Protestantism was more in accord with political economy than was Roman Catholicism. As we have already seen, Newman was harsh in his castigation of political economy as 'a science at the same time dangerous and leading to occasions of sin', and inflexible in his belief that it should be strictly subservient to morality and religion. In his entry in Palgrave's *Dictionary of Political Economy* on the 'Roman Catholic School' of political economists, Charles Gide claimed that by the

> vehemence of its criticism of the economic organisation of the day, more particularly by opposing itself to individualism, self-help, competition, and the inordinate search for gain, also by the sombre picture which it paints of the condition of the working classes, the Roman Catholic school makes common cause with democratic socialism.[153]

And, as we noted, Bicheno saw Catholicism as fostering virtues incompatible with narrow conceptions of political economy. To Horace Plunkett, Catholicism appeared 'in some of its tendencies non-economic, if not actually anti-economic' because of its reliance on 'authority, its repression of individuality, and its complete shifting of what I may call the moral centre of gravity to a future existence'.[154] One author went so far as to speak of 'our unconscious nearness to communism, which did not give way to the individualistic system of industrial production in Ireland until long after the change had come about in most other parts of Europe'.[155] Though almost all writers denied any kind of denominational determinism in Irish society, many of them, consciously or unconsciously, analysed it in terms of the perceived binary opposition of Catholic and Protestant. In general, Protestantism was seen as modern, individualist, rational, utilitarian, self-interested, competitive, libertarian, favouring policies of *laissez-faire* and free trade. So, in terms of the rigours of the binary logic, Catholicism was necessarily traditional, 'social', affective, idealist, altruistic, self-abnegating, co-operative, more centralised in structure, more authoritarian, and more in favour of state intervention in economic affairs. In a phrase neatly conflating country and religion, W.E. Hearn wrote in *Plutology* that there 'is now little risk, at least in any Anglican country, that the old extravagances of State action will be revived'.[156] Needless to mention, positive or negative valuations were placed on these oppositional categories according to taste. By and large, Catholicism was regarded as a force inimical to political economy. So an author like Bicheno, writing just two years before Whately began his great crusade, would have seen the new scientific discipline as totally unsuited to both Irish and Catholic 'character' and 'nature', and so ultimately destined to fail.

Predictably enough, stereotypes of Catholic and Protestant were more-or-less similar to those of the Irish and the English, Celt and Saxon. John Mitchel had canvassed Berkeley as an exponent of *Irish* political economy but the as-yet unregenerate Hancock accused the author of the *Querist* of attributing the evils of Ireland to the 'Celtic Race', by claiming that in Ireland 'industry is most against the natural grain of the people', an error which led Berkeley, in Hancock's view, to 'recommend public interference with private enterprise in utter disregard of the doctrine of *laissez-faire*'.[157] To take but one other example, William Monsell wrote that the most popular British explanation for Irish backwardness was that 'the Celtic race wants these qualities necessary to successful industry; that it has flash but no steadiness; that we have not the depth and perseverance of the Saxon'.[158] This charge Monsell refuted by denying the exclusively Celtic nature of the Irish and by pointing to other lands where Celts were economically progressive. But despite numerous ritualistic denials, the proposition that industry went against the 'natural grain' of both Catholics and Irish, remained the suppressed premiss in the enthymeme of Irish economic argumentation.

Central to the view that both Roman Catholicism and Irishness (an especially impotent force when combined) made for economic backwardness was not only their moral antipathy to economic rationality, but also their perceived opposition to individualism. In Bicheno's terminology, a nation and a religion governed by their affections saw individualism as foreign to them, refusing, for instance, to see land as merely a commodity and regarding the landlord–tenant relation as of a 'social nature', and not just as a contract between buyers and sellers. Unfortunately, in Bicheno's view, 'wealth, prosperity, trade, commerce, manufactures' and their science, political economy, obliterated the 'natural affections', bringing 'independence and selfishness' in their train.[159] From the early 1860s individualism came under increasingly heavy attack. In 1862 Hutton wrote of the 'inadequacy of the theories of property currently received', stating that 'the fundamental principle' was that property was a 'social institution'. Rejecting, in Comtean terms, the 'juridical' and 'economical' theories of property, he advocated the 'sociological' theory, which recognised both the legal and the moral aspects of property. Each of these represented property as 'social' in its origins and in its destination. A just appreciation of the legal aspect of property tended to 'correct the common view, not merely by supplying the social element, but by checking an exaggerated individualism, which, in our day especially, substitutes a false and metaphysical unity for the real complication of human affairs'.[160] Replying to Hutton, Jonathan Pim expressed his satisfaction that the 'moral bearing' of the question had been considered and he saw no necessary coincidence between a landlord's interest and his duty. He believed that the owners of landed property held it in trust for the community.[161] Historical economists, like Leslie, attacked the centrality of individualism in economic thinking, and Ingram pointed out that society had 'passed through states in which the modern economic constitution was so far from existing, that property did not belong to the individual but to the community'.[162]

In 1884, in a work dedicated to Ingram, Posnett wrote of the necessity of seeing land as a 'communal possession', adding that there was a 'growing distrust of individualism in ownership – as in every department of human thought and action – which is bound to make the "rent" problem of the future a relation between the State and its members, and no longer a private relation between class and class'. He saw individualism as 'approaching the limits of its disappointing reign; and socialism, in forms of action and thought' as 'everywhere in the air'.[163] Authors such as Horace Plunkett and 'Pat' regretted the economic consequences of the lack of individualism in the Irish character, but Plunkett hoped that in modern conditions 'our preference for thinking and acting in groups' might not be altogether a *damnosa hereditas*. If, he added, 'owing to our deficiency in the individualistic qualities of the English, we cannot at this stage hope to produce many types of the "economic man" of the economists, we think we see our way to provide, as a substitute, the economic *association*. These 'associative' characteristics happened to have a 'special value' in farming, while the largely industrial England did not possess the associative instincts of the Irish.[164]

In 1829 Robert Southey wrote that 'bad as the feudal times were, they were less injurious than these commercial ones to the kindly and generous feelings of human nature'.[165] Mitchel went so far as to argue that, in theory, slave social arrangements were morally superior to those of capitalism. In a letter to the Revd Henry Ward Beecher in 1854 he wrote that the 'idea of a slaveholder's position' was a 'true patriarchate', being the 'father of a family'. His duties and responsibilities, as such, were much higher 'than those of a mere employer for money wages, between whom and his labourer the sole *nexus* is cash payment'.[166] And indeed it was in the name of the family that the great moral critique of individualism was conducted in Ireland. Its most persuasive exponent was Hancock, once the leading advocate of unfettered individualism and *laissez-faire*. In 1859 Hancock read a paper to the Statistical Society with the coat-trailing title: 'The family and not the individual the true unit to be considered in social questions; with some applications of this theory to poor laws, the employment of women, and the enlistment of soldiers.'[167] The paper was not published. Beginning in 1855 Hancock had objected to the workhouse as a mode of relief for widows and orphans on family grounds and, four years later, he advocated substituting the 'family system' for rearing orphans, instead of the workhouse. In a paper in the same year he condemned the bothy system of lodging farm labourers in Scotland, because it violated 'family principles'.[168] In

1860 he opposed the long hours and Sunday working of journeymen bakers in Dublin as leading to a 'complete destruction of family life'.[169] Later in that year he addressed the Statistical Society on the violation of 'family ties' in Irish workhouses.[170] In a short paper in 1865 he argued that strikes for shorter hours constituted 'primarily a moral and social question, and not an economic one'.[171] In castigating those who relied on 'selfish motives alone as influencing human actions', Hancock cited the 'strength of family affection' of the Irish people who sent remittances from America to their families in Ireland. These economically unmotivated intra-familial transfers deeply moved Hancock, leading him to attach enormous importance to

> cherishing and preserving in the young all the natural family ties and affections; and to resisting, in every possible form, the separation and destruction of families, – whether it appears in Sunday work or night work, – in bothies, or in the workhouse system as applied to widows and to children.[172]

It was, however, the issue of the employment of women which played a central role in Irish opposition to individualism and *laissez-faire*. In August 1861 the Social Science Congress met in Dublin, and several important papers were read on the subject of the employment of women. One result was the foundation of an Irish branch of the Society for Promoting the Employment of Educated Women. Another was that women ('ladies') were allowed to become associate members of the Statistical Society. Not unconnected events were the extention of the objects of the Dublin Statistical Society to 'all questions of Social Science', the change of name to the Statistical and Social Inquiry Society of Ireland, and increased discussion on co-operation as a sort of 'feminine' alternative to the manly strife of competition. The rational, calculating maximiser of utilities of political economy was clearly male; its *homo economicus* was literally that. A woman's place was in the home, in industrial society seen as a place of consumption and leisure rather than of production, while a man's place was in the public arena. However, for the efficient working, reproduction, and growth of capitalism, for the servicing of labour and the investment in human capital, the unpaid labour of women in the home was vital. The values of individual greed and selfishness were crucial to success in the market-place, but a traditional morality of self-abnegation and self-sacrifice was demanded of women in the home. The future of capitalism depended on the unselfishness of parents, especially of mothers, in relation to their children, an investment in human capital for which there was little or no economic return. To enable this division of 'spheres' (one powerful, the other virtually powerless) on gender grounds, recourse was had in the nineteenth century to the celebrated double standard whereby men were regarded as naturally selfish and women as naturally virtuous. So women needed no economic inducement to acting morally, for it was 'natural' and virtue was, quite literally, its own reward. They were the guardians of tradition and of morality, and the transmitters of these values to future generations. In mid nineteenth-century Britain women were seen as taking the lead in the moral regeneration of industrial society. But the tender and altruistic characteristics of women (as of Celts and Catholics) unfitted them for economically-productive roles in the market-place, though they also challenged the universality of self-interest as the necessary and sufficient condition of economic progress. Home and family, the female space, constituted an oasis of community in Victorian ideology, providing, at once, a palliating gloss to and a searing critique of the public male sphere. From the end of the 1850s women, Catholics, and Celts contributed to what one might call a 'feminisation' of values in Ireland which constituted a radical questioning of the English, Protestant, and 'male' discourse of political economy.

Early in 1855 Hancock wrote of the 'spontaneous and universal recognition of the principle that women ought naturally to be supported by men'.[173] The 'natural way of rearing children' was as 'members of a family, with a mother to cherish and a father to control',[174] the conventional gender-based division of duties of female nurturing and male authority. Exactly five years later, in a paper on the employment of women, Hancock stated that 'women are, and must in general be, supported by men, their employment being absorbed in the domestic work, on which so much of the health, comfort, and moral well being of society depends', arguing that the 'domestic employment of women is a necessary consequence of the great fundamental law of our nature – the division of mankind into families'.[175] As a direct result of the Social Science Congress meeting and the foundation of a branch of the Society for Promoting the Employment of Educated Women, Edward Gibson delivered a paper on the 'Employment of women in Ireland' to the Statistical Society in December 1861, arguing, dramatically, that the 'labour market should be thrown open to all comers'.[176] The following year Arthur Houston, the Whately Professor of Political Economy (1861–6) published his important Whately lecture *The Emancipation of Woman from Existing Industrial Disabilities: Considered in Its Economic Aspect*, in which he defended the employment of women on the basis of the principle of 'Unrestricted Competition'.[177] In a paper read before the Statistical Society in 1866 Houston returned to the theme, again calling for the 'unrestrained admission of women to employments'.[178] In both publications Houston vigorously contested the doctrine of confining women's 'proper sphere' to the home. 'The theory', wrote Houston, 'of a proper sphere for women cannot be maintained in principle, and is not maintained in practice'.[179] He also challenged the founding assumption of the separation of male and female spheres, the idea that a 'true womanly life is lived for others', describing it as 'self-immolation', a 'most absurd and abominable doctrine'.[180] Houston, however, did not advocate the entrance of women into all employments 'indiscriminately' for there were 'parts of the battle field of life' for which women were not 'by nature fitted'.[181] So Houston was advocating the 'progressive' case for the employment of women in terms of what was increasingly coming to be seen as 'conservative' *laissez-faire* policies. Faced with this intractable dilemma, Hancock relented on *laissez-faire* in order to defend the doctrine of the gender-based separation of public and private spheres. In reply to Houston's paper Hancock opposed free trade in the employment of women on family and moral grounds. He accused Houston of ignoring the 'family system, which was the one which nature pointed out as that upon which society should be organised'. The basis of that system was that 'men should provide support for the women and the children, and the women manage the domestic economy of the household'. This was a 'proper and natural division of labour'.[182] Domestic economy was a woman's proper study, political economy that of a man. Houston closed the debate by repudiating any intention of ignoring the 'family relation' but hedged his bets by 'neither admitting nor denying that the family system should be made the basis of society'.[183]

Many commentators made reference to what Hancock called the 'wonderful and strong family and clan feeling' of the Irish.[184] Plunkett wrote early in this century of the 'survival in the Celt of the tribal instincts'.[185] His critic, Fr. O'Riordan, condemned the 'spirit of industrialism' which took mothers from their homes and children, and which ignored 'any high mutual relation between employer and employed than that of so much wage for so much work' and so had 'naturally ceased to look upon the family as a sacred thing, and the essential unit of society'.[186] He saw agriculture as more conducive to family life and more 'natural' to Irish people and to Catholics, views endlessly reproduced in manuals of Catholic 'sociology' in twentieth-century Ireland. Citing Marshall that the 'basis of capital' was 'family affection', 'Pat' argued that were it not for the 'unique loyalty of the family unit in Ireland, especially among the peasantry, the economic process must have been degraded among us even more than it is'. And he saw the survival of nationality as being dependent on the 'fine instinct with which the people have always extended the analogy of the family tie to its national application'.[187]

In general, there was agreement that 'family affection', while it was to some extent economically enabling, by subverting individualism, militated against the accumulation of capital. In the words of A.G. Richey, the accumulation of capital, the 'essential condition of a progressive society', had not occurred in Ireland because it was a pastoral country and so the 'ancient system of society was maintained long after it had ceased to exist in the other western countries of Europe'. He claimed that no social or political development was apparent between the fifth and sixteenth centuries in Ireland. Ireland differed from England in being earlier in the evolutionary scale and in therefore being closer to her Celtic and Aryan origins than to English commercial society. Basing his views on the researches of Sir Henry Maine into primitive communities, Richey saw early Irish society as 'a community without a government or executive; without laws, in the modern sense of the term; in which the individual had no rights save as a member of a family', where private property scarcely existed and where social bonding was achieved not through law and contract, but through custom. The family or household, and not the individual, was the basic unit of this society and the tribe and the nation constituted natural extensions of the family. The Irish, according to Richey, 'never advanced beyond the tribal condition and failed to develop into a nation with a central government and executive'. Crucially, the trade of this family-centred society was 'uninfluenced by the laws of political economy'. And as the individual existed only as a member of a family, property belonged only to the collective household.[188]

Even the ultra-orthodox W.E. Hearn came to accept that a household-centred society was not only economically inefficient, but that its existence successfully challenged the universality of the laws of political economy. *The Aryan Household*, which Hearn published in 1878, is the pre-history of modern, economic society which he dealt with in his earlier *Plutology*. Central to his analysis was the oft-repeated statement that the 'unit of modern society is the individual; the unit of archaic society is the Household'. Aryan society was both pre-political and pre-economic, it knew no state or law, it lacked the concepts of the individual and individual freedom, and it operated a regime of custom rather than of law, of status rather than of contract, to use Maine's famous formulation. Paradoxically, it was the coming into existence of the state that enabled the development of individualism, so crucial to economic progress. Not only was the state not inimical to individualism, it was only in a political society and through the agency of the state that individualism was possible. And it was in the proportion, too, that a state advanced towards perfection, that it removed, 'except so far as its own requirements and the limiting rights of others demand, all impediments from the action of the individual. Thus the freedom of individual actions is found in the State, and is not found elsewhere.' Similarly, the 'history of individual property and the history of personal liberty coincide. Both of them result from the disintegration of the Household.' Hearn argued that Christianity extirpated the Lares, the household gods, which were central to Aryan society, and that its precepts were alien to the clan structure. In addition Christianity was a modernising force in that its 'whole theory and practice' implied the 'recognition of the individual man, and the value of the single human soul'. Clearly Hearn had Anglican Christianity in mind rather than Roman Catholic.[189]

Hearn's analysis of archaic society (and Ireland for him was closer to primitive than to modern society) had profound repercussions for political economy, especially for the universality of its laws. In an extraordinary passage in the introduction to *The Aryan Household*, Hearn attempted, at once, to deny and confirm the universal character of economic laws:

> Much of the opposition to political economy has been due to
> the very natural, or at least very British, desire of some of its

earlier teachers to generalize from British phenomena alone. This error has been corrected; but it is evident that there are some societies which the ordinary economic rules do not fit. I think that the reason is, that the conditions of political society alone furnish the postulates of political economy. I believe that political economy is a true science; that is, that its phenomena may be traced to ultimate laws of human nature. These laws are at all times the same, but the conditions necessary for their operation did not exist, or very imperfectly existed, in archaic society. Political economy requires competition, and is hopelessly embarrassed by custom. Competition implies free individual action, and such action is unknown under the clan *regime*. The conclusions of political economy are universally true, but only on the assumption that a certain state of society is present, and that certain beliefs and motives are absent. What can political economy do with a Chinaman, who, for the sake of posthumous worship of himself and his ancestors, is willing to be hanged for the sum of £33?

In like manner, Hearn argued, the 'theory of utility would have been altogether incomprehensible to our archaic forefathers'.[190]

The assimilationist and utilitarian view was that customary practices and the family and clan systems were barriers in the way of individual enterprise, *laissez-faire*, and economic progress in general. But others with a comparative and historical perspective welcomed the challenge to the imperial sway of political economy, to *laissez-faire*, to the absolutist doctrine of private property in land, to the sacredness of contract, and increasingly saw economic virtue in the notions of communality which were undergoing a rehabilitation. It would be difficult to exaggerate the profound effect which the editorial introductions to the first four volumes of *The Ancient Laws and Institutes of Ireland* ('The Brehon Laws') had on debates about Irish land. As Clive Dewey puts it in his outstanding article 'Celtic Agrarian Legislation and the Celtic Revival', this reconstruction of early Irish society popularised the 'historicist approach to the Irish agrarian problem'; it was a sharp lesson in 'historical relativism', demonstrating the 'feasibility, perhaps the desirability of alternative forms of social organisation to those the utilitarians had taken for granted'.[191] Hancock, who converted to tenant rights in 1865, and Richey were engaged for a time in editing and translating (however incompetently) the Brehon Laws, but it was their editorial introductions which were so vastly influential. In terms of the currently fashionable evolutionary theory, Ireland was seen as being at a more rudimentary state of development than England, so laws appropriate to a 'commercial society' were not necessarily appropriate to Ireland. The family was the unit in early Irish society, custom rather than contract prevailed, and land was communally owned. This reconstruction, though highly problematic, gained virtually unanimous assent, although authorities differed as to whether it indicated barbarism or civilisation, noble savagery or just savagery. These 'Irish ideas' mounted a powerful challenge against the most sacred doctrines of political economy: individualism, contract, and private property in land.

As we saw, Bicheno spoke of Ireland as contradicting the 'established doctrines of political economy', although England was attempting to transplant the science in its inhospitable soil. In his book *States of Mind*, Oliver MacDonagh writes of the transfer of English concepts and presuppositions to Irish affairs after the Act of Union, especially the 'gradual transference of the notions of political economy to the sister island', despite Irish resistance.[192] The 'English' ideas of absolute ownership of and free trade in land, and of the sacredness of contract were not effectively challenged until the 1860s. We saw how in 1848 the young Hancock ridiculed the very notion of Irish political economy. But after the Famine there was an increasing awareness that Irish social and economic circumstances differed so radically from English conditions that ideas valid in England were not necessarily so in Ireland. According to one author, the 'two main pillars of English law', the 'absolute rights of property and the sacredness of contract' had, on the whole, worked well in England, whereas in Ireland they had brought 'unmixed evil'.[193] Writing in 1858, Joseph J. Murphy described as an 'established truth of political economy, that the interest of the entire community requires land to become private property, and to be as nearly as possible assimilated to chattels' but admitted that such simple truths appeared not to have been recognised by any primitive people.[194] But four years later Hutton stated as his 'fundamental principle' that property was a 'social institution' and quoted Thomas Drummond's well-known maxim, interestingly addressed to an Irish landlord, that 'property has its duties as well as its rights'.[195] In a paper in 1870 Hutton wrote of the 'impossibility, now recognized, of reforming the relation of landlord and tenant in Ireland by the English system, or economic *laissez-faire*. He suggested instead looking at the ancient tenures and modern land legislation in British India. He noted that tribal ownership of land and status tenure were characteristics of early society in both India and Ireland. It was, stated Hutton, instructive to observe that the 'extreme economic notions' of the English in India had 'gradually yielded to an enlightened, just, and humane regard for native ideas and institutions'.[196] Some years earlier Isaac Butt had opined that the reason why Indian land reform of the 1860s was the envy of Ireland was because 'we have a fixation of an identity with England. The owner of the soil is a "landlord" not a "zemindar" – the occupier is a "tenant", not a "ryot"', and Butt made it clear that even the simple terms 'landlord' and 'tenant' had quite different connotations in England and in Ireland.[197] The previous year an article in the *Westminster Review* stated that it was 'perplexing in the extreme' for English politicians to discover 'after years of important legislation, that Indian zemindars were no landlords, and Indian ryots perversely resisted the process of transmutation by State alchemy, into English tenants'.[198] In his controversial pamphlet of 1868, *Ireland and England*, Mill declared that Ireland should be governed by Irish ideas. India, he wrote, 'was now governed with a full perception and recognition of the differences from England ... What had been done for India has now to be done for Ireland.'[199] Indeed it was a book by an Indian civil servant, George Campbell, which, in large measure, inspired Gladstone to take such action. The difficulty, said Campbell, arose from 'our applying English laws to a country where they are opposed to facts' and, echoing Butt, that 'in Ireland a landlord is not a landlord and a tenant is not a tenant in the English sense'.[200]

Mill's ideas were very much influenced by a remarkable series of articles, nine in all, written by his friend John Elliot Cairnes, entitled 'Ireland in Transition', and published in *The Economist* in 1865. Cairnes rejected the English agricultural model as appropriate for Ireland and he attacked the absolute nature of private property in land, declaring that land was not to be treated as an ordinary commodity.[201] He found that 'English theory' was at variance with 'Irish ideas' about landed property and did not explain Irish 'fact', and he rejected what he called the 'English doctrine' of 'open competition and contract as the remedy for all social disorders arising from land tenure'. The landlord–tenant contract was not, in Ireland, an ordinary one, but one which required from the state 'a large supervision and control'.[202] In a later article Cairnes strongly supported Campbell's scheme, as he had taken 'custom and Irish ideas as his guide'.[203]

By the end of the 1860s most commentators on Irish affairs, especially on land, and those anxious for the pacification of Ireland, felt, in many cases reluctantly, that the price to be paid was either the abandonment or the radical redefinition of political economy. The imperial rule of political economy was over. The O'Donoghue, for example, asserted in the House of Commons in 1868 that in almost every instance in Ireland the occupier had 'ancient prescriptive titles to their farms, and although this might count for little in the arithmetic of the political economist, it should be considered by those who wished to approach the difficulty in a true spirit'.[204] And, as we noted, Richey claimed that in early Irish society trade was carried out 'uninfluenced by the laws of political economy'. Clearly Ireland, suspended somewhere between being a colony of England and a 'sister kingdom', between being a primitive society and a modern one, presented extremely complex problems to political economy. One major result was the methodological revolution in English economics pioneered by Leslie and Ingram. Perhaps even more extraordinary was the case of Cairnes, who produced as searching and comprehensive a critique of orthodoxy, but who remained a methodological deductivist. In a review of Leslie's *Land Systems and Industrial Economy of Ireland, England, and Continental Countries*, Mill drew attention to the subversive effects Ireland and its agrarian problems had on political economy:

> The Irish land difficulty having shown, by painful experience, that there is at least one nation closely connected with our own, which cannot and will not bear to have its agricultural economy ruled by the universal maxims which some of our political economists challenge all mankind to disobey at their peril; it has begun to dawn upon an increasing number of understandings, that some of these universal maxims are perhaps not universal at all, but merely English customs; and a few have begun to doubt whether, even as such, they have any claim to the transcendent excellence ascribed to them. The question has been raised whether the administration of

the land of a country is a subject to which our current maxims of free trade, free contract, the exclusive power of every one over his own property, and so forth, are really applicable, or applicable without very serious limitations; whether private individuals ought to have the same absolute control, the same *jus utendi et abutendi,* over landed property, which it is just and expedient that they should be permitted to exercise over movable wealth.[205]

Mill's review appeared in 1870, the year of the Irish Land Act which qualified the absolute control of landlords over their property. The Encumbered Estates Court set up after the Famine and the 1860 Irish Land Act both attempted to establish free trade in land. The 1881 Irish Land Act, in effect, accepted the co-ownership of land, replaced free contract with status tenancy, and gave the state a permanent role in the fixing of rents. Writing about the 1870 Land Act, 'A Protestant Celt' felt it did not go far enough in the direction of 'Irish ideas'. It still represented a form of 'compulsory Anglification': an 'English statesman now tries to force Irishmen, whether they like it or not, in the English contract system, and to stamp out all ideas of status tenancy'.[206] The 1881 Act conceded the 'Three Fs' (fixity of tenure, fair rent, freedom of sale), a concession justified by the Bessborough Commission on the basis of Campbell's historicist arguments of 1869. This 'wholesale departure from English norms', as Dewey terms it, was defended on the grounds that Ireland had not yet reached the evolutionary stage of contract tenancy.[207] 'That condition of society', according to the Report, 'in which the land suitable for tillage can be regarded as a mere commodity, the subject of trade, and can be let to the highest bidder in an open market, has never, except under special circumstances, existed in Ireland'. The 'economical law of supply and demand was but of casual and exceptional application' and there had 'in general survived, despite the seeming or real veto of the law, in apparent defiance of political economy, a living tradition of possessory right, such as belonged, in the more primitive eyes of society, to the status of the man who tilled the soil'.[208] Indeed Gladstone had expressed similar views when he introduced the 1870 Land Bill. In Ireland, he stated, unlike England and Scotland,

where the old Irish ideas were never supplanted except by

the rude hand of violence – by laws written on the Statute Book, but never entering into the heart of the Irish people – the people have not generally embraced the idea of the occupation of land by contract; and the old Irish notion that some interest in the soil adheres to the tenant, even though his contract has expired, is everywhere rooted in the popular mind.[209]

In effect, indigenous oral custom, which had entered the heart of the Irish people, was to be preferred to imposed, written law. More credence was to be given to the 'popular mind' than to the rational calculus of maximising utilitarians, to national *pietas* than to cosmopolitan enlightenment. To give one final example, Posnett claimed that the economic conditions of Ireland had 'contributed to expose the fallacies of Ricardian theory'. The 'misery of a tenancy left to the ideal freedom or serfage of Ricardo' was, in Ireland, 'exposing the true nature of private monopoly in land' and the 'absurd fallacies of free competition and free contract could not live in the atmosphere of a country in which incumbered landlords and rackrented tenants-at-will, farming for subsistence, give them the lie'.[210]

Needless to mention, 'Irish ideas' were frequently condemned for, in the words of a volume published in 1882 entitled *The Irish Landlord and His Accusers*, threatening to 'unsettle the principles of Political Economy, to shake the stability of contracts as a law of civilised society, and to invade the rights of property'. The 1870 Act had 'violated the sacredness of contract, and destroyed the security of property – the two principles which constitute the essential distinction between a civilised and a savage state of society'.[211] Froude had humorously spoken of murder, violence, and destruction as 'Irish ideas' in his *English in Ireland*; a four-page pamphlet published in 1878 by 'An Irish Proprietor' was entitled *Irish Ideas*, one of which was 'spoliation clap-trap'.[212] There was extreme anxiety in Britain lest 'Irish ideas' should migrate to that country, destroying civilisation as they knew it. But that is another story.

Political economy as a cure-all for Irish ills, as the locus of ideological consensus in Ireland, and as prime agent of social control, failed in all of its ambitious objectives. Irish nationalists were suspicious of an 'English' science used to explain away the Famine, and the people in general were on their guard against a species of knowledge so enthusiastically embraced by their betters and so untiringly propagated by them. Roman Catholicism, Irishness, and engrained familial ideology, all perceived as economically regressive forces, not only resisted the onslaught of political economy but forced the establishment into a moral and sociological critique of its absolutism. In Bicheno's terms rational political economy failed to wean the Irish from their affective, non-rational ways. Contemporary evolutionary views were used to validate the notion that Ireland was insufficiently developed to come under the full rigorous sway of political economy. The attempted imposition of political economy on Ireland for the purpose of assimilating it to England was no more successful. The decline in prestige of political economy was concomitant with the increased emphasis on Ireland's difference from England. Ireland had to be governed by 'Irish ideas'. It was, as it transpired, a short step from historical to 'national' economics. In 1905 Arthur Griffith derived the economic ideas of Sinn Fein from Friedrich List and, most intriguingly, from Henry Carey (the son of an Irish political exile, Mathew Carey) whose views, both Leslie and Ingram agreed, were significantly influenced by a hereditary dislike of England and its political economy. In his youth Ingram himself wrote a patriotic ballad for the *Nation* called 'The memory of the dead', but which achieved lasting popular fame as 'Who fears to speak of '98?' Though Ingram soon abandoned his incipient nationalism, and even opposed Home Rule, Thomas Kettle saw a continuity between his patriotic effusion and his political economy. Kettle, a methodological discipline of Ingram, saw the 'Historical School' as 'under another aspect, the National School', and he was the initial holder of the first and only Chair of National Economics (at University College Dublin) in these islands. He spoke of the 'identity of the human reality' behind Ingram's poem and his 'methodological admonition' of English political economy for, as always, Ingram voiced the 'revolt of the small nations against the Czardom, scientific and political, of the great'.[213] In 1916, the year of the Easter Rising in Dublin, Kettle was killed in action at the Battle of the Somme, fighting for the freedom of small nations.

APPENDIX
Biographical details of Professors of Political Economy at Trinity College Dublin and the Queen's Colleges (Belfast, Cork, Galway) in the nineteenth century

Mountifort Longfield (1802–84) was the son of a clergyman from County Cork. He was educated at Trinity College, where he graduated in 1823 as moderator and gold medallist in science. Two years later he was elected a Fellow of the College, and proceeded to the degrees of MA in 1829 and LL D in 1831. He was called to the Irish Bar in 1828, but never practised. In 1832 he was appointed the first Whately Professor of Political Economy, a position which he held until 1836. Already by 1834 he had become Regius Professor of Feudal and English Law in Trinity College, an office he held until his death. In 1842 he was admitted a Queen's Counsel. When the Encumbered Estates Act was passed in 1849 he was appointed one of the three Commissioners, and he held that office until the Landed Estates Court was established in 1858. He then became a judge of that court until 1867. In that year he was sworn into the Irish Privy Council and left the Landed Estates Court. He became a Commissioner of National Education in 1853, a Bencher of the King's Inn in 1859 and, from 1863 to 1867, he was president of the Statistical and Social Inquiry Society of Ireland, having been one of the original · vice-presidents of the Society from its foundation in 1847. His principal publications included: *Lectures on Political Economy, Delivered in Trinity and Michaelmas Terms, 1833* (Dublin, 1834); *Four Lectures on Poor Laws, Delivered in Trinity Term, 1834* (Dublin, 1834); and *Three Lectures on*

*Commerce and One on Absenteeism, Delivered in Michaelmas,
1834, before the University of Dublin* (Dublin, 1835).

Isaac Butt (1813–79), the second holder of the Whately Chair,
was born in County Donegal, on 6 September 1813, the only son
of Revd Robert Butt, rector at Stranorlar, Co. Donegal. He was
educated at the Royal School, Raphoe, and at Trinity College
where he took his BA in 1835, LL B in 1836, and MA and LL D in
1840. In 1833 he was one of the founding members of the *Dublin
University Magazine* and was its editor from 1834 to 1838. In
1836 he was appointed, as successor to Longfield, to the Whately
Chair of Political Economy, which he held until 1841. Butt was
called to the Irish Bar in 1838, and in 1844 to the Inner Bar. In
1859 he was called to the English Bar at the Inner Temple. His
high reputation as a barrister obtained for him a considerable
practice, and it was also instrumental in involving him in active
politics from the outset of his career. In his early political life he
was considered one of the most formidable defenders of the
conservative position, actively opposing O'Connell's Repeal
Association in 1843. In May 1852 Butt entered Parliament as
member for Harwich, but in the same year, in the course of a
general election, he modified his political allegiance and offered
himself as a Liberal-Conservative candidate for Youghal in County
Cork. He was elected and sat from 1852 to 1865. By 1864 he had
returned to Ireland and got involved in the legal defence of
Fenian prisoners, which engaged all his efforts from 1865 to 1869.
In 1867 he accepted the presidency of the Amnesty Association.
In 1871 the most celebrated part of his political career commenced,
when he was selected to represent the city of Limerick, and to
accept the leadership of the Home Rule Party. It is in this capacity
that he is best remembered in Irish political history. He died in
1879 and is buried in Stranorlar in Donegal. His publications
included: *Introductory Lecture Delivered before the University of
Dublin, in Hilary Term, 1837* (Dublin, 1837); *Rent, Profits and
Labour: A Lecture Delivered before the University of Dublin in
Michaelmas Term, 1837* (Dublin, 1838); *Protection to Home
Industry: Some Cases of Its Advantages Considered: The Substance
of Two Lectures delivered before the University of Dublin in
Michaelmas Term, 1840* (Dublin, 1846); *Land Tenure in Ireland:
A Plea for the Celtic Race* (Dublin, 1866); *The Irish Querist*
(Dublin, 1867); and *The Irish Deep Sea Fisheries* (Dublin, 1874).

APPENDIX

James Anthony Lawson (1817–87) succeeded Butt in the Whately Chair, which he held from 1841 to 1846. A native of Waterford, where he received his early education, he entered Trinity College and was elected a scholar in 1836. He obtained a senior moderatorship in 1837, was a gold medal recipient, and earned a first-class honours degree in ethics and logic. He graduated with the BA in 1838, LL B in 1841, and LL D in 1850. Lawson went on to pursue a distinguished legal career, and a considerably more modest political one. He was called to the Irish Bar in 1840. In 1857 he became a Queen's Counsel, and in the same year he made an unsuccessful attempt to obtain a parliamentary seat as member for Dublin University. In 1861 he was elected a Bencher of the King's Inn, Dublin, and between 1858 and 1859 he acted as legal adviser to the Crown in Ireland. In 1861 he was appointed Solicitor-General for Ireland, and in 1865 Attorney-General. Between 1865 and 1868 he was Member of Parliament for Portarlington, the same seat having been held between 1819 and 1823 by the distinguished, albeit absentee, political economist, David Ricardo. In 1868, when his political career was effectively ended with his defeat in the general election, he returned to his legal career. In that year he was appointed fourth Justice of the Common Pleas in Ireland, a position he held until 1882. In 1870 he became an English Privy Counsellor, and in 1882 he was made a judge of the Queen's Bench division. It was in this latter capacity that he achieved considerable notoriety in a series of political trials associated with the Land League agitation. An attempt to assassinate him in 1882 failed. Lawson was closely associated with the foundation of the Statistical Society in 1847, serving as honorary secretary between 1847 and 1851, and as president between 1870 and 1872. He had the distinction of reading the first paper to the Society. He was Barrington lecturer in the years 1849, 1850, and 1852. He died in Dublin on 10 August 1887. His principal publications included: *Five Lectures on Political Economy, Delivered before the University of Dublin, in Michaelmas Term, 1843* (London, 1844).

William Neilson Hancock (1820–88), the fourth holder of the Whately Chair, was born in Lisburn, County Antrim. He entered Trinity College in 1838 and was originally a student of mathematics, turning to law and political economy only after graduation. He was called to the Irish Bar in 1844. Two years later he was elected Whately Professor, a position he held until 1851. Hancock, like a number of Whately Professors, had the distinction of holding two chairs simultaneously. While still a Whately Professor he was appointed the first Professor of Jurisprudence and Political Economy at Queen's College Belfast, when it opened in 1849, and he held that position until 1853. Hancock's remarkably prolific career was characterised by a commitment to what he called 'Applied Political Economy'. This was reflected in his interest in practical problems, his contributions to various commissions, and his concern for social reform based on a careful statistical analysis of the problems at hand. It was this commitment which led Hancock to establish the Dublin Statistical Society in 1847 and the Belfast Social Inquiry Society in 1851. Indeed after 1851 his career centred on his role as public servant and compiler of social and economic statistics. In that same year, 1851, he was appointed Secretary to the Dublin University Commission, a position he held simultaneously with the Professorship in Queen's College, Belfast, until 1853. In 1854 he filled the same office for the Endowed Schools (Ireland) Commission, which reported in 1858. Hancock was Clerk of the Custody of Papers in matters of Idiots and Lunatics in Court of Chancery from 1855 to 1858 and again from 1859 to 1866. He was Secretary of the English and Irish Law and Chancery Commission in 1861, and of the Irish Admiralty Commission in 1864, while in 1867–8 he was Secretary to the Railways (Ireland) Commission. In 1880 he was made a Queen's Counsel and later in 1881–2 became Keeper of Records of the Irish Land Commission, and Clerk of the Crown and Hanaper between 1882 and 1884. In addition to these activities he was an exceptionally prolific writer, producing numerous reports on different economic and social topics; between 1863 and 1873 he collected and compiled the 'Judicial and Criminal Statistics of Ireland', and he was by far the most frequent presenter of papers to the Statistical Society, delivering more than eighty in all between 1847 and 1882. Hancock was the founder of the Dublin Statistical Society and was its honorary secretary from its foundation in 1847 until 1881, in which year he was persuaded to become president, a position he held for just one year, but he remained a vice-president until his death in 1888. Among Hancock's many publications, the following represent a limited listing of his more significant contributions: *The Tenant Right of Ulster, Considered Economically*

(Dublin, 1845); *Three Lectures on the Questions, Should the Principles of Political Economy be Disregarded at the Present Crisis?* (Dublin, 1847); *Introductory Lectures on Political Economy, Delivered in the Theatre of Trinity College, Dublin, in Trinity Term, 1848* (Dublin, 1849); *Impediments to the Prosperity of Ireland* (London, 1850); *Is the Competition between Large and Small Shops Injurious to the Community? Being a Lecture Delivered in Trinity College, Dublin, in Trinity Term, 1851* (Dublin, 1851); *Report on the Supposed Progressive Decline of Irish Prosperity* (Dublin, 1863); *Report on the State of the Public Accounts between Great Britain and Ireland* (Dublin, 1864); *Report on the Landlord and Tenant Question in Ireland, from 1860 till 1866; With an Appendix, Containing a Report on the Question from 1835 till 1859* (Dublin, 1866); and *The State of Ireland in 1874* (Dublin, 1874).

Richard Hussey Walsh (1825–62), the fifth holder of the Whately Chair of Political Economy from 1851 to 1856, was born in Kilduff, King's County, on 25 July 1825. Having received his early education by private tuition, he entered Trinity College. He graduated with a BA in 1847, after a distinguished academic record in science in which he achieved the highest honours in mathematics and physics. The following year, 1848, he was awarded the first of Bishop Law's Mathematical Prizes. Precluded from pursuing a Fellowship by virtue of being a Catholic, he turned his attention to the study of political economy. In 1850 he was awarded the prize in political economy in the University of Dublin, and as a result was made a Barrington lecturer. The following year he successfully competed for the Whately Professorship, and he was also made an honorary secretary of the Statistical Society, which office he held for six years. In addition to his duties as Whately Professor, Walsh also acted as Deputy Professor of Jurisprudence and Political Economy in Queen's College Belfast, for Hancock during the winter of 1853. His academic career effectively ended on completion of his term of office in the Whately Chair. In 1856 he was appointed Assistant Secretary of the Endowed Schools (Ireland) Commission. As a result of his contributions to that Commission he was appointed Superintendant of the Government Schools of Mauritius in 1857. Walsh's commitment to his work attracted the attention of the Governor, who then appointed him to a Commission to inquire into the administration of the island. In addition, Walsh was made responsible for conducting a Census of Mauritius in 1861. He died shortly after the completion of this work in January, 1862, at the early age of thirty-seven. Walsh contributed several papers to the statistical section of the British Association, and to the Statistical Society. He also wrote frequently for *The Economist*. His principal area of interest was monetary economics, and his most important publication, which was a pioneering study of the subject and was highly regarded by Senior and Mill, was entitled *An Elementary Treatise on Metallic Currency* (Dublin, 1853).

John Elliot Cairnes (1823–75) succeeded Hussey Walsh as the sixth occupant of the Whately Chair, holding it from 1856 to 1861. Cairnes was born in Castlebellingham, County Louth, where his father was a partner in a brewery. After a somewhat indifferent performance in his early education, Cairnes, against the wishes of his father, entered Trinity College in 1842. He graduated with a BA in 1848, and received the MA in 1854. After a period of indecision, Cairnes, having been advised by Professor William Nesbitt of Queen's College Galway, turned his attention to political economy, and was persuaded by Nesbitt to compete for the Whately Professorship. This he successfully did, in 1856, and held it for the regulation five years. In 1857 he was called to the Irish Bar, but never seriously practised; he was for the remainder of his career a full-time academic economist. In 1859 he was appointed Professor of Jurisprudence and Political Economy at Queen's College Galway, while still a Whately Professor. In 1860 he married Eliza Alexander, who was a sister-in-law of his friend Nesbitt. In 1865 he moved to London and settled at Mill Hill, but retained the Galway professorship until 1870. Meanwhile, in 1866, he was appointed Professor of Political Economy at University College London, a position he held until 1872 when bad health forced him to resign. Apart from his major contributions to methodology and economic theory, Cairnes wrote extensively on the Irish land and education questions. At his death, Cairnes was regarded as one of the most outstanding economists of his time. His principal publications included: *The Character and Logical Method of Political Economy* (London, 1857; 2nd ed., 1875); *The Slave Power; Its Character, Career, and Probable Designs: Being an Attempt to Explain the Real Issues Involved in the American Contest* (London, 1862); *Essays in Political Economy: Theoretical* *and Applied* (London, 1873); and *Some Leading Principles of Political Economy Newly Expounded* (London, 1874).

Arthur Houston (1833–1914)   was born in Dublin on 10 August 1833, the youngest son of Timothy Turner Houston, a Dublin merchant. His mother was Mary, the youngest daughter of Henry Banks, MD. He was educated at Dr Wall's School in Dublin and D. Starkpoole's School in Kingstown. He continued his studies at Trinity College Dublin, where he graduated as senior moderator in history, political economy, law, and English literature. He received the BA degree in 1858 and the LL D in 1865. He was appointed Whately Professor of Political Economy in 1861, vacating the Chair in 1866. In 1862 he was called to the Irish Bar. Twenty years later, in 1882, he was made a Queen's Counsel. He was called to the English Bar in 1897. He died, in London, on 11 March 1914. His principal publications included: *The Emancipation of Women from Existing Industrial Disabilities: Considered in Its Economic Aspect* (London, 1862); *The Principles of Value in Exchange, Explained and Expressed in Simple and Comprehensive Formulae. Two Lectures Delivered in the University of Dublin* (London, 1866); *The Fusion of Law and Equity* (Dublin, 1866); and *Daniel O'Connell: His Early Life, and Journal, 1795 to 1802* (London, 1906).

James W. Slattery (1831–97)   was born on 18 August, 1831, the eldest son of Prince Slattery of Carrick-on-Suir, County Tipperary. He was educated at Trinity College being elected a scholar in 1859 and graduating with the BA in 1862. In 1866 he was awarded the MA. He was first senior moderator in classics, and senior moderator in history, political science, and English literature. He was elected Whately Professor of Political Economy in 1866, retaining the Chair until 1872. He was also Professor of Common Law at the King's Inn, Dublin, 1868–70. He was elected to the Council of the Statistical Society for the twenty-fourth session (1870–1). He was president of Queen's College, Cork from 1890 until his death. He was also a member of the senate of the Royal University of Ireland from 1890 to 1897. He died in Cork on 25 April 1897.

Robert Cather Donnell (1839–83)   was born on 25 June 1839, the second son of William Donnell and Isabella Cather at

Ballinamallard, County Tyrone. He was educated at Queen's College Belfast, and was the first gold medallist in jurisprudence and political economy in the Queen's University in Ireland. He graduated in 1860, received the MA in 1863 and the LL D in 1882. He was called to the Irish Bar in 1864. He was elected to the Statistical Society in 1860. He was Barrington lecturer for the years 1871, 1872, and 1873. In 1872 he was appointed ninth Whately Professor of Political Economy at Trinity College Dublin, and held the post until 1877. In 1876 he was appointed Professor of Jurisprudence and Political Economy at Queen's College Galway, a position he held until his death in 1883. His principal publications included: *Practical Guide to the Law of Tenant Compensation and Farm Purchase under the Irish Land Act* (Dublin, 1871); *Chapters on the Leaseholder's Claim to Tenant-Right, and Other Tenant-Right Questions* (Dublin, 1873); *A Scheme of Land Transfer for Small Proprietors, by Local Registry of Title* (Dublin, 1874); and *Reports of One Hundred and Ninety Cases in the Irish Land Courts* (Dublin, 1876).

James Johnston Shaw (1845–1910) was born at Kirkcubbin, County Down, on 4 January 1845, the second son of John Maxwell Shaw and his wife, Anne Johnston. He attended the local national school and in addition received private lessons from the Revd J. Towan, the minister of Kirkcubbin. His secondary education was received at the Belfast Academy which he attended from 1858 to 1861, when he entered Queen's College Belfast. For his first two years he studied classics and English literature, and in his third year, logic and metaphysics. He also studied political economy, but only as a supplementary subject. He graduated with the BA in October 1865, taking first place in logic, metaphysics, and political economy. The following year, 1866, he was awarded his MA in the same subjects. Uncertain as to what career to pursue, he spent the winter of 1866–7 at Edinburgh University studying theology with a view to taking up a career in the ministry of the Irish Presbyterian Church. In the event he did not follow this path and, in June 1869, he was appointed to the Chair of Metaphysics and Ethics in Magee College, Derry. He became increasingly unhappy in this position, and in 1876 he successfully competed for the Whately Chair of Political Economy. He occupied this position from 1877 to 1882. After his term as Whately Professor, Shaw's contributions were mainly to legal and educational matters. In 1878 he was called to the Bar, and in 1889 he was made a Queen's Counsel. In December 1891 he was offered the County Judgeship of Kerry, which he accepted and retained until 1909. In the educational sphere he was a senator of the Royal University of Ireland, a Commissioner of Irish National Education, a member of the Commission on Manual and Practical Instruction, and a Trustee of the National Library of Ireland. His most celebrated contribution to educational affairs was his chairmanship of the Belfast University Commission of 1908–10, which was concerned with elaborating the structures of the new Queen's University Belfast in accordance with the provisions of the Irish Universities Act of 1908. He was appointed one of the first Pro-Chancellors of the new university after its establishment in 1908. He had also been president of the Statistical Society from 1900 to 1902, and in 1909 he accepted the Recordship of Belfast. He died on 27 April 1910. The papers which comprise his principal published work were edited by his daughter Margaret G. Woods. The volume, *Occasional Papers*, included a long biographical introduction by his daughter and was published in Dublin in 1910.

Charles Francis Bastable (1855–1945)   was born in Charleville, County Cork, the son of a clergyman. His early education was obtained at Fermoy College. He entered Trinity College in 1873, and graduated in 1878 with first-class honours in the senior moderatorship in history and political science, which included some study of political economy. After graduation he read law and was called to the Irish Bar in 1881. In 1882 he obtained the degree of MA, and in 1890 the LL D. In 1882 Bastable was appointed to the Whately Chair for the statutory five-year period. On completion of the five-year term, the conditions for holding the Whately Chair were altered, allowing it to be held for longer periods. Bastable was re-elected under the new conditions and retained the chair until his retirement in 1932, by which time he had spent fifty years as Whately Professor. During this period Bastable held a number of positions, both in Trinity itself and in other institutions. In 1883 he was appointed Professor of Jurisprudence and Political Economy at Queen's College Galway, a position he retained until 1903. In 1902 he was appointed Professor of Jurisprudence and International Law, and in 1908 Regius Professor of Laws in Trinity College Dublin. He played an active part in the Statistical Society, of which he was an honorary secretary from 1886 to 1895, and a vice-president from 1896 to 1915. He was one of the original Fellows of the Royal Economic Society, and a member of its first council. In 1894 he was elected president of the British Association, Section F, and in 1921 he was elected a Fellow of the British Academy. When the Irish Free State was established in 1921 he served on the Fiscal Inquiry Committee, which reported in 1923. Bastable retired in 1932 and died thirteen years later in 1945. Bastable published prolifically over an exceptionally long career. His principal works included: *An Examination of Some Current Objections to the Study of Political Economy: Being an Introductory Lecture Delivered in Trinity College, during Trinity Term, 1884* (Dublin, 1884); *The Theory of International Trade; With Some of Its Applications to Economic Policy* (Dublin, 1887); *The Commerce of Nations* (London, 1892); and *Public Finance* (London, 1892).

THE QUEEN'S COLLEGES (1849–1900)

Queen's College Belfast

William Neilson Hancock (1820–88), was professor of Jurisprudence and Political Economy from 1849 to 1853. For further biographical details, see entry under Trinity College Dublin.

Thomas Edward Cliffe Leslie (1825–82) was born on 21 June 1825 in County Wexford, the second son of Revd Edward Leslie and Margaret Higginson. He was educated at King William's College, Isle of Man, and Trinity College Dublin, where he graduated in 1847 with a gold medal in ethics and logic. In 1851 he took the degree of LL B. In 1850 he was called to the Irish Bar, and after further legal studies at Lincoln's Inn, to the English Bar in 1857. Leslie was appointed Professor of Jurisprudence and Political Economy at Queen's College Belfast in 1853, a position he retained until his death on 27 January 1882. Despite the fact that Leslie resided mainly in London, he was an active member of the Statistical Society between 1851 and 1863. He was appointed Barrington lecturer in political economy for 1852 and 1853, and acted as one of the honorary secretaries of the Society from 1857 to 1863. He read a number of papers to the Society between 1851 and 1855. He was a member of both the Political Economy Club and the Athenaeum Club in London. His principal publications included: *The Military Systems of Europe Economically Considered* (Belfast, 1856); *Land Systems and Industrial Economy of England, Ireland and Continental Countries* (London, 1870); and *Essays in Political and Moral Philosophy* (Dublin, 1879); the second revised edition of this work was entitled *Essays in Political Economy* (Dublin, 1888).

William Graham (1839–1911) was born at Saintfield, Co. Down. He was educated at the Dundalk Institution, and later at Trinity College Dublin, where he graduated in 1867 with his BA. In 1870 he was awarded the MA and was elected scholar in mathematics and mathematical physics. He was the Wray prizeman in logic, ethics and metaphysics, and was the vice-chancellor's prizeman in English prose. During 1873–4 he was private secretary to Mitchell Henry, and engaged in literary and private tutorial work in London during the period 1875–82. He was called to the Bar at the Inner Temple in 1892. He was examiner in political economy and philosophy for the Indian Civil Service examinations, and was examiner for the Royal University of Ireland in 1893–4, and again between 1900 and 1909. He was appointed Professor of Jurisprudence and Political Economy at Queen's College Belfast in 1882 and retained this position until 1909. He died on 19 November 1911. His principal publications were: *Idealism: An Essay* (London, 1872); *The Creed of Science* (London, 1881); *The Social Problem* (London, 1886); *Socialism, New and Old* (London, 1890); *English Political Philosophy from Hobbes to Maine* (London, 1899); and *Free Trade and the Empire* (London, 1904).

Queen's College Cork

Richard Horner Mills (1815–93) was born in Dublin in 1815, the first son of Francis Mills, a merchant, and Anne Horner. He was educated at Trinity College Dublin where he graduated in 1838 with the BA. In 1841 he took the MA. He was called to the Irish Bar in 1847. Prior to this he had worked as a merchant. In 1849 he was appointed the first Professor of Jurisprudence and Political Economy at Queen's College Cork, a position he retained until his death in London on 24 August 1893. His main publication was *The Principles of Currency and Banking; Being Five Lectures Delivered in Queen's College, Cork* (London, 1853).

George Joseph Stokes (1859–1935) was born in Sligo on 3 March 1859 and was educated at the Diocesan School, Sligo, Trinity College Dublin and at the Universities of Heidelberg and Berlin. He held the Hibbert travelling scholarship between 1881 and 1883. He received the MA degree from Trinity College and was called to the Bar at Lincoln's Inn. He was for a time a member of the Senate of Dublin University. He was Professor of Mental and Social Science in Queen's College Cork 1894–1909 and Professor of Philosophy from 1909 to 1924. He died on 6 March 1935. His publications, which are mainly philosophical, include, *The Objectivity of Truth* (London, 1884); 'Gnosticism and modern pantheism', *Mind*, n.s. 4 (1895); and 'Logical Theory of the Imagination', *Mind*, n.s. 9 (1900).

Queen's College Galway

Denis Caulfield Heron (1824–81), the first Professor of Jurisprudence and Political Economy at Queen's College Galway, was born on 16 February 1824 in Dublin, the first son of William Heron of Newry, Co. Down and Mary Maguire. He was educated at St Gregory's, Downside, and in 1840 he attended Trinity College Dublin, where, in 1843, he qualified for a scholarship, but as a Catholic was refused election. He graduated in 1845, and in 1857 he was awarded the LL B and LL D. He was called to the Irish Bar in 1848. In 1849 Heron was appointed to the Chair of Jurisprudence and Political Economy at the newly-established Queen's College Galway, a position he held until 1859. Heron was closely associated with the Dublin Statistical Society, being one of the original members. He was also one of the first four Barrington lecturers appointed in 1849, and was a vice-president from 1871 until his death in 1881. After he resigned his chair at Queen's College Galway, Heron devoted himself to his legal career, with a short interlude in active politics. He became a Queen's Counsel in 1860, a Bencher of King's Inns in 1872, and third Serjeant-at-law in 1880. Between 1870 and 1874 he was Member of Parliament for County Tipperary, having narrowly won the seat from Charles Kickham. Heron died while salmon fishing on Lough Corrib at the age of fifty-seven, on 15 April 1881. His major publications included the following works: *The Constitutional History of the University of Dublin* (Dublin, 1847); *Three Lectures on the Principles of Taxation, Delivered at Queen's College, Galway, in Hilary Term, 1850* (Dublin, 1850); *Should the Tenant of Land Possess the Property on the Improvement Made by Him?* (Dublin, 1852); *An Introduction to the History of Jurisprudence* (Dublin, 1860); and *The Principles of Jurisprudence,* (Dublin, 1873).

John Elliot Cairnes (1823–75)   was Professor of Jurisprudence and Political Economy at Queen's College Galway from 1859 until 1870. For further biographical details, see entry under Trinity College Dublin.

William Lupton (1830–76) succeeded Cairnes at Queen's College Galway. He was educated at Queen's College Belfast, where he graduated with first-class honours in mathematics in 1852. The following year he obtained his MA in mathematics and mathematical physics with first-class honours. He was a member of the Inner Temple. From 1853 to 1870 he was Registrar of Queen's College Galway, and in 1870 he was appointed to the Chair of Jurisprudence and Political Economy at the same college, a position he held until 1876. He was the author of *The Reform Bill and the Queen's University in Ireland* (Dublin, 1860) and a series of articles, 'Industrial progress: its causes and conditions', in *Irish Industrial Magazine* (1866).

Robert Cather Donnell (1839–83)   was Professor of Jurisprudence and Political Economy at Queen's College Galway from 1876 until his death in 1883. For further biographical details see entry under Trinity College Dublin.

Charles Francis Bastable (1855–1945) was Professor of Jurisprudence and Political Economy at Queen's College Galway from 1883 until 1903. For further biographical details see entry under Trinity College Dublin.

NOTES AND REFERENCES

1 POLITICAL ECONOMY:
'A SCIENCE UNKNOWN IN IRELAND'

1 J.K. Galbraith, *The Age of Uncertainty* (London, 1977), p. 13.
2 C.F. Bastable, *An Examination of Some Current Objections to the Study of Political Economy* (Dublin, 1884), p. 5.
3 J.A. Lawson, 'Address at the opening of the sixteenth session', *Journal of the Statistical and Social Inquiry Society of Ireland*, 3 (1861-3), p. 291.
4 J. Lentaigne, 'Address at meeting for inauguration of the thirty-first session', *Journal of the Statistical and Social Inquiry Society of Ireland*, 7 (1876-9), Appendix, p. 4.
5 J.A. Lawson, 'Address delivered at the opening of the eleventh session of the Society', *Journal of the Statistical and Social Inquiry Society of Ireland*, 2 (1857-60), p. 147, and 'Address', *Journal of the Statistical and Social Inquiry Society of Ireland*, 3 (1861-3), p. 285. See also Report of the council, *Journal of the Statistical and Social Inquiry Society of Ireland*, 4 (1864-8), p. 1.
6 W.N. Hancock, *Three Lectures on the Questions: Should the Principles of Political Economy Be Disregarded at the Present Crisis?* ... (Dublin, 1847), p. 3.
7 W.N. Hancock, 'Obituary notice of the late Most Revd Richard Whately ...', *Journal of the Statistical and Social Inquiry Society of Ireland*, 4 (1864-8), p. 10.
8 Sir Robert Kane, 'Report of the address at the opening of the fifth session of the Dublin Statistical Society', *Transactions of the Dublin Statistical Society*, 2 (1849-51), p. 16.
9 J. Lentaigne, op. cit., p. 4.
10 R.H. Mills, *The Principles of Currency and Banking* (London, 1853).
11 J. Pim, 'Address delivered at the opening of the eight session of the Society', *Journal of the Statistical and Social Inquiry Society of Ireland*, 1 (1855-6), p. 7.
12 W.J. Fitzpatrick, *Memoirs of Richard Whately, Archbishop of Dublin: With a Glance at His Contemporaries & Times,* 2 vols (London, 1864), vol. I, p. 189.

NOTES AND REFERENCES

13 British Library, Add. MSS 44112, 15 October 1869, quoted in R.D.C. Black, *Economic Thought and the Irish Question 1817–1870* (Cambridge, 1960), p. 58.

14 R. Whately, 'Report of the address on the conclusion of the first session of the Dublin Statistical Society', *Transactions of the Dublin Statistical Society*, 1 (1847–9), pp. 3, 4.

15 W.J. Fitzpatrick, op. cit., vol. I, p. 182.

16 E. J. Whately, *Life and Correspondence of Richard Whately D.D. Late Archbishop of Dublin* , 2 vols (London, 1866), vol. I, p. 142.

17 R. Whately, op. cit., p. 4.

18 Sir Robert Kane, op. cit., p. 16.

19 J.A. Lawson, 'Address at the opening of the sixteenth session', *Journal of the Statistical and Social Inquiry Society of Ireland*, 3 (1861–3), p. 285.

20 ibid, p. 284.

21 W.N. Senior, *Journals, Conversations and Essays Relating to Ireland*, 2 vols (London, 1868), vol. I, p. viii.

22 T. O'Hagan, 'Address by the vice–president, ... at the opening of the nineteenth session', *Journal of the Statistical and Social Inquiry Society of Ireland*, 4 (1864–8), p. 230.

23 *Irish Industrial Magazine*, 2 (1866), p. 73.

24 E.J. Whately, op. cit., vol. I, p. 47.

25 M. Longfield, *Four Lectures on Poor Laws* (Dublin, 1834), p. 1.

26 *Dublin University Magazine*, 4 (1834), p. 33.

27 I. Butt, *An Introductory Lecture Delivered before the University of Dublin in Hilary Term, 1837* (Dublin, 1837), especially pp. 11, 12.

28 J. Haughton, 'The application of machinery to manufactures, beneficial to the working classes', *Transactions of the Dublin Statistical Society*, 2 (1849–51), p. 3.

29 J. Mitchel (ed.), *Irish Political Economy* (Dublin, 1847), p. iv.

30 Revd G.H. Stoddart, *The True Cure for Ireland, the Development of Her Industries*, 2nd edn. (London, 1847), p. 3.

31 S. Laing, *Coercion in Ireland* (London, n.d.), p. 5.

32 An Irish Liberal, *Irish Issues* (Dublin, 1888), p. 46.

33 A.S. Greene, *Irish Nationality* (London, 1911), p. 229.

34 W.N. Hancock, 'On the economic views of Bishop Berkeley and Mr Butt, with respect to the theory that a nation may gain by the compulsory use of native manufactures', *Transactions of the Dublin Statistical Society*, 1 (1847–9), p. 3.

35 M. Longfield, 'Report of the address on the conclusion of the second session of the Dublin Statistical Society', *Transactions of the Dublin Statistical Society*, 1 (1847–9), p. 5.

36 J. Pim, op. cit., p. 6.

37 J.A. Lawson, 'at the opening of the eleventh session', *Journal of the Statistical and Social Inquiry Society of Ireland*, 2 (1857–60), pp. 151–2.

38 J.J. Murphy, 'The relation of the state to the railways', *Journal of the Statistical and Social Inquiry Society of Ireland*, 4 (1864–8), p. 307.

39 Quoted in R.D.C. Black, op. cit., p. 70.

40 J.E. Cairnes, 'Political economy and land', *Fortnightly Review*, 13

(1870), p. 41.
41 R.E. Thompson, 'Prof. Cairnes on political economy', *Penn Monthly*, September 1874, p. 638.
42 C.F. Bastable, op. cit., pp. 20–5.
43 *Dublin University Magazine*, 4 (1834), pp. 33, 42.
44 R. Whately, op. cit., pp. 3–4.
45 E. J. Whately, op. cit., vol. I, p. 180.
46 J. Pim, op. cit., p. 6.
47 J.A. Lawson, op. cit., *Journal of the Statistical and Social Inquiry Society of Ireland*, 3 (1861–3), p. 291.
48 *Fifteenth Report of Commissioners of National Education in Ireland* (1848), p. 243.
49 *Sixteenth Report of Commissioners of National Education in Ireland* (1849), p. 137.
50 *Fifteenth Report of Commissioners of National Education in Ireland* (1848), p. 262.
51 *Twentieth Report of Commissioners of National Education in Ireland* (1853), p. 357.
52 J. Moylan, 'On the impolicy of a revival of protection as a remedy for the present depression', *Journal of the Statistical and Social Inquiry Society of Ireland*, 7 (1876–9), p. 424.
53 Sir Robert Kane, op. cit., p. 16.
54 *Galway Vindicator*, advertisement for lecture series, 23 February 1850.
55 *Galway Vindicator*, 27 February 1850.
56 *Galway Mercury*, 2 March 1850.
57 ibid., 30 March 1850.
58 R. Whately, op. cit., pp. 3,4.
59 Sir Robert Kane, op. cit., pp. 9–10, 16.
60 J.Pim, op. cit., pp. 6,7.
61 J.A. Lawson, 'Address at the opening of the eleventh session', 2 (1857–60), p. 147.
62 J.A. Lawson, 'Address at the opening of the sixteenth session', 3 (1861–3), p. 285.
63 J.A. Lawson, 'Address at the opening of the eleventh session', 2 (1857–60), p. 157.
64 ibid., p. 149.
65 ibid., p. 152.
66 ibid., p. 149.
67 ibid., p. 152.
68 ibid., pp. 152–3.
69 J. Lentaigne, op. cit., p. 4.
70 W.N. Hancock, 'On (i) the value of Adam Smith's "Wealth of Nations"...', *Journal of the Statistical and Social Inquiry Society of Ireland*, 7 (1876–9), p. 281.
71 A.W. Coats, 'The historist reaction in English political economy 1870–90', *Economica*, n.s. 21–2 (1954), p. 143.
72 Quoted by W.S. Jevons in 'The future of political economy', *Fortnightly Review*, 26 (1876), p. 190.

73 J.K. Ingram, 'The present position and prospects of political economy', *Journal of the Statistical and Social Inquiry Society of Ireland*, 7 (1876–9), Appendix, p. 3.
74 ibid., p. 12.
75 S. Haughton, 'Causes of slow progress of political economy', *Journal of the Statistical and Social Inquiry Society of Ireland*, 7 (1876–9), pp. 410–11.

2 THE WHATELY CHAIR OF POLITICAL ECONOMY AT TRINITY COLLEGE DUBLIN, 1832–1900

1 N. Atkinson, *Irish Education: A History of Educational Institutions* (Dublin, 1969), p. 36.
2 H. Hutchinson, 'Essay on Trinity College' (MS T.5 la.f.2, Manuscript Room, TCD).
3 C. Maxwell, *A History of Trinity College, Dublin 1591–1892* (Dublin, 1946); H.L. Murphy, *A History of Trinity College Dublin from Its Foundation to 1702* (Dublin, 1951); W. Urwick, *The Early History of Trinity College Dublin 1591–1660* (London, 1892).
4 *Chartae et Statuta Collegii Sacrosanctae et Individuae Trinitatis Reginae Elizabethae Juxta Dublin* (1844), p. 1.
5 ibid., pp. 307–14.
6 Quoted in H.L. Murphy, op.cit., p. 60.
7 W. Urwick, op.cit., pp. 1–23.
8 N. Atkinson, op. cit., p. 36.
9 Quoted in Atkinson, ibid.
10 ibid., p. 37.
11 H. Kearney, *Scholars and Gentlemen: Universities in Pre-industrial Britain* (London, 1970), pp. 56–70, 172.
12 J. Coolahan, *Irish Education: History and Structure* (Dublin, 1981), p. 112.
13 R.B. McDowell and D.A. Webb, 'Trinity College in 1830', *Hermathena*, 75 (1950), pp. 1–23.
14 ibid., p. 5.
15 *Chartae et Statuta Collegii Sacrosanctae et Individuae Trinitatis Reginae Elizabethae Juxta Dublin* (1884), p. 2.
16 ibid., pp. 31–2, 42, 44–50, 180–3, 372–3, 379–81.
17 See chapter 3.
18 Registers [Minute Book] of the Board, 1627–1928, vol. 7, Mun v/5, p. 7 (Manuscript Room, TCD).
19 ibid., p. 42.
20 *Dublin University Calendar, 1833* (Dublin, 1833), p. 130.
21 R.B. McDowell and D.A. Webb, *Trinity College, Dublin 1592–1952: An Academic History* (Cambridge, 1982) p. 168.
22 E.J. Whately, *Life and Correspondence of Richard Whately, D.D. Late Archbishop of Dublin*, new edn (London, 1868), p. 78.
23 Whately to the Provost of Trinity College Dublin, 30 March 1832, Trinity College Dublin, Mun/p/1/1745(2) (Manuscript Room, TCD).

NOTES AND REFERENCES

24 Whately to the Provost of Trinity College Dublin, 19 May 1832, Trinity College Dublin, Mun/p/1/1745(3) (Manuscript Room, TCD).

25 Whately to the Provost of Trinity College Dublin, n.d. Mun/p/1/1745(6) (Manuscript Room, TCD).

26 R.B. McDowell and D.A. Webb, *Trinity College, Dublin 1592–1952: An Academic History* (Cambridge, 1982), p. 168.

27 R. Whately, 'Report on the address on the conclusion of the first session of the Dublin Statistical Society', *Transactions of the Dublin Statistical Society*, I (1847–9.), p. 4.

28 ibid.

29 *Queen's College Calendar, 1894–95* (Dublin, 1895).

30 J.E. Cairnes to William Nesbitt, 18 August 1861, Cairnes Papers, National Library of Ireland, MS 8941(5).

31 J.E. Cairnes to William Nesbitt, 22 June 1861, Cairnes Papers, National Library of Ireland, MS 8941(5).

32 J.E. Cairnes to Eliza Cairnes, 24 April 1866, Cairnes Papers, National Library of Ireland, MS 8941(13).

33 R. Burrowes, *Observations on the Course of Science Taught at Present in Trinity College, Dublin, with Some Improvements Suggested Therein* (Dublin, 1792), pp. 5, 17, 66–7, 67–8, 69.

34 R.B. McDowell and D.A. Webb, 'Trinity College in the age of revolution and reform (1794–1831)', *Hermathena,* 72 (1948), p. 5.

35 I. Butt, *Rents, Profits and Labour* (Dublin, 1838), p. 7.

36 R.D.C. Black, 'Trinity College, Dublin, and the theory of value 1832–1863', *Economica,* n.s. 12 (1945), pp. 140–1.

37 R.B. McDowell and D.A. Webb, *Trinity College, Dublin 1592–1952, An Academic History* (Cambridge, 1982), p. 152.

38 ibid., p. 173.

39 *Dublin University Calendar, 1839* (Dublin, 1839), pp. 54–5.

40 ibid., p. 55.

41 *Dublin University Calendar, 1842* (Dublin, 1842), p. 71.

42. ibid.

43 *Dublin University Calendar, 1847* (Dublin, 1847), p. 106.

44 R.B. McDowell and D.A. Webb, *Trinity College, Dublin 1592–1952, An Academic History* (Cambridge, 1982), p. 230.

45 ibid., p. 230.

46 *Dublin University Calendar, 1857* (Dublin, 1857), p. 150.

47 *Dublin Univeristy Calendar, 1859* (Dublin, 1859), p. 38.

48 *Dublin University Calendar, 1872* (Dublin, 1872), p. 271.

49 *Dublin University Calendar, 1874* (Dublin, 1874), pp. 279–80.

50 R.B. McDowell and D.A. Webb, *Trinity College, Dublin 1592–1952, An Academic History* (Cambridge, 1982), p. 230.

51 *Dublin University Calendar, 1874* (Dublin, 1874), p. 278.

52 *Dublin University Calendar, 1876,* 2 vols (Dublin, 1876), vol. I, p. 56 and vol. II, p. 108.

53 *Dublin University Calendar, 1881* (Dublin, 1881), p. 1.

54 *Dublin University Calendar, 1884* (Dublin, 1884), p. 54.

55 ibid., p. 65.

56 ibid., p. 122.

57 *Dublin University Calendar, 1890* (Dublin, 1890), P.62.
58 ibid., p. 73.
59. *Dublin University Calendar, 1900* (Dublin, 1900), p. 92.
60 ibid., p. 92.
61 R.D.C. Black, op. cit., p. 141.
62 ibid.
63 J.K. Galbraith, *The Age of Uncertainty* (London; 1977) p. 13.
64 E.R.A. Seligman, 'On some neglected British economists', *Economic Journal*, 8 (1903), pp. 335–63, 511–35.
65 J.G. Smith, 'Some nineteenth–century Irish economists', *Economica*, n.s. 2 (1935), pp. 20–32; M. Bowley, *Nassau Senior and Classical Economics* (London,1937); J. Whittaker, *History of Economic Ideas* (New York, 1940).
66 R.D.C. Black, op. cit., p. 140.
67 ibid.
68 ibid., p. 141.
69 M. Bowley, op. cit., pp. 106–7.
70 L.S. Moss, *Mountifort Longfield: Ireland's First Professor of Political Economy* (Ottawa, Illinois, 1976).
71 E.R.A. Seligman, op. cit., p. 525.
72 R.D.C. Black, op. cit., p. 145.
73 ibid., p. 147.
74 R.D.C. Black, 'Economic studies at Trinity College, Dublin. – I', *Hermathena*, 70 (1947), p. 68.
75 M. Bowley, op. cit., p. 106.
76 R.D.C. Black, 'Economic studies at Trinity College, Dublin. – II', *Hermathena*, 71 (1948) p. 52.
77 T.E.C. Leslie, *Essays in Political Economy* 2nd edn. (Dublin, 1888), p. 140.
78 J. Viner, *Studies in the Theory of International Trade* (London, 1955). Also J.W. Angell, *The Theory of International Prices: History, Criticism, and Restatement* (Cambridge, Mass., 1926).
79 *Economic Journal*, 7 (1897), p. 397.
80 ibid.
81 G.A. Duncan, 'Charles Francis Bastable 1855–1945', *Proceedings of the British Academy*, 21 (1946) p. 3.
82 ibid., p. 2.
83 *Economic Journal*, 13 (1903) p. 226.
84 ibid., 6 (1896) p. 104.
85 ibid., 2 (1892) p. 673.
86 I. Butt, *Introductory Lecture Delivered before the University of Dublin, in Hilary Term, 1837* (Dublin, 1837).
87 R.D.C. Black, 'Economic studies at Trinity College, Dublin. – I', Hermathena, 70 (1947), p. 70.
88 ibid., p. 73.

3 POLITICAL ECONOMY AT THE QUEEN'S COLLEGES IN IRELAND (BELFAST, CORK, GALWAY), 1845–1900

1 *Charta et Statuta Collegii Sacrosanctae et Individuae Trinitatis Reginae Elizabethae Juxta Dublin* (1884), p. 2.
2 T.W. Moody, 'The Irish university question of the nineteenth century', *History*, 42 (1958), pp. 90–109.
3 R. O'Connell, 'The political background to the establishment of Maynooth College', *Irish Ecclesiastical Record*, 85 (1956), pp. 325–34, 406–15; 86 (1956), pp. 1–16.
4 T.W. Moody and J.C. Beckett, *Queen's Belfast 1845–1949: The History of a University*, 2 vols (London, 1959), vol. 1, pp. xli–xliv.
5 ibid., pp. xliv–liii.
6 See entry for Wyse in *Dictionary of National Biography*.
7 T.W. Moody and J.C. Beckett, op.cit., vol. 1, pp. liii–lix.
8 K.R. Byrne, 'Mechanics' Institutes in Ireland before 1855', unpublished MEd thesis, University College Cork, 1976.
9 T.W. Moody, op. cit., p. 95.
10 Quoted in T.W. Moody and J.C. Beckett, op. cit., vol. 1, p. lxi.
11 R.B. McDowell, *Public Opinion and Government Policy in Ireland, 1800–46* (London, 1952).
12 T.W. Moody and J.C. Beckett, op. cit, vol. 1, p. 1.
13 J.C. Beckett, *The Making of Modern Ireland 1603–1923*, 2nd edn. (London, 1981), pp. 328–31.
14 J. Healy, *Maynooth College: Its Centenary History* (Dublin, 1895).
15 G. Ó Tuathaigh, *Ireland before the Famine 1798–1848* (Dublin, 1972), pp. 107–8.
16 T.W. Moody and J.C. Beckett, op. cit., vol. 1, p. 8.
17 G. Ó Tuathaigh, op. cit, p. 107.
18 *Hansard*, 3rd series, vol. LXXX, cols 1155–8 (30 May 1845).
19 J.C. Beckett, op. cit., p. 331.
20 W.J. Hegarty, 'The Irish hierarchy and the Queen's Colleges (1845–1850)', *Cork University Record*, no. 5, 1945, pp. 20–33.
21 T.W. Moody, op. cit, pp. 98–9.
22 T.W. Moody and J.C. Beckett, op. cit., vol. 1, p. 44.
23 W.K. Sullivan, *University Education in Ireland* (Dublin, 1866).
24 T.W. Moody and J.C. Beckett, op. cit., vol. 1, p. 52.
25 *Report from the Select Committee on Legal Education*, House of Commons, 1846 (696), p. x.
26 *British Parliamentary Papers*, vol. L, 1851, p. 790.
27 *Report of the President of Queen's College, Belfast for 1856–57*, *British Parliamentary Papers*, vol. XXI, p. 591.
28 *Report of the President of Queen's College, Belfast for 1856–57*, *British Parliamentary Papers*, vol. XXVI, p. 10.
29 *Report of Her Majesty's Commissioners Appointed to Inquire into the Progress and Condition of the Queen's Colleges at Belfast, Cork and Galway; with Minutes of Evidence, Documents, and Tables and Returns* (1857–8), vol. XXI.
30 *The Queen's Colleges Commission*, 1858, p. 327.

31 ibid.
32 ibid., p. 100.
33 ibid., pp. 325–7.
34 ibid., p. 326.
35 ibid.
36 ibid., pp. 228–29.
37 ibid., p. 289.
38 ibid., p. 230.
39 ibid., p. 290.
40 *Report of the President of Queen's College, Galway for 1851–52, British Parliamentary Papers*, vol. XLIII, p. 474.
41 *Report of the President of Queen's College, Cork for 1856–57, British Parliamentary Papers*, vol. XXI, p. 632.
42 *Report of the President of Queen's College, Galway for 1871–72, British Parliamentary Papers*, vol. XXVI, p. 263.
43 *Constitution and Statutes of the Catholic University of Ireland* (Dublin, 1869), p. 9.
44 ibid., p. 10.
45 J. H. Newman, *The Idea of a University* (London, 1901), p. 86.
46 F. McGrath, S.J., *Newman's University: Idea and Reality* (London, 1951).
47 ibid., p. 322.
48 ibid., p. 356. See also *University Gazette*, 7 June 1855.
49 F.H. O'Donnell, 'On economic science', *Irish Ecclesiastical Record*, 11 (1875), pp. 145–56, 252–66, 355–68.
50 *A Memorial Addressed by the Students and Ex-Students of the Catholic University of Ireland to the Episcopal Board of the University* (Dublin, 1873), pp. 16, 24–5.

4 EASY LESSONS ON MONEY MATTERS: POLITICAL ECONOMY IN THE NATIONAL SCHOOLS

1 D.H. Akenson, *A Protestant in Purgatory: Richard Whately Archbishop of Dublin* (Hamden, 1981), p. 165.
2 P. Corsi, 'Natural theology, the methodology of science and the question of species in the works of the Reverend Baden Powell', unpublished D.Phil. thesis, Oxford University, 1980, part II, chapter VII.
3 ibid., p. 127.
4 R. Whately, *The Duty of Those Who Disapprove the Education of the Poor on Grounds of Expediency, as well as of Those Who Approve It, Pointed out in a Sermon Preached at Halesworth, Oct. 7, 1830: Published by the Desire of the Subscribers, for the Benefit of the Halesworth and Chediston National School* (London, 1830), p. 17.
5 P. Corsi, op.cit ., p. 129.
6 *Edinburgh Review*, 46 (1827), pp. 38–9. The identity of the author of this and other articles in the *Edinburgh Review* is contained in F.W. Fetter, 'The authorship of economic articles in the Edinburgh Review, 1802–47', *Journal of Political Economy*, 61 (1953), pp. 232–59.

NOTES AND REFERENCES

7 W. and R. Chambers, *Political Economy for Use in Schools and for Private Instruction* (Edinburgh, 1852), p. 54.

8 *Westminster Review*, 4 (1825), p. 89.

9 T. Chalmers, *On Political Economy in Connexion with the Moral State, and Moral Prospects of Society*, in *Works* (Glasgow, 1832), vol. 19; R. Whately, op. cit.; R.W. Soloway, *Prelates and People: Ecclesiastical Social Thought in England, 1783–1852* (London, 1969).

10 This topic has generated an extensive literature. Within sociological theory the concept was first used and elaborated by E.A. Ross, *Social Control: A Survey of the Foundations of Order* (New York, 1929). It was further extended in its application by P.A. Lands, *Social Control: Social Organisation and Disorganisation in Process*, Rev. edn. (Chicago, 1956). As a concept applied to nineteenth-century popular education, see J.F.C. Harrison, *Learning and Living 1790–1960. A Study in the History of the English Adult Education Movement* (London, 1961). More recent studies include: A.P.Donajgrodzki (ed.), *Social Control in Nineteenth Century Britain* (London, 1977); P. McCann (ed.), *Popular Education and Socialization in the Nineteenth Century* (London, 1977). See also R. Johnson, 'Educational policy and social control in early Victorian England', *Past and Present*, No. 49, November 1970, pp. 96–119; F.M.L. Thompson, 'Social control in Victorian Britain', *Economic History Review*, 2nd series, 34 (1981), pp. 189–208; S. Dentith, 'Political economy, fiction and the language of practical ideology in nineteenth-century England', *Social History*, 8 (1983), pp. 183–200. For a similar analysis of the eighteenth century, see B. Rosen, 'Education and social control of the lower classes in England in the second half of the eighteenth century', *Paedagogica Historica*, 14 (1974), pp. 92–105.

11 B. Simon, *Studies in the History of Education 1780–1870* (London, 1960), p. 132.

12 H. Silver, *The Concept of Popular Education* (London, 1965), p. 210.

13 J.F.C. Harrison, op. cit., p. 43.

14 G. Claeys, 'The reaction to political radicalism and the popularisation of political economy in early nineteenth-century Britain – the case of 'productive and unproductive labour', in T. Shinn and R. Whitley (eds), *Expository Science: Forms and Functions of Popularisation* (Dordrecht, 1985), p. 119.

15 C. Gide and C. Rist, *History of Economic Doctrines*, 2nd edn. (London, 1948), p. 354.

16 J. Marsh, 'Economic education in schools in the nineteenth century: social control', *Economics*, 13 (1977), pp. 116–18.

17 C. Gide and C. Rist, op. cit., p. 355.

18 For an extended treatment of the contents of school textbooks in the nineteenth century see R.K. Webb, *The British Working Class Reader, 1790–1848* (London, 1955); R.D. Altick, *The English Common Reader: A Social History of the Mass Reading Public, 1800–1900* (Chicago, 1963); J.M. Goldstrom, *The Social Content of Education 1808–1870: A Study of the Working Class School Reader in England and Ireland* (Shannon, 1972). A succinct overview of this extensive

topic is provided in Goldstrom, 'Popular political economy for the British working class reader in the nineteenth century' in Shinn and Whitley, op. cit., pp. 259–73.

19 The most extended treatment of this topic is contained in the excellent study by D.H. Akenson, *The Irish Education Experiment: The National System of Education in the Nineteenth Century* (London, 1970).

20 D.H. Akenson, *A Protestant in Purgatory: Richard Whately Archbishop of Dublin* (Hamden, 1981), p. 172.

21 The administrative structure of the system is discussed in detail in D.H. Akenson, *The Irish Education Experiment: The National System of Education in the Nineteenth Century* (London, 1970), pp. 123–56.

22 D.H. Akenson, *The Irish Education Experiment: The National System of Education in the Nineteenth Century* (London, 1970), pp. 202–224.

23 E. Larkin, *The Quarrel among the Roman Catholic Hierarchy over the National System of Education in Ireland, 1838–41* (Cambridge, Mass, 1965). For the life and times of MacHale, see B. O'Reilly, *John MacHale, Archbishop of Tuam: His Life, Times and Correspondence*, 2 vols (New York, 1890), and N. Costello, *John MacHale, Archbishop of Tuam* (Dublin, 1939).

24 N. Atkinson, *Irish Education: A History of Educational Institutions* (Dublin, 1969), chapter II.

25 D.H. Akenson, *The Irish Education Experiment: The National System of Education in the Nineteenth Century* (London, 1970), pp. 161–202.

26 D.H. Akenson, *A Protestant in Purgatory:* Richard Whately Archbishop of Dublin (Hamden, 1981), p. 167.

27 ibid., pp. 179–81.

28 D.H. Akenson, *The Irish Education Experiment: The National System of Education in the Nineteenth Century* (London, 1970), pp. 197–202.

29 J. Coolahan, *Irish Education, History and Structure* (Dublin, 1981), p. 17.

30 ibid., pp. 18–19.

31 ibid., pp. 15–16.

32 D.H. Akenson, *A Protestant in Purgatory: Richard Whately Archbishop of Dublin* (Hamden, 1981), p. 174. See also W.J. Fitzpatrick, *Memoirs of Richard Whately, Archbishop of Dublin With a Glance at His Contemporaries & Times*, 2 vols (London, 1864), vol. I, pp. 164–5.

33 R. Whately, *Reply of His Grace the Archbishop of Dublin to the Address of the Clergy of the Diocese of Dublin and Glendalough on the Government Plan for National Education in Ireland* (London, 1832), pp. 8–10.

34 ibid., p. 12–29.

35 N.W. Senior, *Journals, Conversations and Essays Relating to Ireland*, 2 vols (London, 1868), vol. I, p. 67.

36 Letter from Richard Whately to Mrs Thomas Arnold, 2 January 1846, reproduced in E.J. Whately, *Life and Correspondence of Richard Whately, D.D., late Archbishop of Dublin* 2 vols (London, 1866), vol. I, p. 92.

37 N.W. Senior, op. cit., vol. I, p. 63, and quoted in E.J. Whately, op. cit., vol. II, p. 243.

38 D.H. Akenson, *A Protestant in Purgatory: Richard Whately Archbishop of Dublin* (Hamden, 1981), p. 175.
39 D.H. Akenson, *The Irish Education Experiment: The National System of Education in the Nineteenth Century* (London, 1970), pp. 227–9.
40 ibid., p. 230.
41 For a succinct account of these developments, see D.H. Akenson, 'The Irish textbooks controversy and the gospel of free trade', *Journal of Educational Administration and History*, 3 (1970), pp. 19–23.
42 R. Whately, 'Juvenile library', *London Review*, 1 (1829), pp. 404–19.
43 For a detailed history of Whately's contributions to the textbooks of the Commissioners of National Education, see *Report of the Commissioners Appointed to Inquire into the Nature and Extent of the Instruction Afforded by the Several Institutions in Ireland for the Purpose of Elementary or Primary Education; Also into the Practical Working of the System of National Education in Ireland* [Powis Report] (1870), vol. VII, pp. 209–10.
44 For a history of the Society for Promoting Christian Knowledge, see W.K.L. Clarke, *A History of the S.P.C.K.* (London, 1959).
45 J.M. Goldstrom, 'Richard Whately and political economy in school books, 1833–80' *Irish Historical Studies*, 16 (1966), p. 133.
46 ibid., p. 134.
47 ibid., p. 100.
48 E.J. Whately, op. cit., p. 302. See D.H. Akenson, *A Protestant in Purgatory: Richard Whately Archbishop of Dublin* (Hamden, 1981), p. 179; J.M. Goldstrom, 'Richard Whately and political economy in school books, 1833–80' *Irish Historical Studies*, 16 (1966), pp. 135–6.
49 *Saturday Magazine*, 3 (1833), p. 182.
50 Powis Report, vol. VII, p. 39.
51 *Eighteenth Report of Commissioners of National Education in Ireland* (1851), p. 70.
52 *Thirty-Second Report of Commissioners of National Education in Ireland* (1865), p. 13.
53 D.H. Akenson, *The Irish Education Experiment: The National System of Education in the Nineteenth Century* (London, 1970), p. 229.
54 J.M. Goldstrom, 'Richard Whately and political economy in school books, 1833–80' *Irish Historical Studies*, 16 (1966), p. 136.
55 ibid., p. 137.
56 The Newcastle Commission was a Royal Commission established in June 1858 to inquire into the current state of popular education in England and to consider and report what measures, if any, were required to provide for the extension of cheap elementary education to all social classes. It was called the Newcastle Commission after its chairman Henry Pelham, Duke of Newcastle. It included among its members Nassau Senior, former pupil and life–long friend of Richard Whately. The Commission sat from 30 June 1858 to 30 June 1861. It published its report in six volumes in 1861.
57 J.M. Goldstrom, 'Richard Whately and political economy in school books, 1833–80' *Irish Historical Studies*, 16 (1966), p. 138.

58 R. Whately, *Easy Lessons on Money Matters: For the Use of Young People*, 14th edn. (London, 1855), pp. 14–15.
59 ibid., p. 15.
60 ibid., p. 18.
61 ibid., p. 21.
62 J.M. Goldstrom, 'Richard Whately and political economy in school books, 1833–80' *Irish Historical Studies*, 16 (1966), p. 134.
63 R. Whately, *Easy Lessons on Money Matters: For the Use of Young People*, 14th Edn. (London, 1855), p. 27.
64 ibid., p. 27.
65 ibid., p. 28.
66 ibid., p. 30.
67 N.W. Senior, *Selected Writings on Economics* (New York, 1966); M.E.A. Bowley, *Nassau Senior and Classical Economics* (London, 1937). For an overview of classical economics see the excellent volume, which is a model of balance, lucidity and scholarship, by D.P.O'Brien, *The Classical Economists* (Oxford, 1975). For a succinct and perceptive account of Senior see the entry by Neil de Marchi in *The New Palgrave: A Dictionary of Economics* (London, 1987).
68 A. Marshall, *Principles of Economics*, 8th edn. (London, 1961), pp. 269–417.
69 R. Whately, *Easy Lessons on Money Matters: For the Use of Young People*, 14th edn. (London, 1855), pp. 31–2.
70 ibid., pp. 32–3.
71 D.P. O'Brien, *The Classical Economists* (Oxford, 1975), p. 106.
72 S.L. Levy, *Nassau Senior 1790–1864* (Newton Abbot, 1970), chapters VII and VIII.
73 R. Whately, *Easy Lessons on Money Matters: For the Use of Young People*, 14th edn. (London, 1855), pp. 34–5.
74 ibid., p. 35.
75 ibid., p. 37.
76 ibid., p. 40.
77 ibid., pp. 40–2.
78 ibid., pp. 42–3.
79 ibid., p. 93.
80 ibid., pp. 95–6.
81 ibid., pp. 102–3.
82 Bowley, op. cit., p. 107. It should be noted that this evaluation differs from Schumpeter's, admittedly somewhat ambiguous, comment that Whately's 'most important service to economics was ... that he formed Senior, whose whole approach betrays Whately's influence'. See J.A. Schumpeter, *History of Economic Analysis* (London, 1954), p. 484.
83 Levy, op. cit., pp. 51, 68–74.
84 Bowley, op. cit., p. 277.
85 Levy, op. cit., Appendix viii, p. 243.
86 ibid., p. 74.
87 See also N.W. Senior, *Historical and Philosophical Essays (1841–62)*, 2 vols (London, 1865). The second volume contains an extremely

detailed analysis, incorporating legal, historical, and economic dimensions, of trade unions (combinations), which contains supplementary material on this topic which he submitted to Lord Melbourne.

88 Bowley, op. cit., p. 278.
89 ibid., p. 280.
90 N.W. Senior, *Historical and Philosophical Essays (1841–62)* (London, 1865), vol. II, p. 164.
91 ibid.
92 Bowley, op. cit., p. 281.
93 On the general position of the English classical economists with respect to trade unions, see D.P. O'Brien, op. cit., pp. 284–5 and the references cited therein.
94 J.M. Goldstrom, 'Richard Whately and political economy in school books 1833–80' *Irish Historical Studies,* 16 (1966), p. 134.
95 R. Whately, *Easy Lessons on Money Matters: For the Use of Young People,* 14th edn. (London, 1855), p. 103.
96 ibid., p. 44.
97 ibid., p. 44.
98 ibid., p. 45.
99 Bowley, op. cit., pp. 137–66.
100 R. Whately, *Easy Lessons on Money Matters: For the Use of Young People,* 14th edn. (London, 1855), p. 45.
101 ibid., p. 46.
102 ibid., p. 45.
103 ibid., p. 46.
104 ibid., p. 47.
105 ibid.
106 ibid., p. 48.
107 ibid., p. 49.
108 ibid.
109 ibid., pp. 50–1.
110 ibid., pp. 52–3.
111 *Eighteenth Report of Commissioners of National Education in Ireland* (1851), Appendix, p. 43.
112 *Fourteenth Report of Commissioners of National Education in Ireland* (1847), p. 488.
113 *Report of the Commissioners of National Education in Ireland from the Year 1834 to 1848* (Dublin, 1848), p. 20.
114 *Appendix to Seventh Report of Commissioners of National Education in Ireland* (1840), Appendix, p. 104.
115 *Twenty-Second Report of Commissioners of National Education in Ireland* (1855), Appendix, p. 192.
116 B.M. Cowie and S.N. Stokes, *Report on the Training Institution* and *Model School in Marlborough Street* (Dublin, 1870), p. 805.
117 *Twenty-Third Report of Commissioners of National Education in Ireland* (1856), Appendix A, p. 303.
118 J.A. Dease and W.K. Sullivan, *Report on Agricultural Schools* (Dublin, 1870), p. 864.
119 Appendix to Dr Kirkpatrick's Report, *Twentieth Report of*

Commissioners of National Education in Ireland (1853), p. 357.
120 *Twentieth Report of Commissioners of National Education in Ireland* (1853), Appendix, p. 137.
121 E. Butler, *Twentieth Report of Commissioners of National Education in Ireland* (1853), pp. 137, 152.
122 Powis Report (1870), vol. VII, p. 172.
123 ibid., vol. VIII, p. 30.
124 ibid., (1870), vol. VIII, p. 61.
125 ibid., (1870), vol. VIII, p. 75.
126 ibid., (1870), vol. I, pt. ii, p. 617.
127 ibid. See also, for example, *Seventh Report of Commissioners of National Education in Ireland* (1840), p. 104 and *Twentieth Report of Commissioners of National Education in Ireland* (1853), p. 160.
128 See, for example, *Twenty-Second Report of Commissioners of National Education in Ireland* (1855), p. 106. There were six head inspectors and they were usually chosen from the ranks of district inspectors, who were approximately forty in number.
129 *Fifteenth Report of Commissioners of National Education in Ireland* (1848), p. 228.
130 ibid.
131 ibid., p. 243.
132 ibid., pp. 250.
133 *Sixteenth Report of Commissioners of National Education in Ireland* (1849), p. 137. These were the results of the oral examination for males.
134 *Seventeenth Report of Commissioners of National Education in Ireland* (1850), pp. 47–8.
135 ibid., p. 48; *Nineteenth Report of Commissioners of National Education in Ireland* (1852), p. 317; *Twentieth Report of Commissioners of National Education in Ireland* (1853), p. 199; *Twenty-Second Report of Commissioners of National Education in Ireland* (1855), p. 15.
136 *Seventeenth Report of Commissioners of National Education in Ireland* (1850), pp. 34–5.
137 ibid., p. 34; *Eighteenth Report of Commissioners of National Education in Ireland* (1851), p. 330; *Nineteenth Report of Commissioners of National Education in Ireland* (1852), p. 303.
138 *Eighteenth Report of Commissioners of National Education in Ireland* (1851), p. 328; *Nineteenth Report of Commissioners of National Education in Ireland* (1852), pp. 301, 315.
139 *Eighteenth Report of Commissioners of National Education in Ireland* (1851), pp. 58–9.
140 ibid., p. 118.
141 ibid., p. 128.
142 ibid., p. 142.
143 ibid., pp. 53–4.
144 ibid., p. 66.
145 ibid., pp. 84–5.
146 *Powis Report* (1870), vol. VII, pp. 539, 545.
147 *Eighteenth Report of Commissioners of National Education in*

NOTES AND REFERENCES

Ireland (1851), p. 114.
148 ibid.
149 *Fifteenth Report of Commissioners of National Education in Ireland* (1848), p. 319.
150 *Seventeenth Report of Commissioners of National Education in Ireland* (1850), p. 66.
151 *Fifteenth Report of Commissioners of National Education in Ireland* (1848), p. 267.
152 *Twenty-Third Report of Commissioners of National Education in Ireland* (1856), p. 74.
153 *Twenty-Second Report of Commissioners of National Education in Ireland* (1855), p. 138.
154 N.W. Senior, *Journals, Conversations and Essays Relating to Ireland*, 2 vols (London, 1868), vol. I, p. 33.
155 *Fifteenth Report of Commissioners of National Education in Ireland* (1848), p. 290.
156 *Twentieth Report of Commissioners of National Education in Ireland* (1853), p. 205.
157 *Fifteenth Report of Commissioners of National Education in Ireland* (1848), p. 299.
158 ibid., p. 290.
159 ibid., p. 303.
160 ibid., p. 305.
161 ibid.
162 *Sixteenth Report of Commissioners of National Education in Ireland* (1849), p. 222.
163 *Fifteenth Report of Commissioners of National Education in Ireland* (1848), p. 165.
164 ibid., p. 311.
165 *Sixteenth Report of Commissioners of National Education in Ireland* (1849), p. 176.
166 *Nineteenth Report of Commissioners of National Education in Ireland* (1852), p. 332.
167 ibid., p. 335.
168 *Fifteenth Report of Commissioners of National Education in Ireland* (1848), p. 305.
169 ibid., p. 314.
170 *Sixteenth Report of Commissioners of National Education in Ireland* (1849), p. 180.
171 *Fifteenth Report of Commissioners of National Education in Ireland* (1848), p. 316.
172 ibid., p. 291.
173 *Twenty-Third Report of Commissioners of National Education in Ireland* (1856), p. 71.
174 *Fifteenth Report of Commissioners of National Education in Ireland* (1848), p. 289.

5 'TO THE POOR THE GOSPEL IS PREACHED': THE DUBLIN STATISTICAL SOCIETY AND THE BARRINGTON LECTURES

1 R.D.C. Black, *The Statistical and Social Inquiry Society of Ireland: Centenary Volume 1847–1947* (Dublin, 1947), p. 16.
2 Report of the council, read at the opening of the sixth session, *Transactions of the Dublin Statistical Society*, 3 (1851–4), p. 8. For information regarding amount of bequest, see Report of the council, *Journal of the Statistical and Social Inquiry Society of Ireland*, 8 (1879–85), p. 153. This sum generated an income for the trust of approximately £120 per annum. See also, S. Shannon Millin, *The Statistical and Social Inquiry Society of Ireland: Historical Memoirs* (Dublin, 1920), p. 43.
3 Between 1834 and 1849 the Barrington Fund, in James A. Lawson's words, seems to have 'lain dormant in consequence of the difficulty of finding persons who would administer a trust of the kind which involved very considerable care and judgement' ('Address at the opening of the eleventh session', *Journal of the Statistical and Social Inquiry Society of Ireland*, 2 (1857–60), p. 148).
4 Report of the council, read at the opening of the sixth session, *Transactions of the Dublin Statistical Society*, 3 (1851–4), pp. 8–9.
5 ibid., p. 9.
6 Report of the council, *Journal of the Statistical and Social Inquiry Society of Ireland*, 3 (1861–3), p. 5.
7 ibid., p. 132.
8 Report of the council, *Journal of the Statistical and Social Inquiry Society of Ireland*, 4 (1864–8), p. 157.
9 ibid.
10 Report of the council, *Journal of the Statistical and Social Inquiry Society of Ireland*, 5 (1868–70), pp. 240–1.
11 Report of the council, *Journal of the Statistical and Social Inquiry Society of Ireland*, 6 (1871–6), pp. 279–80. Under this new system payment was partly by salary and partly by results. (Report of the council, *Journal of the Statistical and Social Inquiry Society of Ireland*, 7 (1876–9), p. 28).
12 According to Lord O'Hagan, in January 1874 this committee was formed 'to establish classes for the systematic teaching of Political Economy, – chiefly to young men engaged in mercantile pursuits'. The committee was composed of the chief magistrate of Belfast and many of the city's 'leading merchants and professional men, and several eminent professors of the Queen's College'. The 'highly informed economist' they were 'fortunate in obtaining the services of' was Revd Samuel Prenter. Of the fifty-five students, three were alumni of the Queen's College, seven were solicitor apprentices, and forty-five were 'engaged in commercial business'. The average attendance at classes was between forty and fifty. The experiment was, in O'Hagan's view, 'very satisfactory' and he remarked that Dublin had followed Belfast's example with the formation of a class

of 'young mercantile men', presumably the Mercantile Clerks' Association (*Occasional Papers and Addresses* (London, 1884), p. 112).

13 Report of the council, *Journal of the Statistical and Social Inquiry Society of Ireland*, 6 (1871–6), p. 366.

14 Report of the council, read at the conclusion of the second session, *Transactions of the Dublin Statistical Society*, 1 (1847–9), p. 22.

15 ibid.

16 Report of the council, read at the opening of the sixth session, *Transactions of the Dublin Statistical Society*, 3 (1851–4), p. 8.

17 According to the council (*Journal of the Statistical and Social Inquiry Society of Ireland*, 1 (1855–6), p. 5), the management of the Barrington lectures was usually entrusted to the Corresponding Societies. There were mechanics' institutes also in Armagh, Belfast, Cork, Galway, Limerick, and Newry, and it is possible that they were involved in organising the Barrington lectures which were given on several occasions at these places. See list of mechanics' institutes in K.R. Byrne, 'Mechanics' Institutes in Ireland before 1855', M.Ed. thesis, National University of Ireland (University College Cork), 1976, p. 3. Byrne lists twenty-two institutes, but there were at least four more: Downpatrick, Lurgan, Navan, and Portaferry.

18 Report of the council, read at the conclusion of the third session, *Transactions of the Dublin Statistical Society*, 2 (1849–51), p. 21.

19 Report of the council, read at the opening of the fifth session, *Transactions of the Dublin Statistical Society*, 2 (1849–51), p. 18.

20 ibid.

21 ibid.

22 Report of the council, read at the opening of the sixth session, *Transactions of the Dublin Statistical Society*, 3 (1851–4), p. 5.

23 Report of the council, read at the opening of the seventh session, *Transactions of the Dublin Statistical Society*, 3 (1851–4), p. 4.

24 Report of the council, *Journal of the Statistical and Social Inquiry Society of Ireland*, 1 (1855–6), p. 4.

25 ibid., p. 152.

26 Report of the council, *Journal of the Statistical and Social Inquiry Society of Ireland*, 2 (1857–60), p. 3.

27 Report of the council, *Journal of the Statistical and Social Inquiry Society of Ireland*, 3 (1861–3), p. 282.

28 Report of the council, *Journal of the Statistical and Social Inquiry Society of Ireland*, 4 (1864–8), p. 157.

29 ibid., p. 249.

30 ibid., p. 370.

31 ibid., pp. 432–3.

32 Report of the council, *Journal of the Statistical and Social Inquiry Society of Ireland*, 5 (1868–70), p. 71.

33 ibid., pp. 240–1.

34 Report of the council, *Journal of the Statistical and Social Inquiry Society of Ireland*, 6 (1871–6), p. 279.

35 ibid., pp. 279–80.

36 ibid., p. 366.

37 Report of the council, *Journal of the Statistical and Social Inquiry Society of Ireland,* 7 (1876–9), p. 28.

38 Report of the council, *Journal of the Statistical and Social Inquiry Society of Ireland,* 8 (1879–85), p. 3.

39 Report of the council, *Journal of the Statistical and Social Inquiry Society of Ireland,* 10 (1894–9), p. vi.

40 ibid., p. vii.

41 ibid., p. 128.

42 Report of the council, *Journal of the Statistical and Social Inquiry Society of Ireland,* 13 (1912–19), p. 607. This statement obviously derives from Lawson. See note 3 above.

43 Report of the council ... sixth session, *Transactions of the Dublin Statistical Society* 3 (1851–4), p. 9. According to Hancock, John Barrington 'had long felt the disastrous results arising from ignorance of political economy amongst the working classes in Ireland' ('Obituary notice of the late Most Revd Richard Whately', *Journal of the Statistical and Social Inquiry Society of Ireland,* 4 (1864–8), p. 10). A series of lectures given by C.H. Oldham (Barrington Lecturer, 1895–1901) in Dublin was advertised as being of 'special interest to the workers of the city, their families and friends' (card advertising Barrington Lectures, National Library of Ireland, Shelf Number LO P 115, 59).

44 For example, Report of the council, *Journal of the Statistical and Social Inquiry Society of Ireland,* 4 (1864–8), p. 249 and *Journal of the Statistical and Social Inquiry Society of Ireland,* 5 (1868–70), p. 71.

45 Report of the council, *Journal of the Statistical and Social Inquiry Society of Ireland,* 7 (1876–9), p. 159.

46 Report of the council, *Journal of the Statistical and Social Inquiry Society of Ireland,* 8 (1879–85), p. 29.

47 Report of the council, *Journal of the Statistical and Social Inquiry Society of Ireland,* 4 (1864–8), p. 370.

48 Byrne, op. cit., p. 2.

49 Sir Robert Kane, 'Report of the address at the opening of the fifth session', *Transactions of the Dublin Statistical Society,* 2 (1849–51), p. 10.

50 T.E.C. Leslie, 'An inquiry into the progress and present conditions of Mechanics' Institutions', part I, *Transactions of the Dublin Statistical Society,* 3 (1851–4), p. 4.

51 ibid.

52 T.E.C. Leslie, 'An inquiry into the progress and conditions of Mechanics' and Literary Institutions', part. II, *Transactions of the Dublin Statistical Society,* 3 (1851–4), p. 4.

53 ibid., pp. 6–7.

54 ibid., 6.

55 ibid., p. 8.

56 Report of the council, read at the opening of the sixth session, *Transactions of the Dublin Statistical Society,* 3 (1851–4), p. 8.

57 ibid.

58 ibid.
59 ibid.
60 R.D.C. Black, op. cit., p. 16.
61 ibid.
62 Report of the council, *Journal of the Statistical and Social Inquiry Society of Ireland,* 2 (1857–60), p. 345.
63 R.D.C. Black, op. cit., p. 16.
64 ibid.
65 Report of the council, *Journal of the Statistical and Social Inquiry Society of Ireland,* 4 (1864–8), p. 8.
66 ibid., p. 249.
67 ibid., p. 369.
68 Report of the council, *Journal of the Statistical and Social Inquiry Society of Ireland,* 5 (1868–70), p. 241.
69 National Library of Ireland, Shelf Number LO P 115, 59.
70 T.A. Larcom, 'Address on the conclusion of the third session', *Transactions of the Dublin Statistical Society,* 2 (1849–51), p. 3.
71 Sir Robert Kane, op. cit., p. 9.
72 J. Pim, 'Address at the opening of the eighth session', *Journal of the Statistical and Social Inquiry Society of Ireland,* 1 (1855–6), pp. 7–8.
73 Lawson, 'Address at the opening of the eleventh session', *Journal of the Statistical and Social Inquiry Society of Ireland,* 2 (1857–60), p. 148.
74 J.A. Lawson, 'Address at the opening of the sixteenth session', *Journal of the Statistical and Social Inquiry Society of Ireland,* 3 (1861–3), p. 286.
75 W.N. Hancock, op. cit., p. 10.
76 T. O'Hagan, op. cit., p. 112 and W.H. Dodd, 'Introductory address', *Journal of the Statistical and Social Inquiry Society of Ireland,* 10 (1894–9), p. 128.

6 'NEXT TO GODLINESS': POLITICAL ECONOMY, IRELAND, AND IDEOLOGY

1 J.E. Bicheno, *Ireland and Its Economy* (London, 1830), pp. 223–4.
2 A.J. Taylor, *Laissez–Faire and State Intervention in Nineteenth-Century Britain* (London, 1972), p. 23.
3 S. Smith, *The Works* (London, 1869), p. 355.
4 ibid.
5 J.E. Bicheno, op. cit., pp. 224, 225, 226.
6 ibid., pp. 275, 289, 266, 300, 301.
7 J.H. Newman, 'The Tamworth Reading Room', Discussions and arguments on various subjects, 4th ed. (London, 1885), p. 292.
8 J.H. Newman, *The Idea of a University* (London, 1901), p. 86.
9 J.H. Newman, 'The Tamworth Reading Room', op. cit., p. 293.
10 W. O'Brien, *Irish Ideas* (London, 1893), p. 22.
11 'Educational Police', *United Irishman,* 8 April 1848, p. 138.
12 'Combinations of Workmen', *United Irishman,* 18 March 1848, p. 88.
13 *Third Report of the Commissioners of National Education in Ireland*

(1836), p. 95.
14 ibid., p. 18.
15 *Fifth Report of Commissioners of National Education in Ireland* (1838), p. 134.
16 *Sixteenth Report of Commissioners of National Education in Ireland* (1849), Appendix, p. 128.
17 *Eighteenth Report of Commissioners of National Education in Ireland* (1851), p. 55.
18 ibid., pp. 238–9.
19 *Twentieth Report of Commissioners of National Education in Ireland* (1853), p. 113.
20 *Report of the Commissioners Appointed to Inquire into the Nature and Extent of the Instruction Afforded by the Several Institutions in Ireland for the Purpose of Elementary or Primary Education; Also into the Practical Working of the System of National Education in Ireland* [Powis Report] (1870), vol. II, p. 211, Report of Assistant Commissioner D.C. Richmond, Belfast District.
21 *Sixteenth Report of Commissioners of National Education in Ireland* (1849), p. 129.
22 *Reports of the Commissioners of National Education in Ireland for the Years 1834 to 1848, Inclusive* (Dublin, 1848), p. 29.
23 *Report from the Select Committee of the House of Lords Appointed to Inquire into the Practical Working of the System of National Education in Ireland; Together with the Minutes of Evidence and Appendix*, (1854), part I, (525) xv, part I, 285.
24 Powis Report (1870), vol. I, part I, p. 350.
25 ibid.
26 *Collected Works of Pádraig H. Pearse: Political Writings and Speeches* (Dublin, n.d.), p. 32.
27 Powis Report (1870), vol. I, part I, p. 351.
28 *Report from the Select Committee of the House of Lords Appointed to Inquire into the Practical Working of the System of National Education in Ireland: Together with the Minutes of Evidence and Appendix* (1854), part I, p. 456.
29 *Twenty-Second Report of Commissioners of National Education in Ireland* (1855), pp. 73, 76.
30 *Second Book of Lessons: For the Use of Schools* (Dublin, 1847), p. 135.
31 *A Catholic Layman [J.W. Kavanagh], Mixed Education: The Catholic Case Stated* (Dublin, 1859), pp. 39–40.
32 R. Whately, *Speech of the Most Reverend His Grace the Archbishop of Dublin, on Presentation of Petitions Respecting Education (Ireland), in the House of Lords, on Tuesday, March 19th, 1833* (London, 1833), p. 3, and E.J. Whately, *Life and Correspondence of Richard Whately, D.D. Late Archbishop of Dublin*, 2 vols (London, 1866), vol. I, p. 378.
33 A. Webb, *A Compendium of Irish Biography* (Dublin, 1878).
34 E.J. Whately, op. cit., vol. I, p. 377.
35 ibid., vol. II, p. 246.
36 Register of the Board, Trinity College Dublin, 24 October 1835, p. 109 (Manuscript Room, TCD).

37 *Seventeenth Report of Commissioners of National Education in Ireland* (1850), Appendix, pp. 108, 109.
38 Powis Report (1870), vol. III, p. 377.
39 ibid., vol. III, pp. 592, 378.
40 ibid., vol. III, p. 377.
41 ibid., vol. III, p. 376.
42 ibid., vol. III, pp. 376, 378.
43 ibid., vol. III, p. 376.
44 *Third Report of Commissioners of National Education in Ireland* (1836), p. 96.
45 Letter of Cullen to Dr Bernard Smith, 8 March 1852, in Peadar Mac Suibhne, *Paul Cullen and His Contemporaries with Their Letters from 1820–1902*, 3 vols (Naas, 1965), vol. III, p. 113.
46 E. Hayes, *The Ballads of Ireland*, 2 vols (London, 1855), vol., I, pp. xxii–xxiii.
47 Quoted in J. Lee, *The Modernisation of Irish Society 1849–1918* (Dublin, 1973), p. 141.
48 P.J. Keenan, *Twenty-Second Report of Commissioners of National Education in Ireland* (1855), p. 73.
49 ibid., p. 74.
50 ibid., pp. 75, 76.
51 R. Whately, *Elements of Rhetoric*, 7th edn. (London, 1870), p. 170.
52 W.J. Fitzpatrick, *Memoirs of Richard Whately, Archbishop of Dublin: With a Glance at His Contemporaries & Times*, 2 vols (London, 1864), vol. I, pp. 53, 221, 244, 243.
53 R. Whately, *Elements of Rhetoric*, 7th edn. (London, 1870), p. 234.
54 W.J. Fitzpatrick, op. cit., vol. II, p. 68 and vol. I, p. 220.
55 e.g. W.H. Newell, *Twentieth Report of Commissioners of National Education in Ireland* (1853), Appendix, p. 162 and J.W. Kavanagh, *Fifteenth Report of Commissioners of National Education in Ireland* (1848), p. 250.
56 J.E. Bicheno, op. cit., p. 173.
57 W.J. Fitzpatrick, op. cit., vol. I, pp. 229, 54–5.
58 W. O'Brien, op. cit., p. 22.
59 *The Poems of Samuel Ferguson*, ed. Padraic Colum (Dublin, 1963), p. 99.
60 *Report of the Commissioners Appointed to Inquire into the State of Popular Education in England* (1861), p. 127. Quoted in J.M. Goldstrom, 'Richard Whately and political economy in school books, 1833–80', *Irish Historical Studies*, 16 (1966), p. 131.
61 *Saturday Magazine*, 3 (1833), p. 182.
62 E.J. Whately, op. cit., vol. I, p. 180.
63 W.J. Fitzpatrick, op. cit., vol. II, pp. 67–8.
64 R. Whately, 'Report of the address on the conclusion of the first session of the Dublin Statistical Society', *Transactions of the Dublin Statistical Society*, I (1847–9), pp. 5, 7.
65 *Minutes of Evidence Taken before the Select Committee of the House of Lords on the Plan of Education in Ireland* (1837), vol. VIII, part II, Appendix I, p. 1408. Hamill's report, from the province of Munster,

was dated 10 January 1833.
66 J. Patten, *Fifteenth Report of Commissioners of National Education in Ireland* (1848), p. 262.
67 *Seventh Report of Commissioners of National Education in Ireland* (1840), p. 104.
68 W. McCreedy, *Fifteenth Report of Commissioners of National Education in Ireland* (1848), pp. 242–3.
69 E.J. Whately, op. cit., vol. I, p. 65.
70 W.N. Hancock, 'On the economic views of Bishop Berkeley and Mr Butt, with respect to the theory that a nation may gain by the compulsory use of native manufactures', *Transactions of the Dublin Statistical Society*, I (1847–9), p. 3.
71 M. Longfield, 'Report of the address on the conclusion of the second session of the Dublin Statistical Society', *Transactions of the Dublin Statistical Society*, I (1847–9), p. 4.
72 J. Pim, 'Address delivered at the opening of the eight session of the Society', *Journal of the Statistical and Social Inquiry Society of Ireland*, I (1855–6), p. 6.
73 R. Whately, 'Report of the address on the conclusion of the first session of the Dublin Statistical Society', *Transactions of the Dublin Statistical Society*, I (1847–9), p. 4.
74 *Journal of the Statistical and Social Inquiry Society of Ireland*, I (1855–6), p. 4.
75 J. Pim, op. cit., p. 6.
76 M. Longfield, 'Address delivered at the opening of the ninth session of the Society', *Journal of the Statistical and Social Inquiry Society of Ireland*, 1 (1855–6), p. 153.
77 J.A. Lawson, 'Address delivered at the opening of the eleventh session of the Society', *Journal of the Statistical and Social Inquiry Society of Ireland*, 2 (1857–60), pp. 152, 159–60.
78 Report of the council, *Journal of the Statistical and Social Inquiry Society of Ireland*, 3 (1861–3), p. 6.
79 T. O'Hagan, 'Address by the vice-president ... at the opening of the nineteenth session', *Journal of the Statistical and Social Inquiry Society of Ireland*, 4 (1864–8), p. 232.
80 Sir Robert Kane, 'Address by the vice-president ... at the opening of the twentieth session', *Journal of the Statistical and Social Inquiry Society of Ireland*, 4 (1864–8), pp. 355–6.
81 J. Pim, 'Address at the opening of the thirtieth session', *Journal of the Statistical and Social Inquiry Society of Ireland*, 7 (1876–9), p. 1.
82 A. Houston, *The Emancipation of Women from Existing Industrial Disabilities: Considered in Its Economic Aspect* (London, 1862), p. 6.
83 J.A. Lawson, 'On the connexion between statistics and political economy', *Transactions of the Dublin Statistical Society*, 1 (1847–9), p. 6.
84 W.N. Hancock, 'On the use of the doctrine of laissez faire, in investigating the economic resources of Ireland', *Transactions of the Dublin Statistical Society*, 1 (1847–9), p. 9.
85 T.E.C. Leslie, 'The self-dependence of the working classes under the

law of competition', *Transactions of the Dublin Statistical Society*, 2 (1849–51), p. 4.

86 W.E. Hearn, *Plutology* (Melbourne, 1863), p. 338.

87 J.E. Cairnes, 'Political economy and laissez-faire', *Fortnightly Review*, n.s. 10 (1871), p. 80.

88 W.E. Hearn, *The Aryan Household* (Melbourne, 1878), p. 10.

89 J.E. Bicheno, op. cit., pp. viii–ix.

90 Revd J. Godkin, *The Rights of Ireland* (Dublin, 1845), p. 56.

91 H. Martineau, *Letters from Ireland* (London, 1852), p. 66.

92 Revd F.F. Trench, *Observations on the System of the Church Education Society (As Applicable to Ireland)* (Dublin, 1852), p. 27.

93 W.N. Hancock, 'On the use of doctrine of laissez faire, in investigating the economic resources of Ireland', *Transactions of the Dublin Statistical Society*, 1 (1847–9), p. 3.

94 W.E. Hearn, *The Cassell Prize Essay on the Condition of Ireland* (London, 1851), pp. 4–5.

95 H.M. Posnett, *The Ricardian Theory of Rent* (London, 1884), p. 84.

96 Chapman to Cairnes, 23 May 1860, Cairnes Papers, National Library of Ireland, MS 8944 (6).

97 H.L. Jephson, 'Irish statute law reform', *Journal of the Statistical and Social Inquiry Society of Ireland*, 7 (1876–9), pp. 376–7, 385.

98 T.E.C. Leslie, 'An inquiry into the progress and present condition of Mechanics' Institutions', pt. I, *Transactions of the Dublin Statistical Society*, 3 (1851–4), p. 6.

99 Sir Robert Kane, 'Report of the address at the opening of the fifth session of the Dublin Statistical Society', *Transactions of the Dublin Statistical Society*, 2 (1849–51), pp. 4, 15–16.

100 T. O'Hagan, 'Address by the vice-president ... at the opening of the twentieth session', *Journal of the Statistical and Social Inquiry Society of Ireland*, 4 (1864–8), p. 235.

101 T. O'Hagan, 'Address at the opening meeting of the twenty-fourth session', *Journal of the Statistical and Social Inquiry Society of Ireland*, 5 (1868–70), p. 221.

102 H.L. Jephson, op. cit., p. 382.

103 Proceedings, *Journal of the Statistical and Social Inquiry Society of Ireland*, 5 (1868–70), p. 106.

104 See note 88 above.

105 Quoted in T.E.C. Leslie, *Essays in Political and Moral Philosophy* (Dublin, 1879), p. 148.

106 *Hansard*, 3rd series, vol. CXC, col. 1525 (16 March 1868).

107 Revd G.H. Stoddart, *The True Cure for Ireland, the Development of Her Industries*, 2nd edn. (London, 1847), p. 17.

108 *Hansard*, 3rd series, vol. CCLX, cols 890–926 (7 April 1881).

109 Quoted in E.D. Steele, *Irish Land and British Politics* (Cambridge, 1974), p. 306.

110 J.K. Ingram, 'The present position and prospects of political economy', *Journal of the Statistical and Social Inquiry Society of Ireland*, 7 (1876–9), Appendix, p. 15.

111 G.M. Koot, *English Historical Economics 1870–1926* (Cambridge,

1987), p. 32.

112 I. Butt, *A Voice for Ireland* (Dublin, 1847), p. 4.

113 W.N. Hancock, 'On the use of the doctrine of laissez faire, in investigating the economic resources of Ireland', *Transactions of the Dublin Statistical Society*, 1 (1847–9), p. 4.

114 E. Lysaght, 'A consideration of the theory, that the backward state of agriculture in Ireland is a consequence of the excessive competition for land', *Transactions of the Dublin Statistical Society*, 2 (1849–51), pp. 5, 6–7.

115 W.N. Hancock, 'On strikes with respect to hours of labour', *Journal of the Statistical and Social Inquiry Society of Ireland*, 4 (1864–8), p. 217.

116 J.A. Lawson, 'Address at the opening of the twenty-fifth session', *Journal of the Statistical and Social Inquiry Society of Ireland*, 6 (1871–6), p. 58.

117 H.D. Hutton, 'Tenures and land legislation in British India', *Journal of the Statistical and Social Inquiry Society of Ireland*, 5 (1868–70), p. 152.

118 J.K. Ingram, op. cit., p. 25.

119 J.E Cairnes, op. cit., pp. 85, 86.

120 S. Haughton, 'Causes of slow progress of political economy', *Journal of the Statistical and Social Inquiry Society of Ireland*, 7 (1876–9), p. 410.

121 J.E. Bicheno, op. cit., p. 296.

122 J.A. Lawson, 'Address delivered at the opening of the eleventh session of the Society', *Journal of the Statistical and Social Inquiry Society of Ireland*, 2 (1857–60), p. 144.

123 J.A. Lawson, 'On the connexion between statistics and political economy', *Transactions of the Dublin Statistical Society*, 1 (1847–8).

124 J.A. Lawson, 'Address at the opening of the sixteenth session', *Journal of the Statistical and Social Inquiry Society of Ireland*, 3 (1861–3), p. 286.

125 ibid., p. 179.

126 Report of the council at the opening of the sixteenth session, *Journal of the Statistical and Social Inquiry Society of Ireland*, 3 (1861–3), p. 4.

127 J.A. Lawson, 'Address', *Journal of the Statistical and Social Inquiry Society of Ireland*, 3 (1861–3), p. 286.

128 Report of the council, *Transactions of the Dublin Statistical Society*, 2 (1849–51), p. 18.

129 Report of the council, *Journal of the Statistical and Social Inquiry Society of Ireland*, 5 (1868–70), pp. 240–1.

130 M. Longfield, 'Report of the address on the conclusion of the second session of the Dublin Statistical Society', *Transactions of the Dublin Statistical Society*, 1 (1847–9), p. 5.

131 Sir Robert Kane, 'Report of the address at the opening of the fifth session of the Dublin Statistical Society', *Transactions of the Dublin Statistical Society*, 2 (1849–51), pp. 4, 9. See also Sir Robert Kane, 'Address by the vice-president ... at the opening of the twentieth

session', *Journal of the Statistical and Social Inquiry Society of Ireland*, 4 (1864–8), p. 356.

132 W.N. Hancock, 'On (1) the value of Adam Smith's "Wealth of Nations" ...', *Journal of the Statistical and Social Inquiry Society of Ireland*, 7 (1876–9), p. 283.

133 J.K. Ingram, op. cit., p. 11.

134 S. Haughton, op. cit., p. 412.

135 E.J. Whately, op. cit., vol. I, p. 65.

136 M. Longfield, *Four Lectures on Poor Laws* (Dublin, 1834), p. 2.

137 S. Haughton, op. cit., p. 411.

138 *Fifteenth Report of Commissioners of National Education in Ireland* (1848), p. 316.

139 Report of the council, *Journal of the Statistical and Social Inquiry Society of Ireland*, 2 (1857–60), p. 344.

140 W.N. Hancock, 'On the bothy system ...', *Journal of the Statistical and Social Inquiry Society of Ireland*, 2 (1857–60), p. 381.

141 ibid.

142 W.N. Hancock, 'A consideration of the discoveries of gold and silver ...', *Journal of the Statistical and Social Inquiry Society of Ireland*, 3 (1861–3), p. 82.

143 W.N. Hancock, 'On the long hours of employment of journeymen bakers in Dublin', *Journal of the Statistical and Social Inquiry Society of Ireland*, 2 (1857–60), pp. 399–405.

144 W.N. Hancock, 'The effects of the employment of women ...', *Journal of the Statistical and Social Inquiry Society of Ireland*, 2 (1857–60), pp. 439–45, and Discussion, *Journal of the Statistical and Social Inquiry Society of Ireland*, 4 (1864–8), pp. 352–3.

145 G.F. Shaw, 'On the use and abuse of apprenticeship', *Journal of the Statistical and Social Inquiry Society of Ireland*, 3 (1861–3), p. 98.

146 H.D. Hutton, 'The land question viewed as a sociological problem ...', *Journal of the Statistical and Social Inquiry Society of Ireland*, 3 (1861–3), p. 296.

147 J.K. Ingram, op. cit., p. 7.

148 J.E. Bicheno, op. cit., p. 266.

149 'Pat' [P.D. Kenny], *Economics for Irishmen*, 4th edn. (Dublin, 1907), pp. 12–13.

150 E.J. Whately, op. cit. vol. I, p. 67.

151 W.E. Hearn, 'On the coincidence of individual and general interests', *Galway Vindicator*, 6 March 1850.

152 T. O'Hagan, 'Address by the vice-president ... at the opening of the twentieth session', *Journal of the Statistical and Social Inquiry Society of Ireland*, 4 (1864–8), p. 233.

153 R.H.I. Palgrave, *Dictionary of Political Economy* (London, 1894).

154 Sir Horace Plunkett, *Ireland in the New Century* (Dublin, 1983), p. 102. First published 1904.

155 'Pat' [P.D. Kenny], op. cit., pp. 75–6.

156 W.E. Hearn, *Plutology*, (Melbourne, 1863), p. 442.

157 W.N. Hancock, 'On the use of the doctrine of laissez faire, in investigating the economic resources of Ireland', *Transactions of the*

Dublin Statistical Society, 1 (1847–9), p. 16.

158 W. Monsell, 'Address at the opening of the twenty-second session', *Journal of the Statistical and Social Inquiry Society of Ireland*, 5 (1868–70), p. 59.

159 J.E. Bicheno, op. cit., p. 258.

160 H.D. Hutton, 'The land question viewed as a sociological problem ...', *Journal of the Statistical and Social Inquiry Society of Ireland*, 3 (1861–3), pp. 295, 296, 297.

161 Discussion, *Journal of the Statistical and Social Inquiry Society of Ireland*, 3 (1861–3), p. 316.

162 J.K. Ingram, op. cit., pp. 18–19.

163 H.M. Posnett, op. cit., pp. 85, 91.

164 Sir Horace Plunkett, op. cit., pp. 166, 167.

165 Quoted in R. Williams, *Culture and Society 1780–1950* (Harmondsworth, 1963), p. 42.

166 Letter of 23 January 1854 to *The Citizen*, reprinted *Galway Vindicator*, 18 February 1854.

167 Proceedings, *Journal of the Statistical and Social Inquiry Society of Ireland*, 2 (1857–60), p. 396.

168 W.N. Hancock, 'On the bothy system', *Journal of the Statistical and Social Inquiry Society of Ireland*, 2 (1857–60), p. 375.

169 W.N. Hancock, "On the long hours of employment of journeymen bakers in Dublin', *Journal of the Statistical and Social Inquiry Society of Ireland*, 2 (1857–60), p. 400.

170 W.N. Hancock, 'The Aberdeen industrial schools contrasted with Irish workhouses: family ties being cherished in the schools, and violated in the workhouses', *Journal of the Statistical and Social Inquiry Society of Ireland*, 3 (1861–3), pp. 6–19.

171 W.N. Hancock, 'On strikes with respect to hours of labour', *Journal of the Statistical and Social Inquiry Society of Ireland*, 4 (1864–8), p. 218.

172 W.N. Hancock, 'The Aberdeen industrial schools contrasted with Irish workhouses: family ties being cherished in the schools, and violated in the workhouses', *Journal of the Statistical and Social Inquiry Society of Ireland*, 3 (1861–3), p. 19.

173 W.N. Hancock, 'The workhouse as a mode of relief for widows and orphans', *Journal of the Statistical and Social Inquiry Society of Ireland*, 1 (1855–6), p. 85.

174 ibid., p. 86.

175 W.N. Hancock, 'The effects of employment of women', *Journal of the Statistical and Social Inquiry Society of Ireland*, 2 (1857–60), p. 439.

176 E. Gibson, 'Employment of women in Ireland', *Journal of the Statistical and Social Inquiry Society of Ireland*, 3 (1861–3), p. 142.

177 A. Houston, *The Emancipation of Women from Existing Industrial Disabilities: Considered in its Economic Aspect* (London, 1862), p. 5.

178 A. Houston, 'The extension of the field for the employment of women', *Journal of the Statistical and Social Inquiry Society of Ireland*, 4 (1864–8), p. 345.

179 ibid., p. 346.
180 A. Houston, *The Emancipation of Women from Existing Industrial Disabilities: Considered in its Economic Aspect* (London, 1862), pp. 10, 11.
181 A. Houston, 'The extension of the field for the employment of women', *Journal of the Statistical and Social Inquiry Society of Ireland*, 4 (1864–8), p. 351; and *The Emancipation of Women from Existing Industrial Disabilities: Considered in its Economic Aspect* (London, 1862), p. 13.
182 W.N. Hancock, Discussion, *Journal of the Statistical and Social Inquiry Society of Ireland*, 4 (1864–8), p. 352.
183 A. Houston, ibid., p. 353.
184 W.N. Hancock, 'On the remittances from North America by Irish emigrants ...', *Journal of the Statistical and Social Inquiry Society of Ireland*, 6 (1871–6), p. 287.
185 Sir Horace Plunkett, op. cit., p. 167.
186 Revd M. O'Riordan, *Catholicity and Progress in Ireland* (London, 1905), p. 93.
187 'Pat' [P.D. Kenny], op. cit., pp. 13, 14.
188 A.G. Richey, *A Short History of the Irish People* (Dublin, 1887), pp. 14, 15, 13, 35, 54, 35, 58–9.
189 W.E. Hearn, *The Aryan Household*, (Melbourne, 1878) pp. 453, 455, 465, 474.
190 ibid., pp. 10–11.
191 C. Dewey, 'Celtic agrarian legislation and the Celtic revival: historicist implications of Gladstone's Irish and Scottish land acts 1870–1886', *Past and Present*, 64, August 1974, pp. 45, 46.
192 O. MacDonagh, *States of Mind* (London, 1983), p. 35.
193 S. Laing, *Coercion in Ireland* (London, n.d.), p. 5.
194 J.J. Murphy, 'On the tenures and taxation of India', *Journal of the Statistical and Social Inquiry Society of Ireland*, 2 (1857–60), p. 214.
195 H.D. Hutton, 'The land question viewed as a sociological problem ...', *Journal of the Statistical and Social Inquiry Society of Ireland*, 3 (1861–3), p. 295.
196 H.D. Hutton, 'Tenures and land legislation in British India', *Journal of the Statistical and Social Inquiry Society of Ireland*, 5 (1868–70), pp. 152, 153, 158.
197 I. Butt, *The Irish People and the Irish Land* (Dublin, 1867), pp. 267–8.
198 'Tenant-right in Ireland', *Westminster Review*, n.s. 30 (1866), p. 1.
199 J.S. Mill, *Ireland and England* (London, 1868). Reprinted in *Collected Works* (Toronto, 1982), vol. II, pp. 507–32. Quotation is from p. 519.
200 G. Campbell, *The Irish Land Act* (London, 1869), pp. 4, 6.
201 J.E. Cairnes, 'Ireland in transition', *The Economist*, 21 October 1865, p. 1269.
202 ibid., 14 October 1865, p. 1238.
203 J.E. Cairnes, 'Political economy and land', *Fortnightly Review*, n.s. 7 (1870), p. 59.
204 *Hansard*, 3rd series, vol. CXC, cols 1617–18 (13 March 1868).

NOTES AND REFERENCES

Quoted in Steele, op. cit., p. 20.

205 J.S. Mill, 'Professor Leslie on the land question'. *Fortnightly Review*, n.s. 7 (1870), p. 642.
206 A Protestant Celt [Robert Macdonnell], *Irish Nationality in 1870*, 2nd edn. (Dublin, 1870), pp. 26, 43.
207 C. Dewey, op. cit., p. 62.
208 ibid.
209 ibid., p. 59.
210 H.M. Posnett, op. cit., pp. 47–8.
211 Political Economy, *The Irish Landlord and His Accusers* (London, 1882), p. 2.
212 An Irish Proprietor, *Irish Ideas* (n.p., [1878]), p. 1.
213 T.M. Kettle, *The Day's Burden* (Dublin, 1937), p. 138.

INDEX

INDEX

labour theory of value 37, 83–4,
95–6, 98–9
Laing, S. 8–9
laissez-faire doctrine xi, 8, 9, 117,
123, 133, 139–40, 143, 146, 151,
154, 156
land question, the xi, 10, 43, 117,
138, 155, 158–9; Irish Land Acts
(1870, 1881) 140, 158
*Land Systems and Industrial
Economy of Ireland, England
and Continental Countries*
(Leslie) 157
Larcom Sir T. 114
Larne Model Agricultural National
School 91
Lawson, J.A. 3, 5, 6–7, 9–10, 11,
14–15, 30, 31, 38, 42, 103, 106,
114, 132, 134, 139, 140;
biographical details 163
Lectures on Political Economy, Five
(Lawson) 38, 42, 163
Lectures on Political Economy
(Longfield) 38, 39, 61
Lectures on Poor Laws, Four
(Longfield) 7, 11, 161
Lectures (Whately) 57
Lentaigne, Sir J. 4, 5, 15
Leslie, T.E.C. 1, 3–4, 34, 40–1, 43,
57–61, 103, 106, 110, 118, 134,
137, 139; biographical details
170–1
Limerick Declaration (1868) 10
List of Absentees of Ireland, A
(Prior) 27
literary societies 48, 103–4
Lloyd, B. 28, 29
London Review 78
Longfield, M. 7, 9, 10, 23, 25, 30–1,
38, 39, 43, 63, 101, 132, 141;
biographical details 161–2
Lowe, R. 138
Lupton, W., biographical details
173
Lysaght, E. 139

McCreedy, W. 11–12, 93, 94, 123,
131
McCulloch J.R. 31, 63, 68–9, 70

MacDonagh, O. 155
Macdonnell, J. 12, 91
McDonnell, R. 31
McDowell, R.B. 28, 32
MacHale, Dr. J. *see* Tuam,
Archbishop of
MacVickar, J. 70
Madden, S. 4–5, 27
Malthus, T.R. 92
Marshall, A. 35
Martineau, H. 70, 135
Maynooth College 22, 46, 50, 64,
71–2; Maynooth Act (1845) 50
mechanics' institutes 48, 103–4,
106, 107, 110, 127
Memoirs (Madden) 27
Menger, C. 37
methodology 42–3, 118–19
Mill J.S. 31, 33, 34, 35, 63, 70, 117,
138, 156, 157–8
'Mill-Bastable condition' 41
Millin, S.S. 109
Mills, R.H. 6, 34, 61–2, 63
Mitchel, J. 3–4, 8, 146, 148
model schools 91, 95, 109
moderatorships, Whately Chair
29–30, 33–6
Moffett, T.W. 13, 103, 106, 107,
118
Monroe, J. 25, 101, 103, 107,
109–10, 113
Monsell, W. 146
Morier, R.B.D. 34
Moylan, J. 12, 16, 105
Munster college movement 48–9
Murphy, J.J. 10, 155
Murray, Archbishop D. 75–6
music in the national schools
122–4, 127–8
mutual improvement societies 104

National Association for the
Promotion of Social Science
113, 141
national schools, political economy
in the x, 4–5, 11, 14, 15, 48, 51,
67–99, 121; commissioners and
the Board 4, 67, 79, 93–9, 124,
161, 169; inspectors 11–12,